Advance Praise

'A rich compilation of essays from stalwarts in the field, revealing how the women in Tagore's varied representations straddle the public/private spheres depicting the myriad moods of the feminine, from the abstract to the concrete, from the empowered to the romantic.'

—**Abhijit Sen, Professor of English, Visva-Bharati**

TAGORE'S IDEAS OF THE NEW WOMAN

TAGORE'S IDEAS OF THE NEW WOMAN

The Making and Unmaking
of Female Subjectivity

Edited by

CHANDRAVA CHAKRAVARTY
SNEHA KAR CHAUDHURI

Los Angeles I London I New Delhi
Singapore I Washington DC I Melbourne

First published in 2017 by

SAGE Publications India Pvt Ltd
B1/I-1 Mohan Cooperative Industrial Area
Mathura Road, New Delhi 110 044, India
www.sagepub.in

STREE
16 Southern Avenue
Kolkata 700026
www.stree-samyabooks.com

SAGE Publications Inc
2455 Teller Road
Thousand Oaks, California 91320, USA

SAGE Publications Ltd
1 Oliver's Yard, 55 City Road
London EC1Y 1SP, United Kingdom

SAGE Publications Asia-Pacific Pte Ltd
3 Church Street
#10-04 Samsung Hub
Singapore 049483

Published by Vivek Mehra for SAGE Publications India Pvt Ltd, typeset in 10/12 pt Calisto MT by Zaza Eunice, Hosur, Tamil Nadu, India and printed at Chaman Enterprises, New Delhi.

Library of Congress Cataloging-in-Publication Data Available

ISBN: 978-93 81345-16-0 (HB)

SAGE Stree Team: Madhuparna Banerjee, Supriya Das and Neha Sharma
Disclaimer:
© Supriya Chaudhuri, 2017, Chapter 5 in this book
© Dipannita Datta, 2017, Chapter 10 in this book

In Memory of Jasodhara Bagchi

Thank you for choosing a SAGE product!
If you have any comment, observation or feedback,
I would like to personally hear from you.
Please write to me at **contactceo@sagepub.in**

Vivek Mehra, Managing Director and CEO, SAGE India.

Bulk Sales

SAGE India offers special discounts
for purchase of books in bulk.
We also make available special imprints
and excerpts from our books on demand.

For orders and enquiries, write to us at

Marketing Department
SAGE Publications India Pvt Ltd
B1/I-1, Mohan Cooperative Industrial Area
Mathura Road, Post Bag 7
New Delhi 110044, India

E-mail us at **marketing@sagepub.in**

Get to know more about SAGE

Be invited to SAGE events, get on our mailing list.
Write today to **marketing@sagepub.in**

This book is also available as an e-book.

Contents

Foreword

Rabindranath Tagore is a writer who contains multitudes, so to speak. The more I learn about his work, the more I am astounded by the breadth and depth of his achievements and the profound and wide-ranging nature of his preoccupations. The task is made difficult not only by his infinite variety and prolific output but also by a mind that was omnivorous and a personality that was ever-restless, ever-evolving.

Tagore's Ideas of the New Woman: The Making and Unmaking of Female Subjectivity, the thought-provoking and rich collection of essays Chandrava Chakravarty and Sneha Kar Chaudhuri have assembled in the pages that follow, based on new research and re-evaluation that took place at Tagore's hundred and fiftieth birth anniversary. A conference was organized by the Department of English of the State University of West Bengal on this occasion. The essays are all on one topic—'Rabindranath Tagore and Woman'. My reading of the book quickly revealed to me how contemporary, innovative and refreshing the perspectives contained in these pages are. These essays also reminded me yet again of how complex and even contradictory were Tagore's views on the 'woman question' in India, how much he was of his time and place in his prejudices and actions at crucial moments, such as his daughters' marriages, and yet how far ahead of his time and space he could be on other occasions in engaging women in creative projects, or in readying them to embrace their future on their own through his school and university. Whether in his poems, songs, prose essays (in English as well as Bengali), letters, autobiographical writings, travel tales, plays, dance-dramas, short fiction and novels, and in his paintings, he depicted, introspected, and envisioned the role of women that was veering slowly but steadily away from orthodoxy and stasis, and progressing climactically and inevitably towards freedom and increased self-expression.

The editors have organized these essays in a way to help the reader move from an understanding of Tagore's dealings with

women in the domestic space, *ghare*, the household, in his short
and long fiction, to women being given agency to proceed beyond
domesticity and enter *baire*, the wider and modernizing world outside their homes. Aware that to encompass Tagore's achievements
in representing and re-visioning women they would have to go
beyond his literary works, Chandrava Chakravarty and Sneha Kar
Chaudhuri have also included thoughtful and probing essays that
take into account his songs, paintings and dance dramas. But a few
of the essayists go even beyond Tagore's works to track their transformation into captivating films.

Chakravarty and Kar Chaudhuri have dedicated their book to
the memory of Professor Jasodhara Bagchi, professor of English
at Jadavpur University and the author of the keynote essay of the
conference that gave the impetus to this volume. Fittingly, her essay
provides the key needed to enter the volume, for she sees Tagore's
works as distinctive in the way they subtly open up more and more
spaces for women, in contradictory and yet compelling positions
that led them to cross boundaries and disrupt conventional expectations of what a woman's place should be.

As Professor Bagchi points out, we now have the advantage
of being able to see Tagore's works on women from perspectives
informed by intense activity in gender, sexuality, and so on, taking
advantage of recent developments in critical and cultural theory. In
the Introduction the editors contextualize a Tagore disturbed on the
one hand, by colonization and modernity, and tied on the other, to
persistent patriarchal attitudes. Helpfully, they reflect on the modernizing Thakurbari, or family home, in which Tagore grew up
and the contrary strains in the larger society that he moved in that
seemed to lead him on many an occasion into ambivalent and even
contradictory positions. Such ambivalence and contradictions are at
times immensely productive for imaginative writers and artists and
thus worthy of sympathetic consideration and not of a historical
denunciation.

Some of the essayists have contextualized Tagore's works
by looking at contemporary epistolary works, essays and polemical tracts and debates reflecting in one way or the other on the
roles women should play in the domestic and the public spheres.
Tagore's ambivalence on some of the issues associated with the

'woman question', the strong stance he takes on a few of them as well as his conservatism in others are thus situated by these essayists through the examination of discursive formations, on issues such as widow remarriage and widow burning, for instance, of the classic Tagore novel *Choker Bali* (Grit in the Eye) and stories such as 'Jibita o Mrita' (Alive and Dead), to name only a couple of the fictional works analysed in its pages. But these essays leave little doubt that even though on occasions Tagore has appeared to be retrogressive about some aspects of women's lives such as early marriage, he has, on the whole, depicted in his works women becoming self-responsible, struggling for alternative spaces and transgressing the roles that patriarchal society had assigned to them. Indeed, as we learn from more than one of the essays of the book, in his final decades Tagore became not only transgressive but also subversive as far as conventional notions of women's status and sexuality were concerned. The essays on the late Tagore included in the book, that is to say, his later fiction, plays and dance dramas, are therefore intriguing forays into what Edward Said had so suggestively focused on in his posthumously published book, *Late Style* (1906), where the Palestinian-American intellectual and theorist sees the very greatest artists as old men (Said does not discuss any woman artist!) who, having had intimations of mortality, forge a unique and disturbing manner of depicting reality. Surely the paintings are instances of such re-visioning!

Throughout *Tagore's Ideas of the New Woman: The Making and Unmaking of Female Subjectivity,* I came across essays that indicate that this book has done what such volumes can or should do at their best: make us reexamine a writer who has achieved canonical status, reveal how his works have become classics because of his ability to delve into contemporary reality and represent what he finds there in arresting words and images, relating them to readers in such a way that we realize that such a writer and his works are classics also because they speak to us—are our contemporaries, as Jan Kott had so famously indicated through the title of one of his books *Shakespeare: Our Contemporary.* Surely the reader will also be as thankful as I am to quite a few of the essayists of the volume because of the ingenuity they have shown in taking the subject of Tagore and women to new and unexpected areas. A captivating essay is of the 'other woman', which is to say European woman, for his travel writings show the acuteness with which he recorded his encounters with them as well as his evolving attitude to them. The essays on the way Tagore's fictional heroines have had an afterlife in their film versions reminded me of Walter Benjamin theorizing on the afterlife of a text in its translations, for they are suggestive of the manner in which Tagore's short or long fiction are being transformed in celluloid, not only brilliantly by Satyajit Ray or ingeniously by Rituparna Ghosh but also quite imaginatively by the gifted but lesser known director Bappaditya Bandopadhyay.

I am quite certain that these essays will be of excellent use for readers in our time. Not only will scholars studying the book be amply rewarded by these diverse essays on a subject that is of enduring interest, but they will also be able to apply the insights and interpretative techniques deployed in them to other Tagore texts. And while his wife and daughters and Kadambari Devi and Victoria Ocampo are mentioned in a number of the essays, the time has come to consider the ways in which his relationship with his mother, sisters and nieces (Indira Devi in particular) and other women such as Lady Ranu Mukerjee, impacted on his creative works. Reading the book was a pleasurable as well as a learning experience and I can only hope it will be widely circulated and read.

Fakrul Alam
University of Dhaka
Bangladesh

Preface

The Department of English, West Bengal State University, offers courses on Tagore's fiction, nonfiction and drama in translation and is thus well positioned to present this collection of Tagore's thoughts on women and their changing selfhood under modernity. An international conference on this very theme was organized by the department as a result of the UGC's directive on commemorating the one hundredth and fiftieth birth anniversary of Rabindranath Tagore in 2011, and this book has in many ways emerged as a result. We have also invited essays on areas which had not been covered, for instance, the essays by Debashish Raychaudhuri and Dipannita Datta.

We were generously supported by the former Vice Chancellor, Professor Ashok Ranjan Thakur and received the support of all other departmental members. We would like to thank, Uma Das Gupta, Malini Bhattacharya, Mandakranta Bose, Sukanta Chaudhuri, Tirthankar Bose, Supriya Chaudhuri, Krishna Sen, Tapati Gupta, Sanjukta Dasgupta, Amita Dutt, Jayati Gupta, Ashok Viswanathan, Sanjoy Mukhopadhyay and Nandini Bhattacharya. The contributors were remarkably generous in holding their essays for this book and patient with delays.

We especially recall the contribution of Jasodhara Bagchi, who sadly is not with us today. Appreciating the concept note of the conference, she had readily agreed to deliver the keynote address and also offered detailed advice on publication. We are honoured to dedicate this book to her. Krishna Sen, former professor of English at the University of Calcutta, was our philosopher and guide. Rajat Kanta Ray and Prabudhha Raha have helped us in various capacities and we offer them our heartfelt thanks.

We are grateful to Vishwa-Bharati for granting permission to reproduce the photographs in Chapter 2, and the plates of Tagore's paintings in Chapter 14.

We thank Stree-Samya for its editorial support. Nothing can belittle the importance of our students whose energy, curiosity and active participation made possible everything that would have remained a far-flung dream, both physically and intellectually. Last but not the least, a sincere note of gratitude to our family members for the emotional support, understanding and encouragement they offer in all our ventures.

Chandrava Chakravarty and **Sneha Kar Chaudhuri**
West Bengal State University
Barasat, North 24-Parganas
West Bengal

Introduction

Chandrava Chakravarty and Sneha Kar Chaudhuri

I

[The] ideal of stability is deeply cherished in woman's nature. She
is never in love with merely going on, shooting wanton arrows of
curiosity into the heart of darkness. All her forces instinctively work
to bring things to some shape of fullness—for that is the law of life.
(Tagore 2004: 224–25)

The essay 'Woman', delivered as a lecture during Tagore's 1916–17
American tours and later published in the collection *Personality:
Lectures Delivered in America* in 1921, was Tagore's attempt to establish a rapport with his American audiences by upholding the unique-
ness of the Indian concept of liberated womanhood in the wake
of the women's liberation movements in the western world. What
he achieved were sweeping generalizations which explained neither the western perception of womanhood nor the Indian notion
of the feminine. On a close reading, the essay reveals that Tagore's
thoughts were inflected by disparate factors: the deep ideological
crisis in which Tagore plunged after World War I, the imperative to
create a cultural bridge between the aggression of western culture
and India, the traditional veneration of the female deity in Indian
(Hindu) culture,[1] the colonial reconfiguration of Indian womanhood which was transcultural in nature, the impact of a strong
patriarchal way of life in a Brahmo family on Tagore, and Tagore's
own belief in woman's emancipation. A close reading of the essay
'Woman' reveals to sensitive readers a confusion of ideas. Tagore
perceptively observes that the history of the world has been that
of a masculine civilization in which woman's presence and voice
has been relegated as marginal. As against this man-made, aggressive civilization, he upholds the increasing importance of woman

as the harbinger of harmony and stability. What Tagore celebrates is the passivity of feminine nature as a balm for the bruises caused by the power-mongering masculine civilization of the world culminating in World War I:

> For woman's function is the passive function of the soil, which not only helps the tree to grow but keeps its growth within limits.... Woman is endowed with the passive qualities of chastity, modesty, devotion and power of self-sacrifice in a greater measure than man is. It is the passive quality in nature which turns its monster forces into perfect creations of beauty—taming the wild elements to tenderness fit for the service of life. This passive quality has given woman that large and deep placidity which is so necessary for the healing and nourishing and storing of life. (Tagore 2004: 27)

Instead of talking directly about the feminine principle in the cosmos who is looked upon as *Prakriti / Shakti* in the Hindu Shastras, Tagore alludes to the feminine as a life-giving, nurturing power which can resist the destructive propensities of the world around. However, instead of regarding this power as active, Tagore regards the feminine nature to be characterized by passiveness, thus attempting to posit it as an antidote to the much celebrated virility of western civilization. Again, when he regards woman as the repository of certain qualities traditionally attributed to her in Hindu patriarchal society such as chastity, modesty, devotion and sacrifice, Tagore seems to conflate two practically irreconcilable ideas—the mystic, metaphysical perception of the feminine as the procreative, natural, life-giving force in the cosmos; and the historically–culturally constructed and inter-pellated gendered category of woman. This confusion appears to inform the entire essay. He observes that while liberating themselves from patriarchal codes, women of the western world have embraced a certain degree of 'restlessness', and have proved untrue to their nature. What then is the true nature of woman? Tagore resorts to an unqualified essentialism by claiming the domestic sphere to be woman's actual domain irrespective of culture, place and history. He presents 'woman' as a homogeneous category characterized by certain qualities that constitute her essence:

> Wherever there is something which is concretely personal and human, there is the woman's world. The domestic world is the world where every

individual finds his worth as an individual, therefore his value is not the market value, but the value of love; that is to say, the value that God in his infinite mercy has set upon all his creatures. *This domestic world has been the gift of God to woman.... God has sent woman to love the world, which is a world of ordinary things and events.* (Tagore 2004: 229) [Chandrava Chakravarty's emphasis]

It would be meaningless to conjecture whether Tagore's views on woman were accepted by his American audience in 1916. A twenty-first century reader would perhaps refrain from being merely judgmental about Tagore's observations and seek to explore the historical factors that shaped the mind of the poet. What needs to be recognized is that the contradictions were ingrained in Tagore partly because of his upbringing in the Jorasanko Thakurbari and partly because of the discursively turgid times that formed the social environment nurturing Rabindranath's mind and soul.

II

The Jorasanko Thakurbari where Tagore was born in 1861 was an abode of contradictions. We can, however, return to the Jorasanko Thakubari and to Tagore's divided consciousness a little later once we recognize that contradictions were also embedded in the colonial construction of modernity (or modernities) in Bengal, many pioneers of which came from the Tagore family. To talk about the historical and ideological significance of the woman's question in colonial Bengal would be a repetitive exercise since such large corpus scholarly works has been produced on it. We can, however, very briefly, mention that the ideological contradictions of the Jorasanko family needs also to be seen in the context of the historical moment. This leads to the recognition that the Tagore family, with all its conservatism and avant-garde initiatives, embodies a vision of India caught up in the cross current of opposing ideologies: the antagonism between reformist and revivalist trends, between the moderate and extremist elements in politics and, most significantly, the changing relationship between the home and the world.

When Dwarkanath Tagore was a minor, the Thakurbari was a devout Vaishnav family. Dwarkanath and his pious wife, Digambari, worshipped Lakshmi and Janardan. As Dwarkanath's business prospered he was drawn to western culture, and indulged in a dissipated life. Digambari never approved of Dwarkanath's anglicized lifestyle and gradually estranged herself from her husband: 'Digambari did not falter in the path of duty. Except for looking after [Dwarkanath's] material comforts (seva) she severed all relations with him. Her devotion to her husband was so great that no outsider ever learnt anything about this step' (Deb 2010: 16). She had such deep disgust for the kind of life Dwarkanath lived that she bathed in seven drums of Ganga water after talking to him on family matters. Even Dwarkanath, who had renounced the orthodox Hindu lifestyle, commented after Digambari's death that Goddess Lakshmi had abandoned him. Nevertheless, it was Dwarkanath who deserves credit for creating a distinct lifestyle for the Thakurbari people. He came out of the narrow groove of religious orthodoxy, blended the orient and the occident in his aesthetic taste and paved the way for his son Debendranath and grandson Satyendranath. Without him the Tagore family would never have emerged as a strong pillar of 'modern' Bengal.

We need to remember that women of the Tagore household were never so rigidly constrained by the patriarchal dictates of Hindu society as other Hindu women. The reason was perhaps that as *pirali* Brahmins, they lived like outcasts in Hindu society, and could easily flout orthodox norms.[2] Maharshi Debendranath's wife, Sarada Devi, was literate and a paid Vaishnavi was appointed to teach her religious scriptures and epics. Maharshi himself, though conservative in several matters, was keenly interested in the education of the women of his household. His daughters were taught at home to read and write. His eldest daughter, Saudamini, was sent to Bethune School and entreated by her father to teach her other siblings. Her memories of her father, *Pitrismriti,* do not depict Maharshi as an iconoclast.[3] In fact, he conformed to several orthodox Hindu customs, strictly maintained the divide between the *andar-* and the *bahirmahal* and did not stand by radical reform movements like abolition of *sati,* or widow remarriage; instead he encouraged traditional customs followed by the women of the Tagore family. However, the education of his daughters was a matter of prime concern to Debendranath and he encouraged them to indulge in literary activities. His daughter Swarnakumari became a successful writer in Bengali.

The first iconoclastic move came from his ICS son Satyendranath who had a mind far ahead of his time. He not only demolished the barrier between the inner and the outer houses, but also trained his wife, Jnanadanandini, to become the very icon of emancipated Bengali womanhood in the heyday of the Bengal Renaissance. Her personality was fashioned both by her husband and herself to mirror a successful blend of the East and the West. Her journey, however, was not without impediments. The Maharshi did not approve of Satyendranath's indulgence towards his wife, but nothing could deter Satyendranath from encouraging his wife to break free from the traditional mould. Jnanadanandini went to England alone with her infant children to join her husband, educated herself, changed her mode of dressing in the traditional saree for public occasions and also pioneered the nuclear family by beginning to live with her husband in a separate house. The trend set by Jnanadanandini continued to inspire and reshape the other women of the Tagore family:

> Dawn was breaking over Calcutta. The first rays of the sun had just crossed the boundary of the sky and fallen on the roof of the mansion.... Two Arab steeds, treading the dew-laden grass, emerged onto the hard surface of the road. Leaving the main entrance behind, they trotted towards the Maidan. Everyone gaped in silence and disbelief. The two men seemed oblivious to all these people. No, an error. Lo! One of the riders was a lady! The erect horsewoman in full riding habit was Kadambari, wife of Jyotirindranath Tagore. (Deb 2010: 1)

It would be wrong to suppose from the examples of the Thakurbari women that most of the women in Bengali society embraced an enlightened outlook. Nevertheless, the influence of the women of Thakurbari in the colonial phase was immense in upholding an alternative female identity that challenged the traditional models of womanhood in Hindu society. They educated themselves braving the fear that the act of reading/writing turns a woman into a widow; they came out of the andarmahal and many of them attended schools; they indulged unhindered in literary compositions, organized house functions and often performed in them, edited journals, managed the works of the zamindari,

while excelling at the same time in several household accomplish-
ments. Chitra Deb writes about Kadambari, 'Kadambari's role in
the Tagore family is memorable for her aptitude in acting and singing. Jyotirindranath, already an appreciator of drama, had been further encouraged by his talented wife. When the Jorasanko Theatre
became defunct, he began composing plays, satires and musical
dramas' (ibid.: 84). These dramatic compositions were performed
in the courtyard of the andarmahal and Kadambari took part in
them. Although the divide between the inner and the outer houses
were much relaxed during Kadambari's time, the Thakurbari still
maintained its peculiar combination of enlightened humanism and
conservatism. As Deb tells us that when Kadambari participated in
the plays, no questions were raised as there was no outsider to see
her (ibid.). We must remember that the same Kadambari rode her
Arabian horse in the Maidan. One can understand that Tagore had
seen in his early days many enlightened *navinas* (the new women)
in his own house. Tagore's wife, Bhabatarini, was transformed to
Mrinalini (she was renamed thus after her marriage) as she was
regularly trained to talk and carry herself like the other enlightened
women of the family under the tutelage of either Neepamoyee, the
wife of Hemendranath, the third son of Debendranath, and thus
her sister-in-law, or Jnanadanandini. She was sent to Loreto school,
given regular lessons in music, piano and English while at home she
received training in the Sanskrit language. Despite being considerably talented, her predominant role in Tagore's family was that of a
housewife, who lived for the well-being of others, and made daring
sacrifices to fulfil the dreams of her husband.

Rabindranath's attitude to his daughters is also marked by
shocking contradictions. The poet's ambiguous attitude to women
and his duality towards womanhood has been explored in Chapter
6, Sanjukta Dasgupta 'Tagore's Docile Daughters: Ambivalence in
Family Life.' The poet was very fond of his daughters, left no stone
unturned in educating them and in trying to attune their minds to
the higher ideals of life. But it remains a mystery why Tagore hast-
ily married such talented girls at very young ages. Madhurilata was
married when she was fourteen; Renuka and Atashi (Mira) at the
young age of eleven. We have to remember that Tagore believed in
woman's emancipation and also in a higher marriageable age for

women. Yet his decisions in regard to his beloved daughters had been contrary to his publicly proclaimed ideals. One reason could be that a hefty portion of the dowry and the expenses for the marriages was borne by Maharshi's zamindari. Hence, the hurry to marry off the daughters when Maharshi was alive. The, otherwise radical Rabindranath, also yielded to social custom and paid a huge amount as dowry to satisfy the demand of Madhurilata's mother-in-law. Later Tagore wrote to a friend: 'There have been many weddings in our family. It is only at my daughter's marriage that there was haggling over every aspect' (cited in ibid.: 208). This is the same Rabindranath who had critiqued the evil customs of society in his literary works and also undertook the courageous task of introducing co-education in Shantiniketan. While as a poet Tagore often idealized feminine power, as a father his advices to Madhurilata prior to her marriage were thoroughly conservative. Madhurilata's response enables us to construct the father's words: 'I shall try my best to carry out your advice. Besides remembering he [her husband] is superior to me in every respect and that I am not his equal, I shall also try to improve his home' (ibid.: 209). In an essay Tagore justifies the system of early marriages in India, despite the fact that as a socially conscious individual he was also aware of the evils of early marriages, especially, for girls. But while defending the Indian marriage Tagore effusively supports the lofty ideals which underlined the custom in 'The Indian Ideal of Marriage':

> There is a particular age, said India, at which this attraction between the sexes reaches its height, so if marriage is to be regulated according to the social will, it must be finished with before such age. Hence, the Indian custom of early marriage. These must have been the lines of argument, in regard to married love, pursued in our country. For the purpose of marriage, spontaneous love is unreliable, its proper cultivation should yield the best results,— such was the conclusion,— and this cultivation should begin before marriage. Therefore from their earliest years, the husband as an idea, is held up before our girls, in verse and story, through ceremonial and worship. When at length they get this 'husband', he is to them not a person but a principle, like Loyalty, Patriotism, or such other abstractions which owe their immense strength to the fact that the best part of them is our own creation and therefore part of our inner being. (Tagore, *Bichitra Online*)

This might explain why Tagore has been particularly conservative in his advices to Madhurilata. He was, perhaps, trying to inculcate the high ideals on which marriages in India were traditionally based. Tagore values it as the foundation of a stable, healthy society and exalts the role of the mother above that of the beloved. He writes in the same essay:

> Woman, let me repeat, has two aspects,— in one she is the Mother; in the other, the Beloved. I have already spoken of the spiritual endeavour that characterizes the first, viz., the striving, not merely for giving birth to her child, but for creating the best possible child,— not as an addition to the number of men, but as one of the heroic souls who may win victory in man's eternal fight against evil in his social life and natural surroundings. As the Beloved, it is woman's part to infuse life into all the aspirations of man; and the spiritual power that enables her to do so I have called charm, and was known in India by the name of shakti.

In upholding the depth and profundity of the Indian tradition Tagore combines the Hindu revivalist view of woman as the builder of *charitas*, and the western conception of woman as a romantic partner, but gives it a typically Indian dimension by interpreting her love as manifestation of her spiritual power or shakti. Although Tagore strongly negates sexual equality, positing marriage as a union based on the devotion of woman towards the abstract ideal of a husband, he also asserts that if a marriage fails to uphold this ideal union then it should be dissolved. Rabindranath's decision to support his youngest daughter Atashilata against an incompatible marriage brings to the fore a radical father who lived up to his own convictions. As a responsible father he felt that it was his duty to protect his daughter from humiliation and disrespect, and wrote to his son-in-law Nagendranath: 'In Madras I saw that Mira was scared of you and was apprehensive of being insulted by you in public. I then realized that your basic natures are not compatible.' Referring to the rupture between Nagendra and his daughter, Tagore further writes: 'It is beyond me to try and heal the breach by threat or force. I cannot imagine anything more cruel and demeaning' (cited in Deb 2010: 223). As a father Tagore seems to have felt guilty for Mira's ill fate and by offering her firm support in her trying times; he expiated his guilt. In a letter to Rathindranath in August 1919 he wrote: 'I dealt the first blow in her life—without proper thought and consideration, I arranged her marriage.... Her life has already been ruined.... I am its root cause' (Tagore 1997: 227). He remained firm in his decision that forcing his daughter to live a life she did not desire would be an act of inhuman cruelty and violence. His courage and grit in trying to make Atashi self-reliant is indeed remarkable in an age when women in Bengali society were mostly treated as a procreative machine, dependant and devoid of individual identity.

Despite severe social opposition Rabindranath had introduced co-education in Shantiniketan at a time when most women in Bengali household were not allowed formal education. In the essay *Prachya Nareer Sadhana* Tagore talks about woman's role in the creation of Visva-Bharati: 'In this mission I want inspiration from the sisters of my nation. This institution should not be the work of men.... In every aspect of this noble endeavour the need for woman's service is strongly felt.' He further elaborates on his faith in the power of womankind: 'In any great mission it is woman who provides inspiration. In the domain of politics and education our power never becomes true and profound without inspiration from women' (Tagore 2015a). This brief excursion into history attempts to bring to the fore that Tagore's 'modern' consciousness, a product of the historical specificities that shaped and reshaped modernities in colonial Bengal, is hard to define.

We also need to bear in mind that despite the external stimuli which constantly charged his mind, Rabindranath was able to create a secluded inner domain of perceptions which were his own. Hence his relationships with Kadambari Devi, Ranu or Vijaya were coloured with hues of Tagore's unique mind. The inner domain, as Sabyasachi Bhattacharya writes in his interpretative biography of Rabindranath, was immensely important to Tagore:

> In many statements about his intellectual evolution, Tagore spoke of his 'inner life'. In 1904, in one such statements, he underlined the importance of the 'inner consciousness'. In 1917 he distinguished between the 'subconscious' (*upachetana*) and conscious level in his mind to point to the emergence of thoughts from below. In 1940 he reflected on 'the mystery of vitality working in me'. (2011: 19)

It is the power and conviction of the inner domain that enabled Tagore to transcend at times the limitations imposed upon him by custom and heredity. The confluence of the inner and the outer minds often made his responses to life unpredictable. As he would sing to his *Jiban Devata* or his muse in 'You Have Made Me Endless' (*Amare tumi ashesh korecho*):

> You have made me endless, such is thy grace, ...
> At that immortal touch of yours my overflowing heart
> Lost in a profound limitless joy, finds utterance.
> Filling just one cup of my hands
> You are pouring your gifts day and night,
> So many ages pass and you are not done
> I remain your receptacle. (Bose 2012, translated by Sugata Bose)

It was only when he had turned to them later that he could discern the continuity of thoughts amidst a superficial sense of fragmentation. We are trying to understand a vibrant mind, responsive to the varied nuances of life's journey. It would be intellectually restrictive if we try to simplify or schematize Tagore's responses to the genus 'woman', and so we shall refrain from seeking a linear development of the poet's thoughts. The vast corpus of the literary creations of Rabindranath Tagore encompasses his myriad responses to 'woman'. Woman's primacy in Tagore's life is well expressed in his own words: 'I have deep respect towards women—the women of all countries. I have always received inspiration from them. My creative and aesthetic inspiration have also come from the women who nurtured me and gave me life. That is why I feel indebted to them' (*Prachya Nareer Sadhana,* translation Chandrava Chakravarty). Besides the influence of several women in Tagore's personal life and creative life, the notion of the 'feminine' has occupied a serious core of Tagore's creative oeuvres.

In Tagore's creative works 'woman' has become the site of conflictual positioning and perceptions, a battleground of the discursive and the real, the sensual and the sublime, the gross and the ideal. One would naturally think that Tagore was deeply confused in his understanding and hence representations of women. What adds to the impression is that his attitude to the 'feminine' and his representations of women vary from work to work, and also differ with the genre of his work. In Chapter 3, Mandakranta Bose 'Gender and Spiritual Quest in Tagore's Poetry' womanhood is manifest in the form and spirit of Radha, the eternal lover searching for her divine consort Lord Krishna. Contrarily, in the domain of fiction, as explored by Tirthankar Bose, Dipannita Datta and Chandrava Chakravarty (Chapters 8, 9 and 10), woman is the very site of contestation, erasure, denial and subversion. In poetry the notion of femininity as a sublime force changes radically to representations of a socially interpellated being, constrained by social norms and often deprived and abject in the domain of Tagore's fictional works. It would not be out of place to say that the distinction between *sheema* and the *asheem* (limit and limitlessness) also informs the basis of Tagore's understanding of 'woman'. She is asheem (boundless, eternal) as the very embodiment of love in *Bhanushingha Thakurer Padavali* or as the cosmic/spiritual force in the poem *Sabala;* contrarily, the women characters of his fictional world are bound by or embedded in societal codes. Hence, they are constrained or *sheemito.* We would not try to liberate 'woman' from the mystical nimbus in which she is often situated by Rabindranath. This is Tagore's inner perception of 'woman' as an ideal. Here she is *asheem*, the very incarnation of *mahashakti,* the embodiment of cosmic *ananda*, the eternal lover *Radhika* searching for her beloved *Krishna.* Referring to Sankaracharya's poem *'Ananda Lahari'* Tagore writes that spiritual, transcendental delight assumes the form of a woman as this universal shakti is present in the nature of woman.

> Let no one confuse this shakti with mere 'sweetness', for in this charm there is a combination of several qualities—patience, self-abnegation, sensitive intelligence, grace in thought, word and behaviour,—the reticent expression of rhythmic life, the tenderness and terribleness of love; at its core, moreover, is that self-radiant Spirit of Delight which ever gives itself up. (Tagore 2015b)

Tagore has situated 'woman' in two separate compartments of his mind: the inner mind has perceived her as a lofty ideal unsullied by man-made laws, codes and institutions. In 'The Religion of the Forest' Tagore explains the significance of the icon of the

Ardhanareeswara: 'This is the God Shiva, in whose nature Parvati, the eternal Woman, is ever commingled in an ascetic purity of love. The unified being of Shiva and Parvati is the perfect symbol of the eternal in the wedded love of man and woman' (Tagore 2015c). He laments that human civilization has not been able to recognize the 'reign of the spirit' (Tagore 2015b), and so it has failed to value the spiritual wealth of woman. Tagore repeatedly sings the glory of her power as he says in 'Woman and Home': 'True womanliness is regarded in our country as the saintliness of love' (Tagore 2015 d). He sees Dharini, the Queen in Kalidasa's play *Malavikagnimitra*, as the signifier of 'fortitude and forbearance that comes from majesty of soul! What an association it carries of the infinite dignity of love, purified by a self-abnegation that rises far above all insult and baseness of betrayal!' (Tagore 2015).

While essentialisms characterize 'woman' in the domain of Tagore's inner mind, women seen in a social context defy such essentialisms by their problematic relation to culture and history. The fictional world of Tagore embodies a vision of India torn between antagonistic values, struggling to constitute an identity of its own. Under the aegis of the British rule clash between traditional and 'modern' values, led to the questioning of several older sanctions and paved the way for newer modes of self-understanding. In the crucible of these troubled times the 'woman' question—her relation to home and the larger world, her position in the eternal struggle between love and sacrifice, her role in consolidating the identity of the Bengali *bhadralok*—the influential educated group who had access to western learning and who straddled the middle and upper castes—acquired primacy. Every grand meta-narrative of any dominant discourse of any period is bound to be assailed by instances of fissures, disjunctions, contradictions and silences in it. Tagore's fictional world creates space for a dialogue with contemporary society. It becomes the battleground of conservative and liberating impulses, of resistance against societal injustice and lame acquiescence to custom and upholds the tentative, vulnerable nature of colonial modernities. Thus, the 'New Woman', appearing in Tagore as *navina,* is posited at the core of the nationalist episteme and the notion of 'synthetic femininity' becomes a signifier for a number of signifieds. This is well brought out in the essays by

Tirthankar Bose, Dipannita Datta, Supriya Chaudhuri (Chapter 5), Sanjukta Dasgupta and Chandrava Chakravarty. The conservative vanguards of Hindu womanhood attacked Rabindranath for his sensitive explorations of woman's predicament in contemporary Bengali society as also for his non-conformist stances. Pointing to the works written after 1909, Sabyasachi Bhattacharya opines that a major ideational conflict in Tagore's works was 'between a "Hindu" notion of womanhood and the idea of self-empowerment of women in Indian society' (2011: 124).

In the novel *Gora,* the transformation of the initial belief of the protagonist, Gora, in woman's confinement to domesticity and his recognition of her potential in the mission of nation building depicts the progression of Tagore's convictions. Tagore envisages the politics of national self-determination and that of woman's self-determination as simultaneous. Yet, in the novel *Ghare-Baire (The Home and the World),* the nature and extent of woman's liberation emerge as vexed issues, especially, when the language of nation-worship is steeped in falsity. The novels *Chokher Bali, Noukadubi* and *Chaturanga* relate to some of the pressing social issues which rocked Bengali Hindu society towards the end of the nineteenth century. In several short stories and novels, Tagore presented a humane understanding of the woman's abjectness and did not hesitate to highlight her normal sexual needs. Both *Chokher Bali* and *Chaturanga* explore extramarital liaisons and subject the traditional sacramental Hindu marriage to a serious challenge. While *Jogajog* examines the issue of incompatibility in conjugal relationship, *Noukadubi* studies the threat posed to Hindu marriage by an accidental change of wife. In all these novels, women characters occupy cardinal positions, and in many they are projected as subversive to the hegemonic structure.

In several short stories published in the journal *Sabuj Patra,*[4] Tagore depicts woman's resistance to a cruel patriarchy. In stories like 'Shasti', 'Didi' or 'Manbhanjan' woman's insecurity and social cruelty have figured explicitly. 'Postmaster', 'Denapaona' and 'Khata' have repeatedly brought to the fore woman's loneliness and deprivation. In 'Streer Patra' patriarchal violence is subtly manifested. Expression of feminist consciousness, as discussed by Nandini Bhattacharya, was articulated in a woman's voice for the first time in Bengali literature through Mrinal's craving for *mukti* or freedom. Tagore's frequent glorification of woman is accompanied by the lament that her great potential has been wasted and corrupted in human societies from time immemorial: 'That is why man, by dint of his efforts to bind woman, has made her the strongest of fetters for his own bondage. That is why woman is debarred from adding to the spiritual wealth of society by the perfection of her own nature, and all human societies are weighed down with the burden of the resulting poverty' (Tagore 2015b). Mrinal's husband in 'Streer Patra' is too feudal to realize this inner poverty, but what about the 'modern' Bengali bhadralok? Tagore presents the cruel nonchalance of an intellectual, modern husband through his own self-analysis in *Poila Nambar* (Number 1). Like Mrinal, Aneela of *Poila Nambar* has also left home to protest against the cold indifference of her husband. Rabindranath could see through the pretentions of colonial modernity with regard to its concern for women. The reiteration of woman's essential humanity, as discussed by Malini Bhattacharya (Chapter 4), has become the theme of *Chandalika* who has demanded respect as a human being; in *Chitrangada* Arjun's ultimate recognition of Chitrangada's inner wealth has made outward beauty irrelevant. Amita Dutt (Chapter 15) talks about how as a choreographer she visualizes this moment of recognition. Despite Tagore's relentless effort to understand the 'feminine', the gap between idealization and actuality had remained irreconcilable. In the domain of extramarital, consensual love Tagore's relationships with real women had been tentative and fragile. His love for Kadambari, his *natun bouthan,* who died prematurely left him shattered to the core. But she still remained vibrant in his imagination, a presence felt in the depth of his soul: 'You are not here before my eye:/ Within the eye you have taken your place.' The ideal is livelier than the real because she has transcended the body to merge with nature: 'You are green among the foliage, blue amid the sky./ My universe in you/ Has discovered its soul's harmony'(Tagore 2015b).

The course of romantic love was mostly beset with uncertainties in Rabindranath's life as he would ask fervently: ... *bhalobasha kare koy!* (What is love?). Tagore met Victoria Ocampo when he was sixty-three, taught her the Bengali word *bhalobasha* (love), and saw in her a possibility of assuaging his need for companionship. The friendship of Tagore and Ocampo is, according to Jayati Gupta

(Chapter 11), a pointer to the platonic relationship that the poet often nurtured with foreign women to redeem a sense of loss. He wrote to Victoria: 'It is difficult for you to realize what an enormous burden of loneliness I carry about me ... my personal value has been obscured. This can be had only from a woman's love ...' (Dyson 1988: 374). According to Dyson, Victoria or Vijaya, as Tagore renamed her, deeply respected and loved the poet. But soon they parted ways, Tagore growing restless with the burden of mutual expectations and realizing that the difference of language and culture would never allow him to give himself away fully to Victoria.[5] She, however, remained a distant inspiration amidst Tagore's restless sojourns and blossomed in his poems.[6]

The examples of Tagore's tireless attempt to understand 'woman' would be endless. In fact, Tagore's songs and dance have also opened up spaces for woman's self-expression. This volume will make a modest attempt to study Rabindranath Tagore's polyphonic engagement with 'woman' and the dialogic nature of her representations. We, however, undertake this journey with the caveat: *Sesh nahi je/ Sesh katha ke bolbe?* (Who will say the last word about that which is endless? translation by Chandrava Chakravarty).

III

A few words on the title might help in understanding the nature of the critical intervention undertaken here and explain the choice of topics covered in the essays. The issues of 'subjectivity' and individual subject-formation have predominated in the history of ideas to connote the ways in which individual subject-formations are enmeshed with and determined by larger socio-cultural and related domains of public experiences. The relative ability of individuals to exert their own free will in their self-fashioning has been a subject of never-ending debate. Western philosophers ranging from Plato to Descartes have emphasized the importance of the freedom of the self and self-construction over the constraints of social construction. Most postmodern thinkers have systematically challenged such positivism. Michel Foucault's discursive analysis of individual subject-formation highlights how every human identity is formed and controlled by a complex intersection of socially discursive practices and institutions. The influence and impositions of society on individual subjectivities can both be formative and destructive to the self and ego. In relation to the emergence of women's subjectivity the issues are even more complicated. Feminist historians have deciphered the traces of extreme repression and denial of female individuality. The making and consequent unmaking of female selfhood have always been a stressful process fraught with gaps and contradictions. Chris Weedon's analysis (1987) of major feminist theorists like Julia Kristeva and Hélène Cixous points to the essential contradictions of women's subjectivity:

> Although the subject in poststructuralism is socially constructed in discursive practices, she nonetheless exists as a thinking, feeling subject and social agent, capable of resistance and innovations produced out of the clash between contradictory subject positions and practices. She is also a subject able to reflect upon the discursive relations which constitute her and the society in which she lives, and able to choose from the options available (125).

Thus, within the construction of female subjectivity there is a strong social pressure to relegate it to the realm of 'otherization' and the consequent counter-discursive practices of resistance and interventions to contest the rigid social boundaries.

This edited volume aims to explore the ways in which Tagore understood and represented the struggles and dilemmas of female subject formation. The title of the book indicates the trajectories of growth and change that women's subjectivity undergoes through the layers that produce complex and mature female subject-positions capable of contesting subjection and gender discrimination. The binary of making/unmaking points to the social forces the female self has to encounter, endure or resist. The essays attempt to critically read the individual fictional instances of female identity-formation that Tagore offers in terms of their dynamic self-articulations, interrogations of societal norms and consequent transformations.

Tagore's works are by no means dated and their appeal will never remain confined to the nineteenth-century alone. It is no exaggeration to claim that the issues regarding gender, womanhood and patriarchy broached in Tagore's writings continue to intrigue and haunt us to this day for their ideological immensity and intellectual profundity All the essays in this volume explore in detail the complex aesthetics and ideologies expressed in Tagore's works. They focus on issues like Tagore's spirituality, gender ideology, aesthetics and morality with a common aim to underscore the importance of Tagore's responsibility as a writer and social thinker. Twentieth- and twenty-first century womanhood and female liberation may appear to have advanced far more than Tagore had anticipated, but the originary moments of female emancipation and gender equality will always have Tagore as one of its pioneering and consolidating contributors in the history of world thought.

There seems to be a very deep trans-historical link as far as Tagore's vision of womanhood and contemporary femalehood are construed. It is, therefore, not very irrelevant to recall the seductive and enigmatic widow character Binodini from Tagore's *Choker Bali* or the progressive and enlightened Sucharita in *Gora* and the feisty Damini from *Chaturanga* (Chapter 9) as nineteenth-century women much ahead of their times and who are capable of inspiring today's woman. On the one hand, Tagore's women are historically rooted and are typical products of nineteenth-century Bengali patriarchy and on the other hand, as symbols of youth, freedom and colonial modernity their presence and influence cannot be confined to any one age or generation. The relevance of Tagore's vision of gender justice, his critique of patriarchal orthodoxies and his sensitive and layered representation of women in all his works cannot be undermined in our times where the fight for gender equality and justice is still not complete in our country. Moreover, if Tagore is seen as the most canonical 'Victorian' writer who encompasses all the representative tendencies of the long nineteenth century in colonial Bengal, his works continue to remind us of the necessity of understanding the nineteenth century as the historical and socio-cultural matrix of the postmodern condition. If our age can be considered an extension of nineteenth-century colonial modernity, Tagore's relevance as arguably the best thinker of his own age is as strong as ever. His proto-feministic re-configuring of patriarchy and the role of women comes down to us as a historical legacy that both inspires and provokes contemporary scholars and readers alike. In fact, Tagore's 'Victorianism' encourages us to engage with a 'neo-Victorian' revival and often subversive critique of the long nineteenth-century world order.

Divided into six parts, Part I: Beyond Essentialism begins with 'Tagore and Women: Some Thoughts' by Jasodhara Bagchi that offers an overview on gender in Tagore's works and acts as a fitting prologue to the rest of the book, exploring the public sphere/private sphere divide as negotiated by Tagore's women to re-orient, re-inforce and sometimes challenge the clearly defined social spaces of the inner and the outer worlds. Chapter 2, 'Shantiniketan Education for Girls' by Uma Das Gupta critically focuses on the consolidation of female education as pioneered by Tagore. She points out that Tagore's conceptualization of female education garnered great enthusiasm within and without Bengal and even sometimes abroad.

Part II Nature and Spirituality begins with Chapter 3, 'Gender and the Spiritual Quest in Tagore's Poetry' by Mandakranta Bose that draws upon Tagore's essential engagement with the Vaishnava literary tradition and his feminization of the quester-figure's search for love and spiritual fulfilment. By focusing mainly on the text of *Bhanusingha Thakurer Padavali* she argues that Tagore locates in woman an idealistic spirituality that makes her the 'most faithful seeker' of love and atonement. Chapter 4 'Rabindranath's Chandalika: Woman as Prakriti and Prakriti in Woman' by Malini Bhattacharya extends this discussion to an intensive analysis of the intrinsic relationship of the female nature with Mother Nature; both being versions of the concept of *prakriti* as articulated in the Tagorean corpus. *Chandalika*, a dance-drama resonates with the nature/culture divide as manifested through women.

Part III Realm of Domesticity opens with Chapter 5 'Domestic Space in Tagore's Fiction' by Supriya Chaudhuri which looks at how physical space and mental space are interlinked in the lives of Tagore's female protagonists re-defining the polyvalent domesticity of the typical nineteenth-century andarmahal. As she says, 'For Tagore and his characters, especially the women who, in all his fiction, feel most intensely the imprisoning confines of domestic space, intimations of infinitude pierce through the constrictions of physical existence'(17). Chapter 6 'Tagore's Docile Daughters: Ambivalence in Family Life' by Sanjukta Dasgupta presents a thought-provoking analysis of the issue of women's marginalization, victimization and systematic subordination by the very patriarchal institution of marriage as discussed by Tagore the thinker and as practised by Tagore the father. Chapter 7 'Re-reading Rabindranath Tagore's 'Streer

Patra' (the Wife's Letter, 1914) in the Light of Epistolary Culture in Colonial India' by Nandini Bhattacharya captivates Tagore's representation of women reaching out to their conjugal partners through letters, and deals with Tagore's utilization of the much publicized vernacular epistolary device as a form shaping conjugality in colonial Bengal. She diligently argues how writing letters became a focal point of female self-expression, implicating freedom, self-autonomy and emancipation that readily destabilized the stable relational hierarchies of an orthodox conjugality.

Part IV Selfhood and Agency opens with Chapter 8 'How to Fool Women: Tagore's Tales of Seduction' by Tirthankar Bose. He discerns the deception inherent in love encountered by Tagore's seduced women who embattle victimhood and refuse to remain at the receiving end of patriarchal sexual politics. It very adroitly brings into focus Tagore's very nuanced and radical textual representation of the so-called Victorian fallen woman located in nineteenth-century Bengal. Chapter 9 'The Dichotomies of Body and Mind Spaces: The Widows in *Choker Bali* and *Chaturanga*' by Chandrava Chakravarty discusses the representation of widows in Tagore's *oeuvre* in the context of the social connotations of widowhood in nineteenth-century Bengal. Chapter 10 'Bimala Is What She Is: Re-reading Bimala and Gender (In)justice in Rabindranath's *The Home and the World*' by Dipannita Datta analyses the interlink between gender and nation as reflected through the character of Bimala in Tagore's novel *Ghare-Baire*.

Part V Women in Travel Writings begins with Chapter 11 'The "Other" Women in Tagore's Travels to Europe' by Jayati Gupta. She brings the focus on Tagore's interactions with European women and how these shaped his attitude towards the opposite sex. Chapter 12 'Rabindranath's Travelogues and the Absent Female Voice' by Amrit Sen, however, critiques Tagore's sidelining of female agency and perspectives in his travelogues when there was a simultaneous emergence of travel-writing by women in Bengal. Both these essays utilize the rich possibilities underscored by the interface of travel theory and gender discourses in Tagore's travelogues.

In Part VI Women in Other Arts Chapter 13 'Gender in Rabindrasangeet' by Debashish Raychaudhuri concentrates upon the feminine space and articulation of gendered emotions, claiming that Tagore's music and lyrics pioneered the balancing of male and female voices, emotions and perspectives. Chapter 14 'Breaking the Mould: The Paintings of Rabindranath Tagore' by Tapati Gupta analyses how Tagore's visual representation of femininity renders women enigmatic and problematizes the male gaze. Chapter 15 'Women in Tagore's Dance-Dramas' by Amita Dutt highlights his major dance-dramas *Chandalika* (1935), *Chitrangada* (1937) and *Shyama* (1939), and argues that Tagore's dance forms and lyrics articulates the performative potential of his multifarious ideologies of womanhood. Chapter 16, 'Tagore's New Woman the Contradictions of Patriarchy: Adapting *Char Adhyay* as *Elar Char Adhyay*' by Sneha Kar Chaudhuri discusses one of the recent film adaptation of Tagore's novel *Char Adhyay* (1934) as *Elar Char Adhyay* (2012) by Bappaditya Bandopadhyay to explore the rich interactions of Tagore's visions of womanhood and nationalism and the uses to which these discourses are put in a cinematic adaptation. This essay also extends the discussion of Tagore and woman beyond Tagore's own works and times by analysing how contemporary intelligentsia re-visits, revives and revises Tagore for the postmodern cultural imaginary.

Tagore's works are still popular with both lay and informed readers because his works contain certain insights that keep intriguing and engaging us across centuries and generations. Moreover, he belongs to the great tradition of the Bengal Renaissance, the intellectual legacy of a period that has continuously informed and sustained our contemporary culture in the ideological and experiential domains. Tagore's legacy and contribution has often been criticised but never ignored in both the centuries. The modernity of Tagore's vision has inspired us to imitate him even today and the richness of his aesthetic explorations has charmed us. The issues that he has engaged with in his works have been of continuous relevance to our generation and we have read Tagore to understand many of our ideological contradictions regarding gender, love, patriarchy and other related ideas. Our presentist understanding of Tagore has lent his works a historical relativism and timeless appeal that allows every reader to compare and contrast his age with ours. As a collection of Tagore scholarship, this volume is an evergreen tribute to our very own Rabindranath Tagore. The essays seek to establish how he is with us and how he remains a prominent and necessary part of our cultural imaginary in the twenty-first century.

NOTES

1 Tagore's lecture in America dwells on the idea of a transcendental Indian womanhood irrespective of caste, class, religious and regional differences, and the many extant Hinduisms. However, he places his concept of womanhood within an overarching Hindu philosophic construction of *Prakriti* and *Shakti* as feminine space. See Ashis Nandy, 'Woman Versus Womanliness in India ' (2007: 32–46).

2 The term 'Pirali' historically carried a stigmatized and pejorative connotation because someone or some individuals within the lineage had converted to Islam. Muhammad Tahir Pir Ali, who served under a governor of Jessore was a brahmin who converted to Islam; his actions resulted in the additional conversion of two of his brothers. As a result, orthodox Hindu society shunned the brothers' Hindu relatives (who had not converted).

3 Saudamini Tagore's *Pitrismriti* is referred to in Chitra Deb (2010): 23, 25–26.

4 The journal (1914–27) was edited by Pramatha Chowdhury and was inspired by Tagore. Though short-lived it was a major force in remoulding Bengali language and literary style for the post-World War I generation.

5 A letter to Ocampo from Tagore, 13 January 1925. See Dyson, 1988: 390–94.

6 For a detailed account of the relation between Tagore and Ocampo see Note 5.

REFERENCES

Bhattacharya, Sabyasachi. 2011. *Rabindranath Tagore: An Interpretation*. New Delhi: Penguin India.

Bose, Sugata. 2012. *Tagore: The World Voyager.* Translated by Sugata Bose. Noida: Random House India.

Chaudhuri, Sukanta (ed.). 2004. 'The Picture'. *Selected Poems: Rabindranath Tagore*. New Delhi: Oxford University Press.

Deb, Chitra. 2010. *Women of the Tagore Household*. Translated by Smita Chowdhury and Sona Roy. New Delhi: Penguin India.

Dyson, Ketaki Kushari. 1988. *Your Blossoming Flower Garden: Rabindranath Tagore and Victoria Ocampo*. New Delhi: Sahitya Akademi.

Nandy, Ashis. 2007. 'Woman versus Womanliness in India: An Essay in Cultural and Political Psychology', in *Exiled at Home*. New Delhi: Oxford University Press: 32–47.

Tagore, Rabindranath, 2015a. *'Prachya Nareer Sadhana'*. Bichitra: Online Tagore Variorum prepared by School of Cultural Texts and Records. Jadavpur University: Government of India, Ministry of Culture.

———. 2015b. 'The Indian Ideal of Marriage.' Bichitra: Online Tagore Variorum: School of Cultural Texts and Records. Jadavpur University: Government of India, Ministry of Culture.

———. 2015c. 'The Religion of the Forest.' Bichitra.

———. 2015d. 'Woman and Home.' Bichitra.

———. 2004. 'Woman', in *Rabindranath Tagore: Selected Essays*. New Delhi: Rupa Publications.

———. 1997. *Selected Letters of Rabindranath Tagore*. Translated by Krishna Dutta and Andrew Robinson. Cambridge: Cambridge University Press.

PART I

BEYOND ESSENTIALISM

CHAPTER 1

Tagore and Woman: Some Thoughts

Jasodhara Bagchi

The works of Rabindranath Tagore have always come to us with new challenges of entering into a dialogic relationship with the maestro. In the varied discussions that have come up, it is made amply clear that the creative space opened up by fresh readings of Tagore in recent times, has been enormous, and there is scope for a great deal more. One of the most fruitful areas that has opened up fresh perspectives on established authors has been, there is no denying, the burgeoning of feminist scholarship that has offered rich interdisciplinary insights into Tagore's writings.

Professor Pradip Kumar Datta's edited volume (2003) of critical writings on Tagore's novel, *Ghare-Baire*, brought feminist critical thinking into easy alliance with insights from history, politics, philosophical and literary studies. The readings glided with ease over the intimate *andarmahal* and the perilous public spaces of *bahir*. That is why perhaps, 'woman' is talked about being the signified of many signifiers. Extending this further, it can be pleaded that that is why we should talk about *women* rather than *woman* in the text and context of Tagore. There is no finality, hence, it is difficult to speak the final word.

While being a demanding author, we must admit, Tagore is also an indulgent one. Being a great champion of the inner world of *mon* (heart), he is against prohibition. There is no bar in getting lost, in my mind. Hence, I would like to begin with my involvement with Tagore. Although I had learnt my Bengali alphabet not from *Sahaj Path* but from *Barnaparichay*,[1] Tagore was my childhood companion through his songs, a very early authentic channel of creative expressivity. From his early involvement with a range of varied and often contradictory musical traditions—hymnic music, Indian classical

music of Jadubhatta and others, *Vaishnava padavali*, western lyrical experiments, especially Scottish and Irish melodies, strong folk
traditions of singing, especially of *bauls*—the most extraordinary
harvest of modernity in colonial Bengal, that is, Rabindrasangeet,
emerged. In Rabindrasangeet, Tagore has combined the androgyny
of our native Bhakti tradition and the fruit of western Romantic
tradition.

The end product is the release of women's voices, women's
subjectivity, women's emotions and women's passions that helped,
with great effectiveness, to bend the wall—the inner and outer—
into a bridge between the two. The significance of the music that
Rabindranath created was not simply in the unique combination
of making music and poetry open out towards women's affective
and expressive features in both the text and context, but the unfore-
seen possibilities of women's space in rendition and reception. It
resulted in opening up a new social space for a new class subjectivity
in which women were not to lag behind men. What started off in the
well-to-do familial space of Tagore's Jorasanko home had enough
generative power to flood the social space of the newly emerging
bhadramahila of Bengal. This revolutionized the class subjectivity
as well as the experience of agency of women in colonial Bengal.
When postmodernists talk about the emergence of modernity in the
lives of colonial women, as the white men saving the brown women
from the brown men, they seem to be oblivious of the spaces of
selfhood which were opened by new forms of self-expression, well
beyond the ken of white masters.

Rabindranath's songs provide one such major arena which
has not yet been exhaustively analysed by feminist performers and
scholars (although the process has begun) nor am I offering such
an analysis myself. Instead of which I may be pardoned if I offer a
slice of personal anecdote from my mother's life. In her generation,
there was something of an unspoken taboo against women singing and performing in public, as it was not freed from a hint of an
illicit female sexuality. When Sarala Devi directed *Mayar Khela* on
a public stage in Kolkata (most probably in aid of my old school,
Gokhale Memorial Girls' School, founded by Mrs. Sarala Ray, to
whom the play was dedicated by Tagore), she had to gather together
girls (it is true from well-to-do families) who could sing, as dance

was still not indispensable to the operatic play, which had an unmistakable dose of the erotic, not only male, but also female. It was an all-female cast, girls playing male roles, as indeed, was done by my mother. Many years later, my mother had vivid memories of Tagore demonstrating the movements that were to make the songs in the drama expressive and the simple devices used by his daughter-in-law Pratima Devi for appropriate make-up for the stage. An interesting social fall out was the rousing of mild erotic interest, which saw two marriages consequent upon the performance. My mother, belonging to a more conservative Hindu family had to escape from a bunch of young men calling upon her by asking the darwan to say that she was not at home! Such was the chemistry of girls singing in public.

However, what caused anxiety to this urban middle-class girl was absent in Tagore's own ashram where it was accepted as part of the freedom and play with which Tagore infused education. Among such performing *Ashramkanyas* were the two famous Amita Sens. The dancer was my father's cousin, Kshitimohan Sen's youngest daughter, who has written very eloquently on her emancipatory experience of dance. The singer was the aunt of Binayak Sen whose songs (among which was *Ogo Bodhu Sundari Tumi Modhu Monjori*) resounded in Shantiniketan and beyond. Both Sarala Devi and Indira Devi, Tagore's nieces from two siblings, were custodians of his songs, and we are indeed grateful to Indira Devi's niece Supurna and her husband Subhash Chaudhuri for having perpetuated her name in the musical organization *Indira Goshthi*.

Tagore's presentation of women has always been subtle, self-contradictory and subversive of the usual politics of gender representation. It is one of the most difficult propositions to generalize about Tagore's creative engagement with women. One pertinent question in this respect is, which Tagore are we thinking of when we try to locate his complex relationship with women? Is it Tagore the poet? Tagore the writer of prose-fiction, both long and short? Tagore the dramatist and actor? Tagore the writer and performer of songs that re-created, the androgyny of our Vaishnava tradition of musical performance and of western Romanticism alike? Tagore the social thinker, the great innovator of new education in Shantiniketan and rural reconstruction in Sriniketan? Tagore, the writer of letters to non-relatives like Hemantbala or Ranu Adhikari, or to the relatives like Indira Devi or *chhuti* Mrinalini? Or, is it Tagore the painter, whose futurist leap brings him closest to our times in the most obvious way? It is not easy to map the source of this multitudinous creativity that leads it to our own times. Woman, in Tagore's lines, both visual and aural, is, indeed a *bichitrarupini*, a multi-faceted polyvalent entity, who cannot be simply contained in one predictable basket.

The one area in which feminist historians and literary critics have thrown a great deal of light is in reading his fictional representation of women as a subtle commentary on the evolving pattern of the Indian polity under the colonial rule of the British. Historians like Tanika and Sumit Sarkar, literary critics like Sutapa Bhattacharya, Malini Bhattacharya, Supriya Chaudhuri, Mihir Bhattacharya or Rushati Sen have brought out, during the past decade and a half, the enormous subtlety and finesse with which Tagore has presented women in the mesh of social relations, which has lit up the inner and outer fabric of an emerging class in colonial Bengal. I would like to add that Tagore was a rare exception in the ways he practised the politics of gendered representation of the nation. There was a remarkable ability on the part of Tagore to be sensitively open to the fissures and ruptures in the stereotyping of gender in the cultural nationalism that prevailed since the end of the nineteenth century and spilt over to the agitations against *Banga Bhanga* that marked the first decade of the twentieth century. Tagore responded creatively in his famous novels, *Gora* and *Ghare-Baire*. *Gora* depicted the earlier streak of Revivalism stoked by Chandranath Basu's *Hindutva* and expounded in his *Savitritatwa* and, of course, Bankimchandra's *Anandamath* which lent a real political signification to *Bande Mataram*. But Tagore's most trenchant critique of its use in the exclusionary politics of Swadeshi nationalism was made in *Ghare-Baire*. In both the novels, the reified essentialisms of a Hindu mother and that of a Hindu wife are displaced by exploring the social dynamics of a family in its rich interiority. There is a point that needs to be mentioned here—the division between private and public that was designated as the gender division of social space since the early days of feminist criticism has to be read in Tagore with considerable complexity.

The gendered division of space is considered as one of the major hallmarks of the patriarchal re-ordering, whereby the 'domestic' or the inner domain came to be perceived as the woman's domain, with little or no social recognition of her contribution. The outer domain was that of paid work, political and economic engagement with society, in which men found the full fruition of their active citizenship. One may recall that though a gendered division of domain was a central perspective of the second wave feminist resurgence in the West since the mid-sixties of the twentieth century, the impact of this feminist theory escaped from the deliberations during Tagore's centenary celebrations. In recent times, there are marked signs of coming to terms with this analytical tool, especially since the world of Tagore's creativity is inconceivable without women. However, as I have been suggesting since the beginning, Tagore's use of women is too multitudinous to be confined to the gender stereotyping of the outer versus the inner, or the political versus the domestic. For Tagore, women are an essential ingredient of the 'social', with all the complex dynamics that this entails, something that cannot be either simplified or reified, in an age where there was concerted attempt to 'fix' Indian womanhood both by the Empire loyalists and by the cultural nationalists.

An ironical echo of this convergence may be seen in Katherine Mayo's choice of the title *Mother India* for her unabashed apology for continuation of the British rule in India, and the Abanindranath/Nivedita combine in the painting *Mother India* and Nivedita's commentary on it. In applying feminist analysis to Tagore's writings, one cannot be over careful with discrimination and finesse, since Tagore cherished with great care a sense of wholeness that was never too shy to negotiate fissures. As I have argued in an article (Bagchi 2011a) women's confinement to the inner spaces was not necessarily a negative phenomenon in the eyes of Tagore. The inner domain or andarmahal was the space of freedom from the oppressive compulsions of the outer domain of the political and the economic relations of ruling. However, this has to be firmly distinguished from the essentialized Hindu family reified by the identity-based nationalists in which women as icons were meant to find their ideal space as wives and mothers, discussed with power and sensitivity by Tanika Sarkar on several occasions (2009; 2003; 2001). For Tagore's creative imagination showed itself open to the pain and fractures with which this freedom was fraught. After all he has captured in his verse the most memorable articulation of the tedium of domestic chores that is more than a match for Simone de Beauvoir's (2009 [1949]) eternal struggle against dust and dirt! There was a shift, in Tagore's imaginary, from what Sutapa Bhattacharya has called the 'Ruskinian' or the domestic orientation of women from his *Sabuj Patra* days in the beginning of the twentieth century.[2] A fuller argument for this has been, in fact, most notably provided by Sumit Sarkar (2003).

With all his celebrations of the andarmahal allotted to women, Tagore had shown poignant awareness of the imprisonment of women within the patriarchal family in many literary creations of which, Mrinal of 'Streer Patra' and Kumu of *Yogayog* are the most widely disseminated (Sarkar 2003; Chaudhuri 2006). As we know, there are many others in his poems, short and long fiction alike. What is noticeable is the absence of any over-simplified presentation of women, often presented through images that are self-contradictory. We will do well to remember that for Rabindranath the woman question was not to be abstracted from the mesh of social relations: it had not been resolved; hence it could only be perceived as woven into a rich understanding of society. That women's exclusion from the main highway of life was an integral part of it has been demonstrated in the complex modes of Tagore's thinking about interrelated social exclusions in which women have occupied major spaces (or, shall we say, non-spaces?). The cinema has been a late medium that has most sensitively brought out this dialectic very effectively. One of the major areas in which Rabindranath's vision of women's capability has found newer possibilities is in ensuring that the human is kept alive within a crisis-ridden civilization. While this general observation may be seen to operate in many of his literary genres, I would briefly like to point to the prominence he has given to girls and young women in his plays. From the dawn of his *natyik* (a far more graphic way of expressing the dramatic) visions of plots, often seen in dreams, he has invented the figure of girls or young women, who have stood for the principle of life, compassion and social justice.

From *Prakritir Pratisodh* onwards the outer worlds riddled with violence and love of power, have been redeemed by girls or young women who have strayed into this perilous space. This is a major part of what the theatre person Soumitra Basu has called the 'inner face' (*antarmukh*) of Rabindranath's plays (Basu 2011). After all, it is Sudha, the flower girl who does not fail to keep her promise to Amal in *Dakghar*. While his sensitivity to the pull of women's andarmahal which he has written about so eloquently in *Jivan Smriti* as well as in many of the poems of *Sisu* and *Sisu Bholanath* and his innate faith in the efficacy of the affective over the merely ratiocinative, Tagore's notion of woman power often follows unconventional directions and opens up new vistas of possibility. The commitment of Tagore to pluralism is being increasingly harnessed in our fight against social exclusion. Together with caste, class and ethnicity, gender is at the centre of social exclusion. Tagore's literary output has presented this intricate process of marginalization of women in its many refractions.

Starting with the *jal-achal* untouchable girl in Chandalika, significantly called Prakriti, whose sense of humanity is restored by Ananda, the follower of Buddha, who moreover acquires her inner sense of human dignity only after a long process of vain sexual appropriation has been abandoned, we have figure after figure of women from different walks of life, struggling with sexuality and a sense of self-worth. The Manipuri Princess Chitrangada, the Queen in *Raja* and *Arup Ratan*, Labanya in *Shesher Kabita*, Charulata in *Nashtanir*, Ela, the fiery defender of social justice in her final moment of love and violence in *Char Adhyay*, to take a few random examples, the struggle of women with their socially defined positions, their sexuality and their complex self-worth defies the oversimplification of the 'inner' versus the 'outer'. The border-crossing women in Tagore's creativity are discovering newer spaces. One such important extension is provided by Malini Bhattacharya (2011) in her article 'Nandini of Jakkhapuri and the Crisis of Civilization'. As Malini Bhattacharya has beautifully argued, the human, and not a reified feminine regenerative role of Nandini in *Raktakarabi*, is potent enough to extend to the 'crisis of civilization' to which Tagore alerted the world many years later, towards the end of his life (ibid.). This was a social role of humanity that does not have to be cramped into the iconic image of the redemptive Mother Goddess with which the Revivalist Nationalists had used gendered representation. It is quite clear, therefore, that the problem of feminist politics in Tagore's creativity has to be treated with considerable care and finesse. His exploration of women has many refractions that need to negotiate many ambiguities and binaries, intimate, as well as covering perilous outer spaces in a society that he knew and felt to be under colonial/imperialist shackles. Being a highly committed intellectual, he harped constantly on the most effective and un-stereotypical ways of resisting the hegemonic. While acknowledging the contribution of great Tagore scholars like Sankha Ghose and that of the recent crop of bright scholars, I hope the challenge in the new millennium will constantly prompt us to explore Tagore's superb delving into the interiority of women's spaces taking on board the intricate challenges in the public spaces—colonial politics, property relations, creativity, the erotic and other such complex demands of Indian modernity.

NOTES

1   In *Barnoparichay* (1854), Iswar Chandra Vidyasagar reconstructed the Bengali alphabet and reformed Bengali typography into an alphabet of twelve vowels and forty consonants. This was used as a primer to teach children Bengali. Much later, Tagore published a primer, *Sahej Path* that proved to be very popular.
2   See Introduction, Note 4.

REFERENCES

Bagchi, Jasodhara. 2011a. '*Rabindra-lekhanite Ma o Matritwa*', in *Rabindranath Bakpati Bisvamana*, edited by Sudhir Chakravarti, vol.1. Rabindranath Tagore Centre for Human Development Studies, 137–52.

——. 2011b. 'Reading Mother/Reading Swadesh: The Case of Rabindranath's *Gora*', in *Rabindranath and the Nation: Essays in Politics and Culture*, edited by Swati Ganguly and Abhijit Sen. Kolkata: Punashcha in association with Visva-Bharati, 205–19.

——. 2010 (1995). 'Representing Nationalism, the Ideology of Motherhood in Colonial Bengal', Review of Women's Studies, *Economic and Political Weekly/Motherhood in India Glorification without Empowerment*, edited by Maithreyi Krishnaraj. New Delhi: Routledge, 158–85.

Bagchi, Jasodhara. 2009. 'Gender Issues in Social Exclusion', N.K. Bose Memorial Lecture, *Geographical Review of India* I, 71, 2, June, 105–16.

———. 2003. 'Anandamath and the Home and the World: Positivism Reconfigured', in *Rabindranath Tagore's* The Home and the World: *A Critical Companion*, edited by P.K. Datta. New Delhi: Permanent Black, 174–86.

———. 1996. 'Secularism as Identity: The Case of Tagore's *Gora*', in *The Nation, the State and Indian Identity*, edited by Madhusree Datta, Flavia Agnes and Neera Adarkar. Calcutta: Samya, 45–61.

———. 1990. 'Women since Independence', in *Calcutta, Living City,* edited by Sukanta Chaudhuri. New Delhi: Oxford University Press, 42–49.

Basu, Soumitra. 2011. '*Rabindranataker Antarmukh*', in *Rabindranath Bakpati Bisvamana*, edited by Sudhir Chakravarti, vol. 2: 159–69.

Beauvoir, Simone de. 2009 [1949]. *The Second Sex*, translated by Constance Borde and Sheila Malovany-Chevallier. Random House: Alfred A. Knopf.

Bhattacharya, Malini. 2011. '*Jakkhapurir Nandini o Sabhyatar Sankat*', in *Eksathe Sharad, 1418*, 63–70.

———. 2003. 'Gora and The Home and the World: The Long Quest for Modernity', in *Rabindranath Tagore's* The Home and the World: *A Critical Companion*, edited by P.K. Datta. New Delhi: Permanent Black, 127–42.

Bhattacharya, Mihir. 1991. 'Rabindranath Tagore and the Oriental Woman: A Reading of *Chaturanga*', in *Literature, Society and Ideology in the Victorian Era*, edited by Jasodhara Bagchi. New Delhi: Sterling Publishers Private Limited, 316–25.

Bhattacharya, Sutapa. 2011. '*Rabindra Upanyashe Prem ebong Premika*', SWS SRTT Occasional Paper no.12, Jadavpur University: School of Women's Studies.

———. 1990. *Se Nahi Nahi*. Shantiniketan Visva-Bharati Gabeshana Bibhag.

Chakravarti, Sudhir. 2011, May and August. *Rabindranath Bakpati Bisvamana*. Rabindranath Centre for Development Studies and IDSK.

Chaudhuri, Supriya. 2006. Rabindranath Tagore *Relationships (Jogajog)*, translated with an Introduction by Supriya Chaudhuri. New Delhi: Oxford University Press.

———. 2003. 'Love and Marriage in *Ghare Bairey*', in *Rabindranath Tagore's* The Home and the World: *A Critical Companion*, edited by P.K. Datta, 45–65.

Datta, P.K. (ed.). 2003. *Rabindranath Tagore's* The Home and the World: *A Critical Companion*. New Delhi: Permanent Black.

Ray, Bharati. 2010. 'Introduction to Rabindranath Tagore', in *Three Novellas* Nastanir, Dui Bon, Malancha, translated from Bengali by Sukhendu Ray. New Delhi: Oxford University Press, xiii–xxxvii.

Sarkar, Sumit. 2003. '*Ghare Bairey* in Its Time', in *Rabindranath Tagore's* The Home and the World: *A Critical Companion*, edited by P.K. Datta. New Delhi: Permanent Black: 143–73.

Sarkar, Tanika. 2009. 'Questioning Nationalism: The Difficult Writings of Rabindranath Tagore', in *Rebels, Wives and Saints. Designing Selves and Nations in Colonial Times.* New Delhi: Permanent Black, 229–67.

———. 2003. 'Many Faces of Love, Country, Woman and God in the Home and the World', in *Rabindranath Tagore's* The Home and the World: *A Critical Companion*, edited by P.K. Datta. New Delhi: Permanent Black: 27–44.

———. 2001. '*Mrinal onno itihaser swakshar*', in *Adhunikatar du-ek dik Dharma, Sahitya o Rajniti.* Kolkata, Camp, 35–46.

Sen, Rushati. 2011. '*Moner Sharir o Shorirer Mon*', in *Rabindranath Bakpati Bisvamana*, edited by Sudhir Chakravarti, vol. 2. Kolkata: Rabindranath Tagore Centre for Human Rights, 2011: 112–22.

Sen Gupta, Pallab (ed.). 2009 [2002]. *Ami Nari, Ami Mahiyashi*. Kolkata: National Book Agency.

CHAPTER 2

Shantiniketan: Education for Girls

Uma Das Gupta

Rabindranath Tagore's Shantiniketan school began as a school for boys in 1901, but in effect it was co-educational throughout because the teachers' daughters were a part of the school and its activities from its inception. Jamuna, who was Nandalal Bose's younger daughter, sat in the school's classes from the age of six when they moved to Shantiniketan in 1919 (see interview of Jamuna Sen by Uma Das Gupta). A dedicated girls' section was added to the Shantiniketan school in 1908. But this had to close down within two years. Rabindranath was sorry to have to send the girls home. Hemlata Gupta (née Sen), sister of Kiranbala Sen, Kshitimohan Sen's wife, was one of the girl students admitted in 1908.[1] She remembered what Rabindranath said when closing down the girls' section in 1910 and sending the girls away. He said this would not have happened if his wife, Mrinalini Devi, were alive because she would have looked after them. Hemlata had added how during that night before sending away the girls, he had sat out on the roof of Dehali singing '*Aro aghat soibe amar*' ['Suffer I can a lot more hurt'] and '*Jibane jato puja holo na sara/ Jani hey jani tao hoyni hara*' ['The prayers I once began/Those lost in hiatus/Aren't all wasted,/This is a realization.'].[2] His nephew Dinendranath Tagore, who was his song keeper and frequently his composer too, was summoned in the morning to write the *swaralipi* or the musical score (see interview of Hemlata Gupta by Uma Das Gupta). Dehali was the house where Rabindranath then stayed, on the top floor. The floor below had been made into a dormitory for the girls. From what we know the girls did not take their classes under trees as did the boys (Image 2.1). They took classes in the clay hut known as Natun Bari close to Dehali. (Tagore 1934: 47–49).

Image 2.1: An early open-air class at the Shantiniketan school with just a single girl student.

Source: Rabindra-Bhavana Collection, Visva-Bharati, Shantiniketan, by permission.

Officially, girls were again admitted with Visva-Bharati's opening in 1921. Let me now take you very briefly through a history of this institution which will also give you an insight into Rabindranath's ideas for a Shantiniketan education. Shantiniketan was discovered as a serene spot by Debendranath Tagore, Rabindranath's father, in the early 1860s. He was moved by the open spaces and bought a plot of land there on which he built a guest house in 1863 which he named Shantiniketan. He wanted the guest house to be used as a prayerful retreat or ashram for Brahmo householders taking time off from their household responsibilities. Shantiniketan's ashram identity and nomenclature go back to that time (Das Gupta 1983: 93). It is useful to recall here that Debendranath was an early leader of the Hindu reformist movement called the Brahmo Samaj who followed Rammohan Roy in giving leadership to the movement (Kopf 1969: 178–83). Debendranath formalized the Shantiniketan ashram by establishing the Shantiniketan Trust which provided annual funds for the ashram and for an annual fair for villagers to sell their ware, what we know today as the famously popular Poush Mela. He also made provision for a future school. This was the school Rabindranath began in 1901 as an experiment in 'con-structive' swadeshi (Das Gupta 2004: 16–24). In some of his early letters he referred to the school as a 'divine' task and to the boys as 'companions for his highest mission' (Tagore to Atulendu Sen, Das Gupta 1977: 8). At the outset it was conceived as an ashram *vidyalaya* in the model of a *brahmacharyasram*, or a school for nov-ices as in an ancient hermitage or gurukul. He wrote, 'Starting the Bolpur school is an endeavour to take education into our own hands and make it as indigenous as possible'(ibid: Tagore to Sen). Away from the colonial classrooms to which the newly English-educated Indian elite sent their children, Shantiniketan was conceived as an ashram vidyalaya in the model of the ancient forest schools of India where the Vedas and the Upanishads were conceived. Rabindranath started the school with his own meagre funds and, at the outset, took no fees from the students on the model of the ancient *guru-sishwa* hermitages. He soon realized the problem of finding teachers and students for such an idealistic school. This early aspiration is best represented in Tagore's own long statement of how he arrived at this goal. He wrote,

In the modern time my turn has also come to dream of that age towering above all ages of the subsequent history in the greatness of its simplicity and wisdom of pure life. While spending a great part of my youth in the riverside solitude of the sandbanks of the Padma a time came when I woke up to the call of the spirit of my country and felt impelled to dedi-cate my life in furthering the purpose that lies in the heart of her history. I seemed choked for breath in the hideous nightmare of our present time, meaningless in its pretty ambitions of poverty, and felt in me the struggle of my motherland for awakening in spiritual emancipation. Our endeav-ours after political agitation seemed to me unreal to the core and pitifully feeble in their utter helplessness. I felt that it is a blessing of providence that begging should be an unprofitable profession and that only he who hath to him shall be given. I said to myself that we must seek for our inheritance and with it buy our own true place in the world...

The voice came to me in the Vedic tongue from the ashrams, the forest sanctuaries of the past, with the call Come to me as the rivers to the sea, as the days and nights to the completion of their annual cycle. Let our taking and imparting truth be full of the radiance of light. Let us never come into conflict with one another. Let our minds speed towards their supreme good.

My heart responded to that call and I determined to do what I could to bring to the surface, for our daily use and purification the stream of ideals that originated in the summit of our past, flowing underground in the depth of India's soil–the ideals of simplicity of life, clarity of spiritual vision, purity of heart, harmony with the universe, and consciousness of the infinite personality in all creation...

Thus the exclusiveness of my literary life burst its barriers coming into touch with the deeper aspirations of my country lying hidden in her heart. I came to live in the Shantiniketan sanctuary founded by my father and there gradually gathered round me, under the shades of sal trees, boys from distant homes. (Tagore 1917a: 18–21)

But Rabindranath's ideas were not static.... the growth of the school was the growth of my life,' he wrote (Tagore 1917b: 132). The brahmacharyasram was short-lived. He found it unsuited to the idea of children learning and assimilating their learning in joy (O'Connell 2002: 134).

The Shantiniketan school was meant to grow into something fundamentally broader. The first foreign student came there as early as in 1902, within one year of the founding of the school. He was Shitoku Hori from Japan (Azuma 1996: 13). Hori was sent by the Japanese intellectual Okakura Tenshin who was a friend of the Tagore family and an activist for Asian unity. Shitoku Hori's coming to the Shantiniketan school so delighted Rabindranath that between him and his close friend, scientist Jagadish Chandra Bose, they thought of a project for Hori to copy the lost Buddhist texts in Sanskrit from the temples of China and Japan and bring copies to the Indian libraries (Tagore to Bose 1902 and Bose to Tagore 1903). Shantiniketan would thus be taken beyond India. The emphasis on Indian cultures had thus from the beginning an in-built urge to explore a wider connection, in this case, historically with the farther East. This was to be developed with time and more resources.

In an essay that followed in 1908, 'East and West', he discussed the ideal of the inclusiveness of India's civilization in comparison with the exclusiveness of the civilization of the West. He wrote: 'The whole world is becoming one country through scientific facility. And the moment is arriving when we must also find a basis of unity which is not political. If India can offer to the world her solution, it will be a contribution to humanity'. (Tagore Ms. 314, 1917)

After the carnage of the World War of 1914–18, when there was a small window of global empathy for the need to bridge the gap between nations, and when Rabindranath himself was travelling widely and delivering lectures with his message of international cooperation, he offered Shantiniketan as 'the guest house of India' wherever he went in the East and the West. In 1916 he wrote to his son Rathindranath,

> The Shantiniketan school must be made the thread linking India with the world. We must establish there a centre for humanistic research concerned with all the world's peoples. The age of narrow chauvinism is coming to an end for the sake of the future, the first steps towards this great meeting of world humanity will be taken on those very fields of Bolpur. (Tagore to Rathindranath Tagore 1916, Bengali Letters)

Preparations began for adding a Centre of Indian Culture at Shantiniketan in 1918–19. This became a centre for the coordinated study of the various cultural streams of Indian history—Vedic, Puranic, Buddhist, Jain, Islamic, Sikh, Christian and Zoroastrian—in the areas of philosophy, literature, art, and music (Neogy 2010: 88–89). In 1921 he added, 'I have taken courage to invite Europe to our institution. There will be a meeting of truths here.' (Tagore to Sen 1920, Bengali Letters) All this was leading up to the founding of Visva-Bharati (Tagore 1927: 3–4). It was offered to the public with an official inaugural on 22 December 1921 presided over by the philosopher Brajendranath Seal (Mukherjee 1962: 190).

In the twenty years from 1901 to 1921 Shantiniketan thus moved from being a collective of educational experiments into a well-knit whole—a school, a college, a department of higher studies and research, a school of art and music, and an institute of rural reconstruction called Sriniketan. In a clear statement in *The Centre of Indian Culture*, Tagore wrote,

> Our centre of culture should not only be the centre of the intellectual life
> of India, but the centre of her economic life also.... This school must
> practice agriculture, dairy keeping, and weaving on the best modern
> methods, calling science to its aid. Such an institution must group round
> it all the neighbouring villages, vitally unite them with itself in all its eco-
> nomic endeavours. (Tagore 1919: 47)

In 'An Eastern University' he added, Economic life covers the whole
width of the fundamental basis of society, because its necessities
are the simplest and the most universal. Educational institutions, in
order to obtain their fullness of truth, must have close association
with this economic life' (Tagore 1922: 199). These very ideas ultimately culminated into the significant development of Sriniketan.
He now used the name 'Visva-Bharati' for the whole institution.

With Visva-Bharati's inauguration in 1921, the doors were
thrown open to men and women from everywhere to collaborate
in intellectual companionship and social action. There were peri-
ods in the 1920s and 1930s when there were active international
communities at Shantiniketan and Sriniketan (Das Gupta 1977: 35;
1978: 365–67). Believing firmly that all problems could be solved
by education, whether of race or ignorance, poverty or pestilence,
Rabindranath lovingly constructed an imagined Indian personality
who would be free from the conflict of communities, as one belonging to a great nation—'*mahajati*'—by representing the best in the
history of humanity (Das Gupta 1983–84: 17–18). Visva-Bharati
would nurture such a personality with its school in Shantiniketan
and its rural work in Sriniketan, an education that was an endeavour
to integrate the city and the village as the basis of a comprehensive Indian culture and unity of diverse peoples. Prepared by this
education the new Indian personality was expected to give enlightened leadership to a people divided and demoralized from ancient
times by caste and creed, and further divided and demoralized in the
modern age by a colonial education which did not reach the village
where the majority of Indians lived.

It is useful to recall here that the urgency of constructing an
integrated Indian personality came to Rabindranath out of a shocking personal experience. It was an outcome of his participation,
heart and soul, in the Swadeshi movement against the Partition of

Bengal in 1905 (Dutta and Robinson 1995: 141–50). At the time he had put his faith in the Hindu Samaj to bring unity to his country's diverse people. He learnt his lesson when the Swadeshi movement broke out into sectarian violence. He was shocked that the Muslims were being attacked in the name of swadeshi. He had not taken into account that the Muslims had not been taken into the fold of Hindu Samaj. He withdrew from the movement in 1906. He developed his concept of a nation comprising Hindus, Muslims and Christians in India. Its most powerful exposition was in his novel *Gora* serialized during 1907–9, but there were earlier references to the idea. In his essays on India's history he wrote,

> To India has been given her race problem from the beginning of history—
> races ethnologically different have in this country come into close contact.
> This fact has been and still continues to be the most important one in our
> history. It is our mission to face it and prove our humanity by dealing
> with it in fullest truth. (Tagore 1902: 384)

He not only withdrew from the movement but decided to transcend the disappointment not by ideology alone but by hands-on work with a humanistic education where the student, not the system, would be the central concern, in all the felicitous conditions of his or her daily life and social surroundings. That lay at the root of the history of his institution. The lesson he taught himself was that politics must not be allowed to divert education from its true course. Education must produce humanists, he wrote, whose learning would enhance their humanity. All else would follow from that. That became his mission for Visva-Bharati. He wrote,

> Visva-Bharati will not be a mere school; it will be a pilgrimage. Let those
> coming to it say, O what a relief it is to be away from narrow domestic
> walls and to behold the universe. (Tagore to Ray 1918: Bengali Letters)

Now, let me quickly examine his thoughts, particularly, on his Shantiniketan education for girls, although as we could see from the archival photos that boys and girls did much the same things at school including training in the martial art of jujutsu. There could indeed have been an exclusive class for girls occasionally, as we can

see in the Images 2.2 and 2.3, or an assembly of boys only, as we can
see in the Image 2.4, but there is no need to conclude that a gender
statement was being made by these arrangements. Organizationally,
there was a more complete move towards co-education at the
Shantiniketan school once Visva-Bharati University was added to it
in 1921. Rabindranath was of course aware of girls' privacy. When
he took them on tour he prearranged for the girls to stay near where
he was put up. The boys were sent elsewhere.

There were group activities of boys and girls such as going
on picnics. They were also required to act in plays. Kiranbala Sen,
Kshitimohan Sen's wife, who came to Shantiniketan in 1910, mentioned these evening assemblies with Rabindranath (Kiranbala Sen to
Uma Das Gupta). In fact, some of the interviews I took of old students
pointedly spoke of their unique experience of finding a 'community'
in Shantiniketan as something they had never experienced before.
The entities were broader than the conventional girl–boy divide. As
Kamala Paduval from Kerala, who later became the wife of the noted
sculptor Prodosh Das Gupta, told me that the unique thing about
Shantiniketan was its community. The school, the college, the Kala
Bhavana, the Sangit Bhavana—all of those as a whole. Kamala came
to Kala Bhavana in 1933–34. 'You could make friends anywhere, she
said, not just in Kala Bhavana' (Kamala Paduval to Uma Das Gupta).

Image 2.2: Girls practising jijutsu at the Shantiniketan school.

Source: Rabindra-Bhavana Collection, Visva-Bharati, Shantiniketan, by permission.

Image 2.3: An early music class at Shantiniketan school.

Source: Rabindra-Bhavana Collection, Visva-Bharati, Shantiniketan, by permission.

Image 2.4: A clay modelling class at Visva-Bharati.

Source: Rabindra-Bhavana Collection, Visva-Bharati, Shantiniketan, by permission.

Nibedita Bose (née Ghosh) also spoke of a sense of community in a different context. Her father, Tanayendranath Ghosh, took a job at the Shantiniketan school to raise Nibedita whose mother had died young. Nibedita was later married to Nandalal Bose's son, Biswarup Bose. Nibedita spoke of the community ideals of Shantiniketan. In the early years 'Tanay da', as he was addressed in Shantiniketan, was employed as a teacher and a hostel warden. He lived in the hostel with his little daughter. But later they moved to the teachers' quarters. However, whenever a warden was needed he would be moved back to the hostel as temporary warden and Nibedita would then be sent to stay in the girls' hostel. Her comment indicated that there was a free flow between hostels and individual teacher's homes thereby emphasizing a sense of community in this sphere too (Nibedita Bose to Uma Das Gupta). Reba Sarkar (née Mahalanobis) was among the first batch of girl students in the Visva-Bharati period starting 1921–22. She was later married to our legendary teacher Susoban Chandra Sarkar. When speaking of her experience Reba also emphasized the community element in the Shantiniketan education. She added how she and her classmate, the later celebrated social worker Malati Chowdhury, made friends with people in the Santal villages. She commented that such behaviour was unheard of socially in the Brahmo Samaj to which she belonged (Reba Sarkar to Uma Das Gupta). She added that the girls were given certain social responsibilities as students such as nursing the younger boys when sick and also helping in the common kitchen in turns.

When the first ever hostel for girl students was established in 1934, named Sree Sadana, what Rabindranath emphasized was that they must learn to govern themselves and thus shoulder their responsibility willingly. A brief extract from his address to the girls at the inaugural of Sree Sadana is cited below.

> Girls in our Ashrama can demand a reasonable amount of liberty in their everyday life. But true liberty is everywhere based upon severe discipline of responsibility. It may be lazily more comfortable to be ruled from outside than to take up the burden of freedom about our own management (Tagore 1934: 36).

This was his position also for the education of all of Shantiniketan's students. The founder's premise was that his school would be a self-governing republic of boys and girls.

NOTES

1   Kshitimohan Sen spent his early years in Benaras, his birthplace. He joined the Education Ministry of Chamba after completing his Masters at the Benaras University. In 1908, he was invited by Rabindranath Tagore to join the *Brahmacharyasrama*. He continued to be associated with Shantiniketan and became the Principal of Vidya Bhavana, Visva-Bharati, and later, the Vice-Chancellor of Visva-Bharati.
2   The translations have been cited from 'Gitabitan in English', gitabitan-en.blogspot.com; last accessed on 8 June 2016.

REFERENCES

Interviews

Hemlata Gupta by Uma Das Gupta: Interview: Shantiniketan, 1 November 1980. Sister-in-law of Kshitimohan Sen, Hemlata joined the first batch of the first girl's section of the Shantiniketan school at the age of 11 in 1908. Kiranbala Sen to Uma Das Gupta: Interview, Shantiniketan, 5 October 1978. Wife of Kshitimohan Sen, Kiranbala joined him in Shantiniketan in 1910.

Jamuna Sen by Uma Das Gupta: Oral Interview: Shantiniketan, 14 August 1980. Younger daughter of Nandalal Bose, Jamuna came to the Shantiniketan school with her family at the age of 6 in 1919.

Kamala Paduval by Uma Das Gupta: Interview, Shantiniketan, 20 July 1979. A student of the Madras School of Art, Kamala came from Kerala to study in Kala-Bhavana, Shantiniketan, during 1937–38.

Nibedita Bose by Uma Das Gupta: Interview: Shantiniketan, 23 August 1980. Daughter of Tanayendranath Ghosh, teacher of the Shantiniketan school 1926–58, Nibedita joined the Sisu Bibhaga, children's section, in 1926 at the age of 6.

Reba Sarkar by Uma Das Gupta: Interview, Calcutta, 31 May 1977. Student of Visva-Bharati's first batch Reba was at Shantiniketan during 1923–25.

Letters

Rabindranath Tagore to Atulendu Sen, 20 Asvin 1318 (7 October 1911),
Bengali Letters, File: Sen, Atulendu, Rabindra-Bhavana Archives
[RBA]. Atulendu Sen, student of the Shantiniketan school, 1910–11.

Rabindranath Tagore to Jagadish Chandra Bose, 20 June 1902 in *Chitthipatra*,
vol. vi, Kolkata: Visva-Bharati, 1993: 49; Jagadish Chandra Bose
to Rabindranath Tagore, 1 January 1903, in *Dui Bondhu-r Chitthi,
Parasparik o Paramparik,* 1899–1936 Kolkata: Monfakira, date not
given, [2010]: 112.

Rabindranath Tagore, 1917, Ms. Accession no. 314, 'National Unity', in
English, Rabindra-Bhavana Archives [Hereafter, RBA].

Rabindranath Tagore to Rathindranath Tagore, 11 October and 28 October
1916, Bengali Letters, File: Tagore, Rathindranath, [RBA]. Translation
mine. Also see, *Chitthipatra*, vol. ii (Kolkata: Visva-Bharati, 1942):
pp. 54–56. Rathindranath Tagore (1888–1961), the poet's elder son,
first student of the Brahmacharyaasram, 1901–06, worked for the
Shantiniketan school and Visva-Bharati, 1909–53.

Rabindranath Tagore to Kshitimohan Sen, 30 November 1920, Bengali
Letters, File: Sen, Kshitimohan. [RBA] Translation mine. Kshitimohan
Sen (1880–1960), teacher of the Shantiniketan school from 1908, and
one of the pillars of Visva-Bharati. He was a renowned scholar of the
history of medieval mysticism in India.

Rabindranath Tagore to Nepal Chandra Ray, 3 November 1918, Bengali
Letters, File: Ray, Nepal Chandra, RBA. Translation mine. Nepal
Chandra Ray (1867–1944), teacher of the Shantiniketan school from
1910–36.

Books

Azuma, Kazuo. 1996. *Hori'r Deenapanji.* 9th ed. Calcutta: Visva-Bharati.
Das Gupta, Uma. 2004. *Rabindranath Tagore: A Biography*, New Delhi:
Oxford University Press.
———. 1983–84. 'Rabindranath Tagore and the Nineteenth-Century
Renaissance', *The Calcutta Historical Journal* 8, 1 and 2.
———. 1983. 'Shantiniketan and Sriniketan', *Introduction to Tagore*,
Calcutta: Visva-Bharati, 1983.

Das Gupta, Uma. 1978. 'Rabindranath Tagore on Rural Reconstruction: The Sriniketan Programme, 1921–41', *The Indian Historical Review* 4, 2.

———. 1977. *Shantiniketan and Sriniketan: A Historical Introduction.* Shantiniketan: A Visva-Bharati Quarterly Booklet.

Dutta, Krishna, and Andrew Robinson. 1995. *Rabindranath Tagore: The Myriad-Minded Man,* London: Bloomsbury, 1995.

Kopf, David. 1969. *British Orientalism and the Bengal Renaissance,* Berkeley: University of California Press.

M.O'Connell, Kathleen. 2002. *Rabindranath Tagore: The Poet as Educator,* Kolkata: Visva-Bharati.

Mukherjee, Himangshu Bhushan. 1962. *Education for Fullness: A Study of the Educational Thought and Experiment of Rabindranath Tagore,* London: Asia Publishing House.

Neogy, Ajit K. 2010. *Shantiniketan and Sriniketan: The Twin Dreams of Rabindranath Tagore,* New Delhi: National Book Trust.

Neogy, Ajit K. [1934] 2000. 'To The Girls', *Shantiniketan Vidyalaya 1901–2000,* Calcutta: Visva-Bharati.

——— [1902] 1975. 'Bharatbarsh-er Itihas' (India's History), *Rabindra Rachanabali,* iv, Calcutta: Visva-Bharati. Translation mine.

———. 1919. *The Centre of Indian Culture,* Bolpur: The Shantiniketan Press.

———. 1922. *Creative Unity,* London: Macmillan, 1922.

———. 1917a. 'Foreword', in W.W. Pearson's *Shantiniketan: The Bolpur School of Rabindranath Tagore,* London: Macmillan.

———. 1917b. 'My School' in *Personality,* London: Macmillan, 1917.

PART II

NATURE AND SPIRITUALITY

CHAPTER 3

Gender and the Spiritual Quest in Tagore's Poetry

Mandakranta Bose

Although Tagore has a strong affinity with the abstract godhead of Brahmoism, he also personalizes the deity, to the extent of imagining an intense emotional relationship between the worshipper and the worshipped. This impulse towards personalizing God arises largely from Tagore's immersion in Vaishnava poetry and music, and also from his interest in Kabir's vision of the intimacy between the bhakta and the deity. Here again, Tagore's image of the seeker is open-ended in that the seeker is not circumscribed by the usual social identities, particularly that of gender. In the bulk of his poetry of spiritual quest, the 'I' could be either man or woman. When, however, Tagore shifts from an intellectual approximation of the human–divine connection to an emotional yearning for an immediate personal relationship, he tends to feminize the seeker. The literary signifier of this shift is his adoption of the imagery and rhythm of Vaishnava poetry, initiated in his early and experimental *Bhanusingha Thakurer Padavali*. Although he later dismissed *Bhanusingha Thakurer Padavali* as a mere exercise in style devoid of the sincerity of the classic Vaishnava padavali, the impulse behind it is real and substantial, for the questing Radha of *Bhanusingha Thakurer Padavali* travels throughout Tagore's work. This chapter examines how and why this feminizing of the seeker invigorates Tagore's fundamental spiritual perception of love as the key to existence.

'It is he, the innermost one, who awakens my heart with his deep, hidden touches,' writes Tagore. Is 'he' the personal and abstract Brahman who awakens Tagore's heart? And who is the speaker? Given that in the traditional rhetoric of devotional love poetry, the seeker of the divine beloved assumes a female persona, there is good reason to take the speaker, whether it is Tagore's heart

or the human soul itself, as a feminized persona pining for that 'he',
the divine spirit. It is a position that Tagore takes in his poetry, con-
sistently and passionately, as here, or is it the human soul in a feminized persona pining for 'he', the divine spirit? Perhaps it is both. He
heard the spirit's awakening call all through his life:

> *Amar raater svapane*
> *amar hiyay hiyay baje akul andhar jamini*
> *se je tomar bansari*
> *ami suni akas parer tarar ragini, amar sakal pasari*
> (*Gitabitan, Puja:* 36)
> In my dream at night,
> Through my heart rings the endless music of the night
> That your flute plays,
> And I hear the music of the stars beyond the sky, forgetting myself.[1]

The intimacy animating these lines is, as I shall argue, fundamental
to Tagore's spiritual quest and woven throughout his poetical oeuvre
as well as his many philosophical writings. This study will focus on
his poetry and songs across his long productive life. But first, we
may briefly recapitulate his spiritual history.

As we know from his memoirs, Rabindranath's education
in religious ideas began very early, during his Himalayan sojourn
with his scholarly father who not only trained him systematically
in the knowledge of the Vedas and the Upanishads but implanted
in the young boy the thrill of contemplating the Infinite. As
Rabindranath tells us in *Jibansmriti*, the high mountains and long
vistas of Dalhousie filled him with a joyful sense of the power
pulsing through the universe. This sense of inexplicable joy came
to an epiphanic climax later in Rabindranath's life as he watched
the sun rise over the palm fronds in his brother's Calcutta garden.
Throughout his long life Rabindranath's constant citations of Vedic
and Upanishadic verses and ideas testify to their profound influence
in forming his religious and moral philosophy. Another deep influence on him was that of Buddhist thought, especially its confrontation with *duhkha* and the entropic nature of existence. A different set
of ideas came from Christianity, although he was perhaps attracted
more by the message of Christ's self-sacrificing ministry of love than

with theological issues, as reflected in several poems, particularly those written in times of war, and in lectures.

An altogether different set of ideology came to exert as much authority as Upanishadic beliefs on Rabindranath's spiritual and poetical life in the form of what I might broadly term the spirituality of love. This was represented, as mentioned earlier, by the Vaishnava poetry and art that Rabindranath discovered, again at an early age, but also by the passionate spiritual quest he found in Kabir and to a lesser extent in Rumi's poetry. This strain of spirituality, which may be termed as the spirituality of love, by no means supplanted Rabindranath's absolute subscription to Upanishadic beliefs and ideas but ran parallel to it, the two strands often intertwining in his writings. It is tempting to label one as a philosophical impetus and the other as emotional, but it is a distinction to be made with strong qualifications because for Rabindranath philosophy was never unemotional nor emotions unphilosophical. His multiple vision of the human–divine relationship included in its scope the Upanishadic Brahman, an abstract and formless idea that nevertheless included a father-like figure, as well as the human soul, conceived as a woman, who seeks a direct and passionately personal relationship with the Divine Spirit as a man.

As with his introduction to Upanishadic thought, Rabindranath came to Vaishnava poetry early in his life. He was eleven when he discovered Jayadeva's *Gitagovinda* and at about the age of fourteen he found other Vaishnava poetry of the padavali tradition through his elder brother Jyotirindranath's literary friends. At about the same time, he came upon his grandfather Dwarakanath's collection of Rajput, Pahari and Mughal paintings, predominantly on the Radha–Krishna legend. For Rabindranath, the discovery of these passionately human statements of spiritual yearning was an event that opened up a whole new world of imaginative and emotional perception. Radha's passion for Krishna became for him the most powerful trope for the fundamental unity of the human and the divine, with the endless forms of nature supplying its concrete signifiers. It was from Jayadeva as well as the padavali poets, especially of the period spanning the twelfth to fourteenth centuries, that he derived the initial energy for his own poetry of love and nature (*prem* and *prakriti*), and his belief in the inalienability of the human/divine

relationship. So pervasive is this belief that it is often difficult to dif-
ferentiate between earthly and divine love in his songs and poems.
It is a measure of Rabindranath's breadth of sensibility that even
with his philosophical roots deep in the Vedas and Upanishads, he
should have developed into the finest Vaishnava poet after the age of
the padavali poets. This cultural heritage of Rabindranath has been
examined in several articles over the past twenty years.[2]

A direct result of Rabindranath's encounter with Vaishnava
poetry and art was his *Bhanusingha Thakurer Padavali*. Written at
seventeen, *Bhanusingha Thakurer Padavali* celebrates Radha and
Krishna's love set in a landscape of conventionally romanticized
nature, with storm clouds, dark woods and flowing streams, singing
birds and springtime flowers. Later in life, as a mature craftsman,
Rabindranath dismissed this group of twenty poems that make up
Bhanusingha Thakurer Padavali as a boyish attempt to play with the
phrasing and style of Jayadeva's Sanskrit work as well as medieval
Bengali padavalis, and lacking in the spirituality of the padavalis.
That he did emulate Jayadeva's play on words is obvious in the following comparison of alliterative verse:

> *Lalitalavangalata parishilana malayasamire* . . .
> (*Gitagovinda*: 1.27)
> Soft sandal mountain winds caress quivering vines of clove . . .
> (Miller: 74)
> . . .*kesarakirna kadambabane,*
> *Marmara mukharita mridu pavane.* . .
> From '*Keno pantha e chanchalata*'
> (*Gitabitan, Prakriti, Varsha* 93)
>
> In the pollen-filled kadamba forest,
> The gentle breeze murmurs.

But Rabindranath owed much more than stylistic virtuosity to
Jayadeva and the padavali poets, for their idealization of devotion as
a woman's longing for her beloved saturated his own poetry. Despite
his disclaimer, his youthful effort laid the basis of his mature work,
for the imagery that forms the backdrop to Radha's unfulfilled longing keeps reappearing in his poetry both of love and of devotion,

especially in his poems and songs on *varsha* and *vasanta*, that is, the monsoon and spring. We must also remember that Rabindranath's admiration for the padavalis was sustained enough to lead to the publication of a collection of poems under the title, *Padaratnavali*, jointly edited with Srishchandra Majumdar when he was twenty-four (Tagore [1885]1990).

But far more substantially than in stylistic influences, the stamp of Vaishnava spirituality on Rabindranath can be seen in the humanizing of the spiritual quest to the extent that the quest becomes a lovers' narrative. Of the 617 songs that make up the *Puja* section of *Gitabitan*, at least half are written in this mode and the same emotional value recurs in many of the poems on love, *prem* (395 songs) and nature, *prakriti* (283 songs). The speaking voice in such songs is a woman and the bulk of the metaphors used are derived from Vaishnava padavalis. The seeker's beloved is ever elusive and yet ever present at the edge of the seeker's vision, which invests the quest with the thrill of an ever-renewed promise. As in typical Vaishnava poetry, Rabindranath's seeker assumes the persona of a lovelorn woman set within the conventions of both space and speech that Rabindranath found in Vaishnava poetry, painting and music. The seeker braves the dark and stormy night to go on a tryst with her beloved, awaits him in her lonely dwelling and calls out to him from the flowering landscape of springtime. In all this, the seeker's passionate longing is as intense as is her total surrender to her beloved, the two juxtaposed to construct a conventionally feminized image. The only element of the Vaishnava scenario missing is the betrayed heroine's *abhimana*, a word that in Bengali usage stands for her vexation at her injured self-esteem. This world of the feminized seeker's continuous search is an emotionally charged one, evoked by the verbal imagery of waiting, longing and invitation, and by the Radha–Krishna paintings that open window after window upon the landscape of love. Word and picture frequently go together, as in the following image of *abhisarika* Radha in *Bhanusingha Thakurer Padavali*:

Shangana gagane ghora ghanaghata nishitha jamini re /
kunjapathe sakhi kaise jaoba, abala kamini re //
(*Gitabitan, Prakriti, Varsha:* 31)
Dark is the night and rain clouds rumble in the monsoon sky
O friend! How can I, a helpless woman, reach the tryst?

This could have been written as an explication of any of the numerous Pahari miniatures on the theme, or a reworking of Radha's journey to her tryst in the *Gitagovinda*:

> *Tvadabhisaraṇarabhasena valanti /*
> *patati padani kiyanti chalanti / /*
> *natha hare sidati Radha vasagrihe / /*
> (*Gitagovinda*, vi. 3)
> Rushing in her haste to meet you,
> She stumbles after a few steps and falls,
> Lord Hari, Radha suffers in her retreat.
> (Miller 1984: 96)

Like these lines, Rabindranath's song expresses the same anguish of a woman heartsick in separation—the typical *virahakatara* heroine—who seeks union with her beloved. Both in manner and message, Rabindranath's song is aligned with Jayadeva's translation of worship into the idiom of human love.

So powerful was Rabindranath's urge to correlate human and divine love that even in his *brahmasangitas* he often uses the imagery of human desire, as here:

> *Hridaya nandanabane nibhrita e niketane*
> *esho he anandamaya esho chirasundara.*
> (*Gitabitan, Puja:* 168)
> To the pleasure grove of my heart, to my secret abode,
> Come, spirit of joy, come you of eternal beauty!

In the poetic tradition of India, phrases such as *nandanabana* (pleasure grove) and *nibhrita niketana* (secluded abode) are powerful signifiers of romantic episodes, especially evocative of Radha's expectation of her tryst with Krishna. Further into the song, the phrase to express the seeker's anguish at separation is '*viraha katara tapta chitta*' (a heart burning with the anguish of separation), locating the speaker within the conventions of the Indian romantic tradition in art and poetry by the image of a burning heart drooping from the pain of separation. This directly humanized relation between the human seeker and the divine spirit sets the song's tone even though it goes on to acknowledge the divine spirit in the characteristic idiom of Brahmo worship as the one and indivisible ruler of the universe from whom all good flows, in the certainty that *'jharibe jibane mane diba nishi sudha nirjhara'* (my life and my mind will be showered with nectar day and night) A breathtaking conjunction indeed of private intimacy and public homage!

As we see in this example, God imagined as the Supreme Being who can be worshipped only as the devotee's infinite superior and, therefore, a distant figure coexists in Rabindranath's imagination with one who is the human soul's closest, immediate and intimate companion. In this relationship, the human soul is imagined by Rabindranath invariably as a woman who waits for, calls out to and invites her lover, as in the following:

> *Patha cheye je kete gelo kata dine rate,*
> *aj tomay amay praner bodhu milbo go ek sathe*
> *(Gitabitan, Puja: 159)*
> So many days and nights have I spent awaiting your coming,
> My beloved! You and I will come together today.

This quest is given a more specific Vaishnava colouring by the motif of Krishna's flute (*banshi* and *benu*) calling Radhā to abandon all other tasks:

> *Amar hriday tomar apan hate dolao, . . .*
> *Banshir dake sakal badhon kholao . . .*
> *(Gitabitan, Puja: 57)*
> Sway my soul in your own hand,
> Untie me from all chains by the call of your flute.

There is no question, of course, that Rabindranath subscribes to the idea of the One as a father figure of the Old Testament variety, as the following examples show:

> *Tumi amader pita tomay pita bole jeno jani,*
> *tomay nato hoye jeno mani,*
> *tumi koro na koro na rosh.*
> *(Gitabitan, Puja: 392)*
> You are our Father,
> Let us remember that you are our Father
> Let us bow to you and obey,
> Do not look upon us in anger.

The idea here is that of submission before a remote being who is too great and too far above the speaker to be claimed as a personal companion. In this impersonal connection with superhuman authority, the speaker's gender is irrelevant:

> *amar matha nato kare dao he tomar charana dhular tale*
> *sakala ahankara amar dubao chokhero jale*
> (*Gitabitan, Puja:* 492)
> Let me bow my head under the dust of thy feet
> Let me drown my pride in my tears.

The worshipper may only wonder at such power, render homage and give thanks:

> *Sara jiban dilo alo surya graha chand*
> *Tomar ashirbad he prabhu tomar ashirbad*
> (*Gitabitan, Puja:* 355)
> The sun, the planets and the moon have given me light all my life
> All of this is your blessing, my Lord!

The celebrant locates the Lord in all that is joyous, good and true:

> *Anandaloke mangalaloke biraja satyasundara*
> (*Gitabitan, Puja:* 476)
> Beauty and Truth pervade the world of joy and benevolence.

These are declarations of faith in the absolute truth, beauty and goodness of an intellectually conceived divinity, but they lack the emotional energy of intimacy of a love relationship between the seeker and the sought. The feminization of the seeker in that relationship intensifies the emotional need of the seeker by adding an undercurrent of eroticism. Often implicit in Vaishnava poetry, this intensification was even more explicitly modelled for Rabindranath by Kabir's poems, to which he came later in life through his friend Kshitimohan Sen's effort to collect Kabir's poems scattered over much of India. When Rabindranath studied them he was so overwhelmed that he took on the proselytizing task of presenting Kabir to the greater world beyond India by translating and putting out an edition of a hundred poems by Kabir.

As I have demonstrated in a paper (Bose 2011), Rabindranath found a deep resonance between himself and Kabir despite their very different rhetorical practice. As Linda Hess has remarked, Kabir's was a 'rough' voice, quite different from Rabindranath's elegance. A basic alignment between them was that both were philosophically inclined to what in Kabir's case is termed *nirgunabhakti*, i.e., devotion to a Formless God, which was also Tagore's position as a Brahmo. Yet both humanize God in their poetry, imagining Him in male form and the devotee as female. Even when the relationship is not imagined as between lover and beloved, Kabir addresses God as Ram and Tagore addresses God as Pita. But in both poets, the most powerful expression of the human longing for the divine is unambiguously gendered, its idiom feminine and the human–divine relationship conceived as eternally ordained and unbreakable. Kabir is far more explicit than Rabindranath in imagining the relationship in sexual terms, as here:

> *Balama au hamanrai greha re*
> *tuma bina dukhiyā deha re.*
> *sab koi kahai tumhari nari mokaun yah andeha re,*
> *ekameka hvai seja na sobai taba lagi kaisa neha re.*
> (Callewaert, ed., 2000 poem no. 357)
> Beloved, come to my dwelling,
> My body aches in your absence.
> Everyone says I am your woman but I have doubts about that,
> For if we do not lie as one on the bed, then what kind of love is this?

This is the voice of consuming desire, plainly stated in the common metaphor of human union. Rabindranath too asserts union, as in,

> *Tomay amay milan habe bole,*
> *Yuge yuge visva bhuvantale*
> *Paran amar badhur bese chale svayambara*
> (*Gitabitan, Puja:* 34)
> Since you and I are destined to be together,
> In every eon, in the entire world,
> My soul travels like a bride to marry you.

Like Kabir, he represents the seeker as an expectant bride, though in a far less earthy manner:

> *Iccha chilo baranmala parai tomar gale,*
> *nai ba tomar thaklo prayojan.*
> (*Gitabitan, Puja:* 59)
> I want to put on the bridal garland on your neck
> Even though you may not want it.

These being just two of countless examples available in Rabindranath's poetry labelled both as of devotion and of love.

Theologically, the most exciting concept that Rabindranath shares with Kabir is the unconditional and eternal interdependence of seeker and sought, which Kabir expresses thus:

> *Mohi tohi lagi kaise chuṭe |*   *jaise hira phoryo na phute ||*
> *mohi tohi jiva siva ka basa |*   *aho prabhu tum sahib myai dasa ||*
> *mohi tohi kiṭa bhringa ki nay |*   *jaise siddhahi bunda samai ||*
> *myai ananta kahun nahi laga |*   *jaise tute kacha dhaga ||*
> *kahe kabira mana laga |*   *jaise sono miley suhaga ||*
>
> (Callewaert no. 369)

Here is Rabindranath's translation:

> How could the love between Thee and me sever?
> As the leaf of the lotus abides on the water; so thou art my Lord, and I
> am Thy servant.
> As the night-bird Chakor gazes all night at the moon: so thou art my
> Lord, and I am Thy servant.
> From the beginning until the end of time, there is love between Thee
> and me; and how shall such love be extinguished?
> Kabir says: 'As the rivers enters into the ocean, so my heart touches
> Thee.'
> (Tagore no. 34)

Admittedly, this is a toned down version and inexact in places, replacing for instance the concrete precision of Kabir's '*jaise sono miley suhaga*' (as gold is annealed with borax) with a misty geographical simile. But the concept of inalienability remains unchanged. At the same time, Rabindranath signifies the romantic nature of the love between the Lord and His servant by invoking the emblematic *chakor*. The fundamental agreement between the two poets can hardly be missed or their similar rendition of the devotee as a woman.

It is worth noting that in thus feminizing the spiritual seeker Rabindranath is part of a rhetorical practice that seems only too common both in his own culture and that of the West. From South Asia we have the examples that I have noted earlier and much more, including of course the poems of Mirabai and other women poets such as Akka Mahadevi. But the trope is equally common in western devotional thought. The most obvious example is the reference to Christ and the Christian church as bridegroom and bride (Ephesians 5:22) and the more frequent mention of Christ as the bridegroom (Matthew 9:15, Mark 2:19, Luke 5:34, John 3:29). Whether Rabindranath knew the Bible closely or not, he certainly seems to have used the parable of the wise and foolish virgins who fall asleep as they wait for the bridegroom with their lamps. The biblical view of all humanity as ideally espoused to Christ is not far from Rabindranath's image of the woman seeking God as her lover. The theme of God's human lover is iterated by several Christian mystics, notably St. Theresa and St John of the Cross. A full discussion of Rabindranath's reflections on Christianity appears in Shyamal Ray's *Rabindranather Khrishtachinta* (1994).

Closer to Rabindranath is the poet John Donne whom Rabindranath certainly knew, as we find from his well-known quotation of Donne's line: 'For God's sake hold your tongue and let me love' in *Sesher Kavita*, a particularly effective reference whose cross-cultural implication has been noted by a recent critic (Frontain 2011). What is perhaps less readily acknowledged is the parallel between Donne's position in his sonnet: 'Batter my heart, three-personed God' ('Holy Sonnet' 14) and a number of Rabindranath's songs in which Rabindranath's speaker implores his Lord to purify him through suffering. To cite only two examples

Aro aro prabhu aro aro,
Emni kore, emni kore amay maro.
(*Gitabitan, Puja* 228)

My Lord! Again and again
Punish me the same way.

Ei korecco bhalo, nithur he, nithur he, ei korecco bhalo,
Emni kore hridaye mor tibra dahan jalo.
Amar e dhup na porale gandha kiccui nahi dhale,
Amar e dip na jalale dey na kicchui alo.
(*Gitabitan, Puja:* 223)

O heartless One! You have done the right thing.
Ignite my heart in this way . . .
If my incense is not burnt, it gives no fragrance.
If my lamp is not lit, it does not give light.

In both the urgency of need and the assurance of satisfaction, these statements match Donne's lines. As I have outlined earlier, much of religious poetry tends to cast itself in the idiom and form of romantic love and Rabindranath is a particularly persuasive exemplar of that tradition. His spiritual imagination was by no means confined within that tradition alone, as I have pointed out by noting his powerful invocation of the Lord as a limitless persona transfusing all that the human mind and heart can conceive or experience. The emotion aroused by contemplating such a person is one of awe and admiration. Quite different from this and no less moving in its emotional intensity is the idea of the Lord as the lover, the bridegroom, the seeker's very own companion, whose nearness is felt with all the fervour of personal, nearly erotic love. For Rabindranath, that kind of love sings most movingly in the female voice. Biological gender has nothing to do with this; one might recall Rabindranath's reference to the 'woman within all of us' in one of his Shantiniketan sermons (Tagore 1974: vol. 13, 474–75).

Why and how across time and cultural space poets such as Jayadeva, Kabir, Donne and Rabindranath should elect the female persona as the truest embodiment of the quest on which they launch the poetical 'I' is a speculation that would take us into the realms equally of psychology and sociology. What is not subject to speculation is that their gendered idiom resonates with readers. Perhaps life's experience tells them that the most faithful seeker is a woman.

NOTES

1 All translations are mine, unless otherwise noted.
2 Beginning with Bose (1999).
3 In collections of Pahari paintings around the world, e.g., the National Museum, New Delhi, and the British Museum, among many others. For scholarly discussions, see Archer (1973) and Randhawa (1963).

REFERENCES

Archer, W. G. 1973. *Indian Paintings from the Punjab Hills: A Survey and History of Pahari Miniature Painting*. London, New York: Sotheby Parke Bernet.

Bose, Mandakranta. 2011. '"Where He Lies, I Lie:" Tagore Meets Kabir', *Journal of Hindu Studies* (Oxford) 4 (2): 165–75.

———. 1999. 'Rabindranath and the Poetic Heritage of *bhakti*', in *Studies in Early Modern Indo-Aryan Languages, Literature and Culture*, edited by Alan Entwistle, Carol Saloman with Heidi Pauwels and Michael Shapiro. Delhi: Manohar.

Callewaert, W. M. (ed.) 2000. *The Millennium Kabir*. Delhi: Manohar.

Frontain, Raymond J. 2011. 'Donne, Tagore, and Love's Passing Moment', *Papers on Language and Literature*, 47, 1 (Winter): 45–62.

Miller, Barbara Stoller (ed. and trans.). 1984. *The Gitagovinda of Jayadeva: Love Song of the Dark Lord*. Delhi: Motilal Banarsidass.

Randhawa, M. S. 1963. *Kangra Paintings of the Gīta Govinda*. New Delhi: National Museum.

———. 1962. *Kangra Paintings on Love*. New Delhi: National Museum.

Ray, Shyamal. 1994. *Rabindranather Khrishtachinta*. Calcutta: Prabha Prakasani: Paribesaka Progressive Book Forum.

Tagore, Rabindranath. 2002. *Gitabitan*. Calcutta: Visva-Bharati Press.

———. 1974 '*Prarthana*', in *Santiniketan, Rabindra Rachanabali* (Collected Works). Calcutta: Visva-Bharati Press, 13: 474–5.

Tagore, Rabindranath, and Srishchandra Majumdar (eds.) [1885]1990. *Padaratnavali*. (New edition by Anathnath Das and Visvanath Roy.) Calcutta: Ananda Publishers.

CHAPTER 4

Rabindranath's *Chandalika*: Woman as Prakriti and Prakriti in Woman

Malini Bhattacharya

In Tagore's play *Chandalika* (1933), as well as in the dance-drama with the same title later composed by him (1938), the pivotal character is a woman from an untouchable caste named Prakriti. The narrative core in these texts and also the name of the woman go back to *Shardulakarnabadana*, a Sanskrit-Buddhist fable from Nepal in a translated edition of such fables by Rajendralal Mitra published by The Asiatic Society in 1882. It is likely that Tagore had read it long before he composed the earlier-mentioned texts; but the story, together with the name, must have stuck in his mind.

In his early years, Tagore composed a verse-play titled *Prakritir Pratisodh* (1884) which seems to contain some resonances from Shelley's 'Alastor'. Interestingly, in this romantic play, a young girl who is said to be the daughter of *mleccha* untouchable parents, seeks affection and shelter from the mendicant who has renounced the world of Nature with its 'monstrous' propensities in his search for the boundless. In this play, ironically for the mendicant, it is in this young girl that Nature or *prakriti* with its small everyday graces seems to be incarnated. Having spurned the affections of the girl, the mendicant realizes after her death what precious gifts of ordinary life are now lost to him. It is this term 'prakriti' that may be seen as an implicit link between this early effort and his later reconstructions of the Buddhist narrative.

His earliest attempt to reconstruct the Buddhist story had been in 1932 in a poem called 'Jalapatra' where the name Prakriti does not appear; the lowly woman whom the 'lord of her life' saves by accepting a drink of water from her hands does not mind being left behind by him. She is content to make her distant offering to him each morning by turning the water pot touched by him into a thing of beauty through her paintings. In 1932–33, untouchability became a thematic preoccupation with Tagore and he wrote a number of poems, often in free verse, on this theme, taking his cue from 'Bhakti' literature. His play *Kaler Jatra* where the ceremonial chariot refuses to move until the 'shudras' put their hands to the rope was also composed in 1932. In 'Jalapatra', the woman's presence is more-or-less symbolic; she is more of the gender-neutral *bhakta* (devotee) rescued from a state of degradation by the touch of the saviour's compassion and endowed with creative powers that give her a new life. However, like many other poems on the issue of untouchability of the period, 'Jalapatra' too, highlights and valorizes the humble manual labour of the 'untouchable' which is anathema for the 'elite' culture. I would like to argue that this orientation has some relevance for *Chandalika* as well.

Prakriti, the chandal's daughter reacts differently from the woman in 'Jalapatra', both in the original narrative and in Tagore's dramatic representations.[1] Struck by the physical beauty of Ananda, the monk, and consumed by desire for him, she urges her mother to carry out magical rituals so that he may be irresistibly drawn to her. These wiles are defeated through the Buddha's intervention. In the original story, Prakriti is eventually purged of her lust for Ananda and is inducted into the fold of the order by being offered the saffron robe. In Tagore's version, however, Prakriti relinquishes her efforts to ensnare the monk when she realizes that having succumbed to earthly desire through her magic spells, Ananda has lost the very aura that had drawn her to him inexorably. The dramatic representation demands a more complicated response to the theme than the earlier poem by centralizing the trope of Prakriti's womanly desire for Ananda, Ananda's failure to resist it and Prakriti's ultimate renunciation of her efforts to seduce Ananda so that he may fulfil the higher purpose of his life.

At one level, the representation coincides with a very old, somewhat essentialist idea about man–woman relationship that we find recurring in many of Tagore's writings; it pertains to woman's specific 'nature' (prakriti) relative to man's and is expressed through the well-known binaries of nature/spirit, blind instinct/enlightened intelligence, body/mind, bonding/freedom, home/world, and so on. It finds typical expression in a very personal letter written to Victoria Ocampo in 1925:

> You have often found me homesick,—it was not so much for
> India, it was for that freedom. It becomes totally obscured
> when for some reason or other my attention is too much directed
> upon my own personal self.... My mind must have a nest to which
> the voice of the sky can descend freely, the sky that has no other
> allurements but light and freedom. Whenever there is the least sign
> of the nest becoming the jealous rival of the sky[,] my mind, like a
> migrant bird, tries to take its flight to a distant shore.... (Pal 2004: 169)

Within this structure of feeling, the woman represents the world of Nature (prakriti) enmeshing the man within the distracting bonds of personal affections while it is for the man continually to resist all attachments and to move ahead to a higher plane. There is something in common between woman and Nature according to this view in so far as the Spirit, obviously male in essence, has to overcome Nature in order to come to its own. I am not discussing here the old monistic philosophical sources that articulate and reinforce this view, but there is no doubt that this also coincides to some extent with the moral of the Buddhist fable, that is, the source of *Chandalika*, and expounds the importance for the monk in search of salvation to overcome the temptations and tests set before him by the material world of which the woman is a living incarnation.

But in the fable, another complicating factor is introduced by the fact of Prakriti being an untouchable girl from the chandal caste from whom Ananda receives drinking water without hesitation. When the Buddha accepts her within the fold of his order, it creates a scandal in Shravasti and to explain the untenability of caste discrimination, the Buddha has to narrate the story of an earlier life when Prakriti had been a brahmin's daughter of great beauty and merit, and Ananda, then the wise and virtuous son of a wise and virtuous chandal chieftain, had claimed her hand in marriage and won it. Thus, even in the fable, Prakriti is not just the 'natural' lustful woman seeking to ensnare Ananda; she is not merely to be abhorred and discarded, but one who may inspire an equalizing compassion having been wrongfully cast into a state of degradation in this life by the society to which she belongs.

It is this duality in the story that makes it interesting. Tagore, in his own treatment of the Buddhist narrative of Prakriti and Ananda, seems to be fully sensitive to the theme of an equalizing compassion that forms a major element in it and he endows Prakriti with a subjectivity that transcends her stereotypical role of seduction. Her desire for Ananda is imbricated in her newly found realization that she is as much of a human being as he is. But it also dislocates her from her familiar sphere of daily loving and giving, essential labour like bathing the calf, drawing water, reaping the harvest and starting the home fire, that her passion for the impossible makes her neglectful. Ananda's mission is high and therefore attractive to her, but it is completely impersonal. Reading the play against the grain, we may find elements in the text justifying Prakriti's desire, though it does not admit any resolution. Her refusal to seduce Ananda when the moment comes is a conscious acknowledgement of the paradox that her desire can have no resolution. And this is because Tagore's version of the narrative not only moves a step beyond its original source in making Prakriti a conscious agent, but lends a value, not less than that of Ananda's renunciation, to the labours of everyday life, the loving service that she embodies as a mere untouchable woman.

Throughout Tagore's writings, there are many references to this grace of everyday life, of Nature, being the proper sphere of femininity. It is interesting to note that in both *Europe-Jatrir Diary* written at the time of his first trip to England and in *Paschim-Jatrir Diary* written in 1924–25 while travelling to South America, he accordingly speaks of the specific space allotted to woman in Nature's dispensation. In the former text, he goes to the extent of saying that in Europe, women in search of 'civilization', have been dislocated from their proper sphere of caring and affection, which is not lost to the 'backward' women of our country. In the latter text, he says that women are rooted in life (*pran*) while men are driven by the mind (*mon*); in Nature's system, women have been given a fixed space, while men are always searching restlessly for a space of their own. He justifies the manner in which women use *maya* to fulfil their assigned role in this 'natural' order. Of course, a perspective somewhat contradictory to this may be found elsewhere. Tagore shows great sensitivity in questioning the image of fixity embodied in women in many of his own creative writings, for example, through his peripatetic Vaishnavi Anandi, or Mrinal (of the short story 'Streer Patra') who breaks all attachments with her marital home and family. At the same time, his conception of the boundaries of woman's nature or of Nature's dispensation for woman turns to some extent into an ideological limitation in his portrayal of women like Bimala in *Ghare-Baire* or Ela in *Char Adhyay*.

Both these women assume a destructive role in the texts where they appear, having broken out of the social-political space assigned to them by their very nature. Women being closer to Nature are perceived as partaking of its elemental force; they are creatures of instinct generating a dark and irrational momentum in their unaccustomed trajectory into the public sphere. We may recall here how the nationalist Sandip in *Ghare-Baire* talks of the need to find an image for the turbulent and all-consuming love for one's country not in the motherliness of a woman, but in her erotic, fearsome and asocial essence. He wishes to substitute *Bande Mataram* (Let us worship the Mother) by *Bande Priyam* (Let us worship the Mistress). In their destructiveness, women like Bimala and Ela, as represented in Tagore's novels, resemble Prakriti craving for Ananda. But, unlike Prakriti, they remain undeserving of authorial grace.

To some extent, indeed, it is possible to read Bimala against the grain in certain parts of the text. She is indeed not seen as wholly a tool in Sandip's hands; the object of her attraction at times seems not Sandip, but something larger than him, the great mission of freedom for the country, whatever that may mean. Standing alone in the outer darkness she visualizes her country as a woman like herself; she appears as the archetypal *abhisarika* forgetful of her role as housewife and mother, rushing on her perilous path towards an unknown destination to meet her lover.[2] This powerful attraction of something larger than any individual is a potent justification of her negligence of her regular domestic duties. Bimala's destructiveness does at such crucial points suggest a liberation which is again negated by the pressure of the text. On the other hand, her rebellion against Sandip's power over her takes the form of retreating inside the domestic stronghold, and finding relief in feeding Amulya with *pithes* (popular Bengali pancakes) made with her own hands. But this is an escape which bears no hints of liberation, such as we may perhaps find in Prakriti's labours of love.

In other fictional renderings of the problem by Tagore, the essentialist interpretation of the feminine essence is fractured by irony penetrating through the text. We may find examples of this in *Chaturanga* (1916), a novel, and in 'Sesh Katha', one of Tagore's last short stories. In both texts, there is a male narrator, but although both appear as main actors in the narration, they are differently located. While Sribilas in the earlier text shares the authorial perspective of irony, Nabinmadhav in 'Sesh Katha' lacks this ironical perspective which is, however, reflected indirectly through the narration in the prelude. In both texts, the familiar pattern of the woman offering bonds of caring and affection and the man seeking release from these appears in the structure of the narration, but with effects surpassing the stereotypical binaries of man–woman relationship.

Damini, the woman in *Chaturanga*, is described as one who 'refuses to have any truck with death, engaged with life in total enjoyment' (*'Se nari mrityur keho nohe, se jibanraser rasik'.* translation author); but even with this fullness of life she fails to make peace with Sachish, who in his search for spiritual fulfilment, repudiates all her efforts to bring him physical and emotional succour. To Sribilash's comment that Sachish is so preoccupied with his mind that his need for bodily care has been reduced, Damini responds by saying that it is her *swadharma* as a woman to provide care for and nurture the body and she cannot tolerate Sachish penalizing his own body. Sachish, however, implores her to let him be; he has only one need, he says, that is to be in uninterrupted communion with the 'boundless'. In Sachish's nightmare inside the cave, the 'natural' or the 'physical' is an abhorrent presence, a 'primitive animal', soft and with mane, without well-defined head, torso or tail, an alien cumulus of slobbering hunger wrapping itself around his legs and swallowing him gradually. He is only half-aware that this creature of his nightmare is actually Damini seeking his proximity in the darkness of the cave and getting hurt in the chest as he kicks at the imagined monster in horror and disgust. It is through Sribilash's balancing presence that the narration acquires an alternative perspective when the 'monster' changes into a living woman and the horror we had shared with Sachish is transformed into compassion.

As for 'Sesh Katha', we may refer to the earlier version of the story published in *Desh* (1939); here, even as the man–woman binaries appear much more clearly than in the later version in the conversations between Achira and Nabinmadhav, the two principal characters, the irony that fractures these binaries comes out in the prelude to the story. Here the narrator refers to the myth of the ascetic Rishyashringa and the break in his hard penance caused by an ordinary woman; at one level, in Tagore's story, this has a parallel in the 'tapasya' of the scientist, Nabinmadhav, and the temporary break caused in it by Achira, who lives in a state of self-exile from civilization in the forested area where Nabinmadhav is prospecting in search of mineral ore. Achira herself also refers to the myth of Kacha's repudiation of the love of Debjani, his preceptor's daughter, which results in his acquired knowledge becoming accursed. But she refuses to act like Debjani. Rather, it is she who tells Nabinmadhav that in this state of exile from civilization, it seems to her that the blind force of life (*pranprakriti*) in human beings gets the better of their intelligence (*manaprakriti*). The forest is like a huge multi-limbed primitive animal, a 'land-based octopus' hypnotizing its prey with its fixed gaze; she points out that in being drawn towards each other in this unusual milieu, they have both succumbed to its hypnotic influence. The man has been disturbed in his scientific work which is his tapasya while the woman has faltered in her loyalty to her impersonal 'ideal of love'. Like Prakriti in *Chandalika*, Achira is seen as coming to the realization herself that the desired man would lose the aura through which she sees him if he gets distracted from his high mission, his tapasya. So Nabinmadhav gets his release, but carries a little bit of the 'broken chain' inside like a pain in his memory.

However, the author-narrator who distances himself from this 'short story' in the prelude, also subtly undermines Nabinmadhav's perception of his mission and Achira's sacrifice. Nabinmadhav is the modern man trained in Europe. He resembles a European not only in his looks, but in the habits he has acquired as scientist and prospector. His love for his country is articulated in the belief that it is not through political movements alone but through a modernizing, industrializing mission that the country can be made self-reliant. The primitive forest with rich mineral ore hidden in its depths is for him a location which must be exploited to carry forward his mission. When one sees this in the context of Tagore's extremely critical approach to western civilization in the second half of his life, of which *Sabhyatar Sankat* (1941) becomes the ultimate statement, the irony undermining Nabinmadhav's sense of his own mission can be better understood. We may recall that the prosperity of the King in the earlier play *Raktakarabi* (1926) also lies in mines through which the ransacking of the earth goes on. Achira may look at the primitive forest as identical with the blind life force of the female, but on the other hand, the civilization that Nabinmadhav represents is the domain modelled on the West—that of the exploiting, marauding male. Achira, as a woman, may admire it, but she also represents values which this civilization has lost.

In Tagore's critique of western civilization, articulated through many of his writings particularly from 1915–16, the pattern of configuration of man–woman binaries seems to have come full cycle. The male essence of selfish restlessness characterizes this civilization; compassion seen as a human but now a feminine virtue has been marginalized. It is in tune with this perspective that Achira proves to be elusive to Nabinmadhav. We may, on a superficial glance, say that the same essentialist approach to man–woman relationship, which gets problematized in many of Tagore's earlier creative writings, is here resumed at a new level to critique the predatory character of western 'male' civilization. Nature and woman are identified with each other in their nurturing aspect. To that extent, this position seems to anticipate what would in our own time be designated as environmental feminism, but for the fact that the identification in Tagore's case does not go beyond the figurative. This is evident in the fact that in the mature Tagore's writings, nurturing is often referred to as a basic human quality which has only been ascribed to woman in her marginalized role. Ananda assures Prakriti that she is a part of the same humanity to which Ananda belongs, just as in the earlier play *Raktakarabi* (1924), Nandini is not just the archetypal woman, she is also the 'daughter of man'. On the other hand, the self-destructive aspect of humanity, male and female, is also derived from 'Nature' as Tagore sees it. Sandip in *Ghare-Baire* calls himself a 'realist' as being a worshipper of 'Nature red in tooth and claw'.

Among Tagore's English writings, obviously intended for a non-Indian (specially an American-European) public, there are two essays: 'Woman' and 'Woman and Home' published respectively in 1917 and 1922, where the stereotyped framework of man–woman relationship is recast in the context of the nature–civilization binary that also gets intertwined in his thought with the polarities of the West and the East. Thus, it is said in the first essay that 'in the vital department of humanity woman still occupies the throne given to her by Nature' while 'man in the mental department has created and extended his own dominion'. The present civilization is said to be 'almost exclusively masculine, a civilization of power, in which woman has been thrust aside in the shade'. At the present moment, then, her role has universal implications; it has to surpass the sphere of domesticity and reach into the bruised and maimed world of the individual; she must claim each one of them as her own, the useless and the insignificant.... The world with its insulted individuals has sent its appeal to her. These individuals must find their true value, raise their heads once again in the sun, and renew their faith in God's love through her love' (Das 1996: 416).

In the second essay, the present civilization is said to have developed from primitive nomadic life with its 'predatory instinct of exploitation'. Once again, this is a predominantly 'male' civilization located in the West where the author finds women being 'hustled out of their shelter'. Against that, an agricultural civilization like that of India or China is 'essentially a civilization of human relationship, of the adjustment of mutual obligations'. It is based on 'co-operation, not competition', that is, the 'principle of home', but home in a larger sense. Woman's role here is seen once again as that of restoring 'the spiritual supremacy of all that is human in the world of humanity' (ibid.: 555).

While it is evident that this position involves a degree of idealization not only of the woman, but also of the imagined 'East', it is also true that in Tagore's inventory of 'insulted individuals', those who suffer from such 'insult' and exploitation within the paradigm of the 'East' are not excluded. Side by side with the colonized people, women subjugated by 'the brutal pride of an exclusive possession' through their economic helplessness and human beings degraded by caste discrimination have a distinctive place in this list.

Thus, even while working with the stereotypes common to his own milieu and his own times, Tagore is able to bring into his creative writings diversified and even contradictory resonances.

This brings us back to the poignancy of *Chandalika*, where one of the most insulted of individuals, who is also a woman, gains a new subjectivity through her desire for Ananda. At the same time, her separation from Ananda is made tolerable by the fact that she discovers the value of her own daily life and labour consisting of indispensable acts of love and service. Ananda's high mission of salvation is certainly not to be compared with the predatory mission of western civilization as Tagore sees it and as he represents it in the character of the mineralogist in '*Sesh Katha*'. But a nuanced reading of *Chandalika* does seem to point to the perceived incompleteness of Ananda's high mission which is totally impersonal and self-absorbed like the pursuits of modern science and ignores the day-to-day creativity of human labour that is embodied in Prakriti. She is not just a passive object salvaged by Ananda, but represents an active value that civilization seems to have lost, which needs to be recovered.

NOTES

1   Chandals are untouchables engaged in the cremation of dead bodies.
2   A female quester undertaking a secret journey in search of her beloved. Radha, the consort of Lord Krishna in Vaishnav literature, is the archetypal figure of an abhisarika. Hence, the motive of such a quester is imbued with spirituality and aims at gratification beyond the carnal.

REFERENCES

Das, Sisir Kumar. 1996. *The English Writings of Rabindranath Tagore*, vol. 2. New Delhi: Sahitya Akademi.

Pal, Prashanta Kumar. 2004. *Rabijibani*, vol. 9. Kolkata: Ananda Publishers, 2002.

Tagore, Rabindranath. 1980–2001. *Rabindra Rachanavali*, vols.1–16. Kolkata: Government of West Bengal, 1961.

———. 1909. *Chaturanga. Rabindra-Rachanavali*, vol. 4. Kolkata: Visva-Bharati.

PART III

REALM OF DOMESTICITY

CHAPTER 5

Domestic Space in Tagore's Fiction

Supriya Chaudhuri

In a letter written to his wife, Mrinalini, in 1901, the year he began publishing *Nashtanir*, as well as *Chokher Bali*, in the journal *Bharati*, Rabindranath wrote: 'My inmost being continually craves emptiness, not just the emptiness of sky, air and light, but an emptiness within the home, an emptiness of furnishings and arrangements, an emptiness of effort, thought, fuss [*alternatively*—empty of furnishings and arrangements, empty of effort, thought, fuss].'[1] This desire for a void within the home projects a cleansed, empty interior, an absolute simplicity or clarity, as against the filled and arranged space of our ordinary lives. The domestic reform it envisages is different from, but not unrelated to, the longing for absolute freedom or release outside the home, which we may think of in terms of the infinite, or *asim*, that Rabindranath refers to repeatedly in his poetry. A European equivalent is perhaps the 'intimate immensity' that Gaston Bachelard wrote of in his phenomenological classic *The Poetics of Space* (1957), an immensity that he described in terms of the sacredness and unboundedness of nature, and illustrated from Rilke, though we find it everywhere in Rabindranath's poetry and in the letters of *Chhinnapatrabali*, written in the 1890s.[2] In his poetry, as in his letters and shorter fiction, Rabindranath does indeed communicate his yearning for that intimate immensity, that 'emptiness of sky, air, and light': but in his novels, dealing directly with the domestic interiors of the bourgeois house in nineteenth-century India, the relations between space and mental life must be differently configured.

For Bachelard, 'the topography of our intimate being' was best understood in terms of the inhabited spaces of the house, for him a site of memories, dreams, reflections. His excavation of the spatial

imaginary, of what he repeatedly calls the oneiric house, organized
like an intimate universe from cellar to attic, and stored with the
private spaces of corners, nooks, crannies, bedrooms, chests, draw-
ers, wardrobes, constitutes an important moment in western phenomenological discourse. His work became a late-modern classic,
influencing postmodernist architecture as well as theoretical and
critical studies of literary texts. Yet looking back at this book today,
we cannot fail to be struck by the distance that separates the spatial
experiences of Indian cultural history from the European domestic
spaces that form the subject of Bachelard's rapturous celebration.
The contrast is particularly visible in texts that seek to negotiate an
emergent notion of psychological interiority within the physical
confines of the home, and do so, moreover, through a literary form,
the novel, whose phenomenological orientation is initially derived
from the West.[3]

Tagore's calculated destabilization of the interiors of the bourgeois house, which provides the settings for all his major novels,
suggests a completely different experience of domestic space. For
his women, particularly, the domestic interior presents itself as a
site of lack at the very same time that its crowded, substantial presence is recorded. Rabindranath himself, looking back at the external and internal compulsions that brought him to the writing of
longer fiction at the turn of the century (though his historical novel
Bouthakuranir Haat had been published as early as 1883), spoke of the
'harsh touch of domesticity' [*samsarer rurha sparsha*] that moulded
his writing during this period, the necessity of engaging directly
with—as he saw them—the cruel facts of household life. Writing
in 1940, the year before his death, of his composition of *Chokher
Bali* ('Grit in the Eye', 1902; serialized in *Bangadarshan* 1901–02),
he links it, in an intricate chain of material and mental relations,
to the new print world addressed by the revival of *Bangadarshan* (of
which he was joint editor) and Bankimchandra Chattopadhyay's
novel *Bishabriksha* ('The Poison Tree', 1872), which, for him, decisively marked the literary universe of the earlier, greater phase of
Bangadarshan's publication history. It is almost impossible to over-
state the influence of *Bishabriksha* on Bengali literature of the suc-
ceeding decades, particularly on Rabindranath's own fiction from
Chokher Bali (1901) to *Jogajog* (1929), both novels that recall and echo

the controlling themes of the earlier work. It could indeed be argued that it is Bankimchandra who, in this study of a young widow who brings disaster into the household of Nagendra and Suryamukhi, provides the impetus for a deconstruction of the interiors of the bourgeois home. Yet Rabindranath, while acknowledging Bankim's place, claims for himself the privilege of being the first to carry out that ruthless examination of the human heart and its domestic arrangements, not just in his novels, but also in the shorter fiction of the period: he mentions *Shasti* ('Punishment') and *Nashtanir* ('The Broken Nest') as examples of a literature without pity (*nirmam sahitya*). As he notes, it is the task of literature in this new phase not simply to describe, but to analyse the terrifying interior life of the household.[4]

In the Bengali novel of the nineteenth century, the furnishings of the bourgeois dwelling cannot be taken as notations of a 'self', as in the European novel of the same period. Rather, they function as an alienating environment for a new sense of personhood, itself marked by the contradictions and imbalances of the colonial encounter. This is as evident, I would argue, in the very first Bengali novel, Pyarichand Mitra's *Alaler Gharer Dulal* [The Spoilt Son of a Rich Family, 1858] as in the highest achievements of the genre in the nineteenth century, the social novels of Bankimchandra Chattopadhyay, such as *Bishabriksha*, published in 1872, as mentioned above, and *Krishnakanter Will* [Krishnakanta's Will, 1878], and Rabindranath's novels of a slightly later period The disjunction between the interior and interiority is marked, above all, through the representation of the furnishings of the bourgeois home. I will not repeat those arguments here. My focus in this essay is on Rabindranath's opening up of the domestic interior itself, his constitution of it as a site of lack, especially for women, and his effort to represent either a subterranean (and subversive) excavation of inner life, or a willed escape from the confines of the home into an imagined 'external' space where the boundaries of the self, and distinctions of outside and inside, are elided.

It is my feeling that Rabindranath is above all the writer who, while configuring mental life in terms of physical and metaphorical space, is most distrustful of the restricted, narrow interiors of the bourgeois house, and he translates this distrust into a way of understanding or representing character. That is, Rabindranath not only locates his characters in specific settings, but employs spatial images to represent personal or affective life, so that the precise contours of a character's inner life or aspirations may be viewed against their *placing* in a material *habitus* or in the public domain. Satyajit Ray, who was a careful and perceptive reader of Tagore, made remarkable use of this aspect of Tagore's representational technique, virtually never seeking a simple translation of Tagore's metaphors into visual forms, but substituting them with a range of cinematic frames within which space, interiority, affect and self-image receive distinct treatment.

The house in colonial India constituted a space roughly divided into outer and inner precincts, the outer areas reserved for the men of the house, for male visitors, and for business, and the inner or women's quarters, referred to in Northern India as the *antahpur*, andarmahal or *zenana*. The separation was reflected in the architecture of the traditional dwelling, though the distinction could only be strictly maintained in households above a certain economic level (that is, if the dwelling was substantial enough to be divided). Moreover, it was open to modification in the heterotopic sites constituted by religion or pleasure—for instance, in the transgressive space of the brothel, or through the socially sanctioned practice of pilgrimage. For women, this demarcation of household space allowed for a degree of freedom as well as privation, both characteristically internalized to become a norm of virtuous conduct. Domestic confinement was constituted not only by external restrictions but also by proscriptive fear or 'shame' (*lajja*). The East Bengal housewife, Rasasundari Devi (1810–99), writing the first Bengali prose autobiography in the second half of the nineteenth century, comments that even her children would not be able to understand the prohibitory shrinkings that formed their mother's consciousness. In a remarkable passage, she describes herself as retreating to an inner room to avoid being seen by her husband's horse when it came into the courtyard to be fed.[5]

Rabindranath's 1916 novel *Ghare-Baire* (At Home and in the World) deals directly with the relation between the inner and outer precincts of the bourgeois home, and chronicles the disastrous entry of outer into inner, as well as the perilous transition of its heroine from andarmahal to *baithak-khana*. Satyajit Ray's 1984 film, *Ghare-Baire* translates the journey to a striking visual sequence, prefaced by the narratorial voice of the film's protagonist, Bimala, showing the young mistress of the zamindari of Sukhsayar, for the first time in the family's history, stepping out of the inner, women's quarters of the house to entertain a guest in its outer apartments. The moment itself belongs entirely to the film's field of vision; it is missing in the novel, which contains no textual counterpart to Bimala's voiced commentary. With the exception of that voice, the filmed sequence is silent. The pale green doors of the andarmahal swing open, and two graceful, formally dressed figures—Bimala and her husband, Nikhilesh,—emerge into a light-filled gallery. The camera's eye focuses for a moment on the pair's feet, shod in decorative slippers, then moves up to track their transit through the corridor, panelled in stained glass that casts an unearthly radiance on the scene. As they reach the open doors at its end and emerge into the long, pillared verandah, with its slender European statues on raised pediments, the pace diminishes to lyrical slow motion. In a series of overlapping shots, the director focuses on their deliberate, self-absorbed, thoughtful steps, making them appear to float rather than walk, like characters in a dream. Two sets of doors remain open behind them, but they do not look back. In the last shot of this wordless sequence, they stand framed by the curtains until Bimala crosses a final threshold into the sitting-room (baithak-khana) of her marital home.

The sequence occupies just over one minute of screen time, though it may seem longer because of the leisurely, poetic movement of the camera as it records the pair's progress through the verandah. Ray might appear to be quoting here the first seven-and-a-half minutes of his own earlier, greater film, *Charulata* [The Lonely Wife, 1964]. There too, as Charulata crosses the long verandah from the inner apartments to her husband's study and sitting-room, screen time and real time coincide. But while the 'realistic' tracking camera here follows Charu's own rhythms—busy, preoccupied, curious, idle—the camera work in *Ghare-Baire* is completely different: time is elongated, non-naturalistic, made to fill the recessive, overlapping shots and dream-like motion. In both films, though, Ray offers a highly self-conscious use of the lens's gaze to assert 'the symbolic functions of the frame and the scene as spatial orders', at the same time he establishes the spatial economy within which relationships and characters must be understood.[6] *Ghare-Baire*, with its contrast of *ghar* (home) and *bahir* (outside), is firmly articulated in terms of this spatial economy.

In the kind of fiction that Rabindranath sees himself as inaugurating around the turn of the century, his women characters are usually located within the domestic spaces that contain and therefore *place* them. Place, in this sense, is a materially and culturally determined region that must be physically traversed. At the same time, there are frequent references to a mental or metaphoric space which is accessible to thought or feeling, but cannot be contained by it. Such space may be ideologically constructed, like the *bahir* into which Nikhilesh seeks to release Bimala in *Ghare-Baire*, or it may be viewed as an infinite solace briefly touched through music or meditation, as with Kumudini in *Jogajog*. These works, it could be argued, offer a much more extensive treatment of the geography of the home, but even in his early novella *Nashtanir*, Charu's idleness and loneliness within the inner apartments of their house is contrasted with Bhupati's preoccupation with his newspaper and his intellectual associates in the public apartments. Rabindranath does not describe the interior of the house apart from a few references to Bhupati's wealth, which would imply opulence, and to architectural features like the verandah. One point that is clearly made, however, is the geographical separation of the inner quarters from the outer rooms of the house where Bhupati entertains his guests or attends to his work. Later in the narrative, Bhupati specifically makes the journey into the antahpur at unaccustomed hours during the day to seek solace, which he does not obtain, from Charu.

Adjacent to the inner quarters is a plot of waste land, and the first extended treatment of Charu's efforts to amuse herself is through the garden plans she shares with her husband's young cousin Amal, already a resident in the house as he pursues his college studies. It is worth noting that the antahpur described far more negatively in 'Streer Patra' (written some thirteen years later in 1914, and the first work in which Tagore saw himself as decisively taking the woman's part), lacks even a scrap of waste land, but contains, as here, a solitary tree of no particular ornamental or utilitarian value.[7] In his 1964 film *Charulata*, Ray deliberately omitted the elaborate fancy of the garden and its design, introducing Amal as a newly arrived relative who sits with Charu in a *locus amoenus* somewhere between a garden and a wilderness. But for Charu in *Nashtanir* the idea of the laid out, elaborately planned garden is itself a place of repose and peace. Even unrealized, it becomes a space shared between her and Amal; the fact that it can never be transferred from the imaginary to the real world is no barrier to its conceptualization and the solace it provides. When the garden is finally abandoned as too ambitious and uneconomic, its place is taken by writing as the intimate, private space of communion between Charu and Amal. The fanciful plans devised for the laying out and beautification of the projected garden and its ornamental pond may remind us of Bankimchandra Chatterjee's novel *Krishnakanter Will,* where both pond and garden function within an elaborate symbolic register: but Bankim is not mentioned at this point by Rabindranath, and if there is an analogy at all, it is the merest of traces producing, in the inter-textual weave, the name Charu chants in Ray's film as she searches for Bankimchandra's novel *Kapalkundala* on the bookshelf. It is worth arguing, however, that the specular dynamics of Ray's film incorporate the serial presence of several women protagonists of Bengali fiction, as well as, of course, the figure unmistakably present in *Nashtanir*, Rabindranath's sister-in-law Kadambari.

In terms of the treatment of actual physical space, there are no descriptions in the novel that really match the detail of the opening sequence of Ray's 1964 film. But there is an affective link to the long verandah at one side of the house, and a classically inflected image of Charu sitting by the window in a state of deep withdrawal and melancholy. The house itself, apart from these images, is never used by Rabindranath to figure in physical terms the interior spaces of Charu's heart. Rather, the journey into the physical interior of the house, undertaken at untimely moments by Bhupati who hopes to gain solace from communion with his wife, becomes an agoniz-ing trajectory of frustration and disappointment: Charu does not respond, he sits by her side in silence, he cannot draw her out or win a consolatory word from her. Meanwhile, the unhappy Charu, who has in a terrible moment left her bedroom and gone outside to weep over Amal's departure, is described as finally reconciling her-self to her loss by constructing a wholly private mental space like a dungeon or a tunnel or a cell, where she can yield herself entirely to her grief and love. The impulse to retreat is one that Rabindranath returns to in his late novel *Jogajog* [*Relationships*]: but its spatial configuration is most fully developed here:

> In this way, Charu dug a tunnel under the entire structure of her domestic tasks and duties, and in that unlighted silent darkness she built a temple of secret grief, adorned with the garlands of her tears. Neither her husband nor anyone else in the world had any claim there. That place was as secret as it was deep, as it was beloved. At its entrance she would abandon all the disguises of her household and enter in her unadorned true form, and when she left it, she would put on the mask again and present herself in the theatre of the world's work, laughter and conversation.[8]

If there is a parallel between this passage and the account of Kumudini's withdrawal in *Jogajog*, there is also, in the later novel, a desperate need to suppress and deaden the inner self:

> In that region of the self where Kumu existed as a person—however much her mind was filled with contempt and revulsion and distaste, however much her domestic life insulted her with the harsh claim of its physical dominance—she began to create a covering for herself. Such an integument, indeed, might efface from her mind the truth of her likes and dislikes—that is, reduce her awareness of herself.[9]

What we have here is metaphor rather than the metonymy of realist object-description. One problem Satyajit Ray must have encountered when he tried to create a visual equivalent for the text of *Nashtanir* is that all the action takes place in the minds of the characters, at the level of assumption, inference and aversion. It must have been immediately obvious to Ray that the mental landscapes of *Nashtanir* were unrealizable in cinematic terms, since film is an iconic medium that offers the illusion of real space, of a world of objects disposed and arranged in a physically verifiable order. This world would require precise and detailed spatial configuration in his film: but what Ray adds is a kind of spatial tracking of affect, as though the camera were setting out to produce character as an effect of space. Ravi Vasudevan, for example, cites 'the highly self-conscious deployment of the camera' in the travelling shots of the opening sequence, and its assertion of the symbolic functions of the frame and the scene as spatial orders. Visually, Vasudevan suggests, 'the verandah running along the house's first floor is recurrently used to define relations between people, and to provide the spectator with a perspective, across the landing, other than that of the characters.'[10]

Those seven-and-a-half minutes of cinema, unforgettable as a real-time experience where our perspective is forced to coincide with that of a shifting viewer *within* the setting but *outside* the frame, establish the interior of Bhupati's house, not constructed as a *montage* but tracked by the camera as it follows Charu's movements through the rooms and the verandah. Spectatorship is divided between our viewing of Charu and her playful, idle viewing of the street scene below, and of her unmindful husband, with the opera glasses. The glasses distance and frame the spectacle of the street for Charu, emphasizing her separation from the ordinary life that passes below her windows, a process culminating at the point where Charu subjects her own husband to 'the ironic, exteriorizing gaze of the opera glasses'.[11] Charu's own subjectivity is linked in the film to a literary domain shaped by her playful invocation of Bankim, while her husband is placed, decisively, outside this region of fictional solace.

The camera's gaze establishes Charu herself as the beautiful object of our loving connoisseurship and concern, while her own gaze is turned away to the life of the street which, like her husband, does not see her. But what overwhelms the scene and constructs itself as a site of alienation, I would suggest, is the elaborately furnished set of rooms through which she moves, and towards which the camera is also turned. The detail and richness of the wallpaper, the small statues lining the verandah, the room's furnishings, the book bindings, the shutters, constitute the physical register of an interior which is not, and can never coincide with, interiority. Ray's deliberate and sumptuous use of space and furniture here to encode the bourgeois way of life in the mid-nineteenth century, constructing the house, like Charu herself, as something that Bhupati owns but does not care for, implicitly produces the domestic interior as a rich, substantial, but alienating setting for a subjectivity not yet fully understood. The scene's irony lies in Charu's *dis-identification* from the furniture (by the production of her own alert, inquisitive, ironic gaze) at the very same time as she is caught in the same frame with it. It is evident from her casual, idle fingering of objects in the room, her detached drifting from point to point within it, that this is not Charu's own set of rooms. By contrast to its magnificence, Charu's own sari is of the common handloom variety; unlike Bimala in *Ghare-Baire*, she is not routinely clad in fine clothes.

Ray cannot have been unaware of Rabindranath's dislike of the lavishly furnished bourgeois interior, even of furniture per se. (There is a story about his getting rid of all the European furniture in the Jorasanko house after returning from a lecture by Brahmabandhab Upadhyay. It was brought back by Debendranath who, of course, had in a similar fit of asceticism given all Dwarakanath's furnishings away after his death.)[12] For the cinematographer, by contrast, the material excess of a setting invites the camera's scrupulous—not necessarily sympathetic—gaze. In an interview recorded by Shyam Benegal, Ray spoke of his fascination with 'the visual aspect of opulence' and specifically mentioned both *Charulata* and 'Monihara' (*Teen Kanya*), with *Jalsaghar*, in this context. In many respects the camera's treatment of the rich, substantial, furnished domestic interior in 'Monihara' matches that in *Charulata*. In 'Monihara', however, that early framing is instrumental in a different narrative of desire: Moni desires, not so much the bourgeois luxury of domestic interiors, but what she can hold or grasp to herself: jewellery. When her husband, Phanibhushan, is threatened with financial ruin, she escapes into the river-dominated landscape with her jewels, as fetishized objects of a yearning that neither the house nor its contents can contain. The tone of 'Monihara', a skilful domestication of the gothic, differs considerably from that of *Charulata*; yet there are resemblances in the camera-work as in the employment of 'the visual aspect of opulence' to define character (in both films, that of lonely and childless wives). In a much later film, *Ghare-Baire*, whose protagonist Nikhilesh expresses, in Rabindranath's text, distaste for the expensive furnishings of his zamindari mansion, Ray shows his discontented couple sitting uncomfortably on the lavishly upholstered chairs of their living room as though it were an unpleasant duty. But in *Charulata*, the useless luxury of the domestic setting that frames and *places* Charu almost seduces the gaze into regarding Charu herself as the same kind of commodity: the camera threatens or invites this conclusion, then dispels it by elaborating Charu's own spectatorship within the scene.

If the interior does not stand for interiority, what does? Having de-legitimized the bourgeois interior, even before it is robbed of its material substance by Umapati/ Umapada (to the strains of Rammohan Roy's stirring Bengali version of *Dies irae*–'*mone karo, sheshera shei din bhayankara*') and of its moral self-assurance by Charu, Ray needs to provide us with a cinematic staging of interiority that might compensate for the hollowness of the house. Such interiority can only be located in the exterior, in the open, empty world, in mental space rather than physical place, in a free-ranging or movement of affect. Ray, therefore, constructs the remarkable sequence of images that passes through Charu's mind as she sits on the swing, culminating in her beginning her first literary composition, 'My Village' ('Amar Gram'). In these village scenes, as in the street life glimpsed by Charu through her opera glasses, Ray recalls a world that cannot be mobilized in the narrative except through the sensibility of the woman protagonist, standing always at a slightly oblique angle to the wealth and power of the bourgeois household she inhabits. Here, as in the scene with the opera glasses, we have a 'modernist framing of a history through devices of spatial staging and distantiation'.[13] Charu's memories, passing over the screen as images that flicker and slide into each other, construct a different history of the nation from that which is being debated by Bhupati in his study. And this repository of images, from the mother spinning cotton to the entertainers at the fair, is finally the source, the film claims (like the novella) of a more authentic literary consciousness, not only gaining critical acclaim but putting Charu's male mentors to shame.

But the film does not stage or create a separate space for desire, because desire is everywhere, it has no precise location, and in this respect it is like space. Charu's desire—for solace, for company, for Amal—fills the film from the beginning, and what we trace through its movement is not so much a trajectory of transgression as an unqualified longing that at some point has become confused with a particular person. The discovery scene is placed indoors, and the end of the film returns us, even more oppressively and painfully, to those heavily over-furnished interiors and enclosed spaces with which we had started. Bhupati comes home in a hackney carriage, trapped in his thoughts as he is shown confined in the coach's dark interior, and Charu, again seen in the bedroom and the verandah, listening for the sounds of her husband's return, is framed with him, trapped in the freeze-shot, in the vista of the long passage. I have no wish to debate the excellence or otherwise of this ending and its adequacy to the literary text. *Nashtanir* and *Charulata* are different works, not linked in the relation of original and copy. It would be useless to attempt to recover, at this remove of time, the notion itself of an original. Ray, who builds his film on his understanding of *Nashtanir* as of other texts, attempts to stage, with the material at his disposal, a spatial disposition of affect and interiority that can be referred to Tagore but is not determined by his example.

It is my feeling that Rabindranath returns, over and over again in the fiction of his maturity, to the intractable differences—of desire, of motive, of self-understanding—that lie at the heart of household life, examining them in terms of relations that are as much symbolic as actual: the domestic triangles of *Chokher Bali* (1901–2) and *Ghare-Baire* (1915–16), the chance-ridden romantic history of *Naukadubi* (1903–5) and the moral fable of nativity in *Gora* (1907–10: both, in different ways, subjecting the notion of the Hindu family to unbearable strain), and the extraordinary quest-narrative of *Chaturanga* (1914–15), which rejects the institution of the family entirely, only to reaffirm faith in an eccentric version of marriage at the close. In several of these novels, what appears to be a triangulated relationship is founded upon an inseparable bond between two men—Mahendra and Bihari, Nikhilesh and Sandeep, Gora and Binoy, Shachish and Sribilash, sometimes presented as a rational–emotional or spiritual–material dyad, sometimes as a deeply exploitative partnership in which one partner appropriates, in a sense, the other's emotional and erotic life. But what is common to virtually all of them is the placing of the woman protagonist as both subject of desire and desiring subject, the locus of an impossible longing that can never, given the nature of household life itself, be satisfied. It seems to me that the form that this representation takes is shaped by Rabindranath's own deep convictions regarding women's lives and their regulation by a special form of desire, a hunger directed not so much towards the world and its objects as towards the self's own image in consciousness, that becomes in some cases, such as that of Bimala in *Ghare-Baire*, a kind of narcissism. *Jogajog*, more or less the last novel in this sequence, offers perhaps the harshest and most unsparing examination of family life, and it is also virtually the only one in which the two partners in a marriage stand directly opposed to one another, unsupported by the partnerships Rabindranath had used in his earlier works. In its treatment of domestic space—the separation of outer and inner apartments in the bourgeois dwelling—the desperate withdrawal of the heroine into ever-more confined spaces in her marital home to escape her husband's attentions, the figurative representations of that impulse to retreat and the longing for release or transcendence, expressed as much through phrases of music as through images of the divine, *Jogajog* is undoubtedly the most complex and finely articulated of Rabindranath's novels, not excepting *Ghare-Baire* (despite its obvious spatial configuration).

But I think it might be more interesting here, given the historical moment I began with, a moment that Rabindranath himself saw as a point of departure, to look briefly at the earliest novel in this sequence, *Chokher Bali* (1901–2), an astonishingly assured exposure of bourgeois marriage and domesticity that echoes and refashions the governing tropes of Bankimchandra's *Bishabriksha* (a book that Binodini is herself shown to be reading in the novel's course). Rabindranath, in his later comments on the novel, sees it as formed by the possessive violence of Rajlakshmi's maternal love, her jealousy (*irsha*), which incites and makes dangerous space for Mahendra's sexual rapacity. Interestingly, he does not here refer to Binodini at all, though in the novel itself and earlier debates about it, it is Binodini—memorably described as *kshudita-hridaya*, hungry-hearted—who is the focus of both readerly and writerly anxiety.

Binodini's hunger consumes both her and others in the novel, yet it is Rabindranath's remarkable achievement that he never represents the operation of desire as hers alone, assigning equal, if not greater agency in the plot to Mahendra and the profoundly self-deceiving Rajlakshmi. For the most part, the novel is set in the stifling confines of the bourgeois home, and the developing relationship between Asha, Binodini, Mahendra and Bihari is articulated through complex negotiations of internal space, Binodini choosing when to appear before the male members of the household and when to withdraw herself, and finally regulating Mahendra's access to her even when she has left the house with him; Asha tongue-tied and embarrassed in Bihari's presence, fleeing abruptly when he turns up in Benares, but gaining in self-presence after she takes charge of the household during Rajlakshmi's illness. Spatially, the novel is ordered around the contrast of the lower floors of the house, which contain both the public apartments and Rajlakshmi's bedroom, and Mahendra's second-floor room with its marital bed and couch on the floor (*nicher bichhana*) which becomes, in a sense, the locus of illicit desire. Contrasted with this oppressive but luxurious domestic interior are Binodini's impoverished village dwelling, Bihari's conversion of his living-space to an exercise in philanthropy, Annapurna's simple residence in Kashi, and the occasional release and solace that the protagonists find on the terrace in the quiet of the evening. In this novel, as in others, arguably, Rabindranath appears to view sexual desire as a function of egotism and self-absorption, a need directed as much towards the self as towards the other. This is evident in Mahendra's careless appropriation of Asha from Bihari, his growing desire for Binodini, and in Binodini's own need to be revenged upon the world for its neglect of her. Most unusually, given the male pairings we find here and in Rabindranath's other novels, the relationship of two women, Asha and Binodini, functions as a conduit through which Binodini can become a secret sharer, even a voyeur, at the scene of Asha's marriage.

Chokher Bali too has received influential, but more recent, cinematic treatment at the hands of the director Rituparno Ghosh, whose version (2003) presents a highly charged cinematic treatment of domestic interiors, the camera's gaze focusing especially on floors, staircases and furniture. The film's use of colour to impart a rich, warm glow to surfaces and skin is instrumental in creating the effect of bourgeois prosperity, if not opulence, in Mahendra's house. But it adds to this, we may recall, such elaborations as the extraordinary scenes with the jewellery, and the Mahendra–Binodini episode in the carriage, which can only be understood as directorial allusions to scenes in 'Monihara' or *Charulata*, and which offer, instead of the finely nuanced critiques of desire, especially material desire, in the earlier films, a complete surrender to the lure of the world and its objects. It is my feeling that Ghosh's transformation of the novel's text to this form of postmodern kitsch, however much it may serve a modern ethic of desire and sexual agency, is deeply unfaithful both to Rabindranath's discomfort with the material embodiments of bourgeois domesticity and his understanding of desire as ultimately self-consuming, founded in the ego rather than directed towards the world.

A longer and more detailed examination might make the necessary connections between this negotiation of internal space, the architecture of the bourgeois dwelling and a projected reform of the interior. Swati Chattopadhyay notes a change in domestic architecture from the eighteenth to the nineteenth centuries:

> Pre-colonial architecture emphasized the experience of the interior spaces and the many thresholds that connected the rooms with the interior open space, be it a courtyard or a garden. The eighteenth-century buildings of Calcutta designed for affluent Indians shared this tradition. They ignored a prominent street entrance, and lavished attention on the four interior faces of the courtyard.... In other words the envelope was de-emphasized to celebrate the interiority of domestic space. This focus on interiority would change in the nineteenth century for two reasons. One was the popularization of the European notion of a façade, and the second was the desire to *connect* with the increasingly busy street life, rather than withdrawing from it.... This interest in generating a 'front' was symptomatic of the new urge to outwardly *display* residences as symbols of wealth and status.[14]

Rabindranath's grandfather, Prince Dwarakanath, built a house in the new style in 1823, a *baithak-khana bari* consisting of reception rooms and offices erected next to the eighteenth-century family mansion in Calcutta's Jorasanko district. After his death, as the artist Abanindranath Tagore recalls in his memoirs, the second floor of the house was reconfigured to accommodate the andarmahal, with screens, curtains, and shutters, as well as extensions, verandahs and passageways on multiple levels. Complex rules governed the shutting of doors and window-blinds, scrupulously maintaining the separation between the andarmahal, inhabited by the women, the children and their servants, and the offices and salon on the first two floors, ruled over by the men of the house.[15] For the poet, as for his nephews Abanindranath and Gaganendranath, who repeatedly return to it in their paintings, the Jorasanko house, with its intricate gradations of interior space, its internal boundaries, the multiple frames of windows, doors and shutters, the possibilities both of *looking out* and *looking in*, became a mysterious and haunted place. It is this interior space, the space of early childhood that is for them the site of creative imagination.

Yet there are within that enclosed space remembered from early childhood, profoundly important moments of looking out, of experiencing the 'intimate immensity' of nature. Even in a novel like *Jogajog*, the grinding detail of realist representation, focusing upon bourgeois interiors, is countered by the affective power of a remembered landscape where the world is not so much a collection of objects in use, as a set of images imprinted on Kumudini's consciousness. That 'other space', a *heterotopia* implicit in religious devotion, music and childhood memory, sustains her in the soulless luxury of her marital home as in her stifling marriage, and constitutes a form of infinitude.

Tagore's revulsion from the crowded interiors of the nineteenth-century colonial mansion, fictionalized in the experiences of his characters, may be related to the real changes he sought to effect in domestic architecture. When he visited the Bauhaus on his sixtieth birthday in 1921, he was still in search of an ideally pared-down, cleared-out living space. Over a period of time, through a series of experiments with furniture, design, and ways of living, he affirms the style of an Indian modernity. The artist Surendranath Kar designed (roughly between 1919 and 1935) five houses for Tagore in his ashram at Shantiniketan, drawing upon Pan-Asian (primarily Japanese), traditional Indian and primitivist-folk sources of inspiration, and rejecting colonial models for a local and nationalist aesthetics, especially in the mud house called Shyamali.[16] In a letter to Andrée Karpelès written on 14 May 1935, Rabindranath spoke of this last space in the following terms: 'Suren has built for me a mud house—a mud casket beautifully worked, for enshrining in it the last few days of my life. All our dwelling places contain various partnerships of love but this last one will only offer me a perfect solitude of a final departure which will not have the time to allow life's trespassers to invade its loneliness.'

We may link this final reform of the interior to the desire for infinitude expressed in so much of Rabindranath's poetry, the yearning for the intimate immensity of 'sky, air, light'. Tagore's 'asim' [unlimited], not identical with Rilke's 'open', is equally invested in a voiding of the world. In Rilke's eighth Duino Elegy, the feeling for space becomes an existential determination: the creature-world, gazing at the 'open', is unaware of death or limitation.[17] Human beings can never be 'unworlded' in this way: for them the familiar contours of land and sky, imbued with love, loss, or longing, are limited by the consciousness of mortality. Yet for Tagore and his characters, especially the women who, in all his fiction, feel most intensely the imprisoning confines of domestic space, intimations of infinitude pierce through the constrictions of physical existence. This is felt most strongly, I would suggest, in the letters of *Chhinnapatrabali* and in much of the short fiction produced in the same period. But Kumudini too, recalling 'the empty sprawling fields, the copses of wild tamarisks, the tow-path', like the young girl Subha, sitting under a tree, at noon, looking out at the immense silence of nature, feels the pull of that infinitude.[18]

NOTES

1   Cited from Rabindranath Tagore, *Chithipatra*, 1: 58, letter 29, in Pal (1990) *Rabijibani*, 5: 19. Translation author's.

2   Bachelard (1994) 183–210.

3   See my essay, 'Space, Interiority and Affect', JMI 6 (2008).

4   See Tagore (1940) '*Suchana*' [Introduction] to *Chokher Bali*, in *Rabindra Rachanabali*, 3: 283–84.

5   Rasasundari Devi, *Amar Jiban* [My Life], in N. Jana et al. (eds.), (1981), 1: 33. On Rasasundari Devi, see also Sarkar (1999).

6   Ravi Vasudevan, 'Nationhood, Authenticity and Realism in Indian Cinema: The Double-Take of Modernism in Ray', in Moinak Biswas (ed.), (2006): 101.

7   In *Nashtanir*, the fruit trees are a *bilati amra*; in *Streer Patra*, a *gab*.

8   *Nashtanir*, Chapter 15, in Tagore (1957), in *Rabindra Rachanabali*, 22: 254.

9   Tagore, *Relationships/Jogajog* (2006): 131.

10   Vasudevan, 'Nationhood, Authenticity and Realism in Indian Cinema', in Moinak Biswas (ed.), (2006): 101.
11   Ibid.: 102.
12   See Pal (1990): 5: 19; Debendranath Tagore, *Svarachita-jibancharit*, in N. Jana et al. (eds.), (1981), *Atmakatha*, 1: 8.
13   Vasudevan, 'Nationhood, Authenticity and Realism in Indian Cinema' in Moinak Biswas (ed.), (2006): 102.
14   Swati Chattopadhyay (2005), *Representing Calcutta: Modernity, Nationalism and the Colonial Uncanny*: 157.
15   Abanindranath Tagore (2005), *Apan Katha* [My Story]: 25–26.
16   See Tagore's letter to Andrée Karpelès, 14 May 1935, in Krishna Dutta and Andrew Robinson (eds.), *Selected Letters of Rabindranath Tagore*: 448.
17   See Rainer Maria Rilke (1968), 'Mit allen Augen sieht die Kreatur/das Offene', J. B. Leishman and Stephen Spender (transl and eds.), *Duino Elegies*: 77.
18   See Tagore, *Relationships/Jogajog* 53; and Tagore, '*Subha*' (1893), in *Selected Short Stories*, ed. Chaudhuri (2000): 105–6.

REFERENCES

Bachelard, Gaston. 1994. *The Poetics of Space*. Translated by Maria Jolas, with foreword by J. R. Stilgoe. Boston: Beacon Press.

Biswas, Moinak. ed. 2006. *Apu and After: Revisiting Ray's Cinema*. London: Seagull Books.

Chattopadhyay, Swati. 2005. *Representing Calcutta: Modernity, Nationalism and the Colonial Uncanny*. London: Routledge.

Chaudhuri, Supriya. 2008. 'Space, Interiority and Affect in *Charulata* and *Ghare-Baire*', *Journal of the Moving Image* 6: 12–35.

Devi, Rasasundari. 1981. *Amar Jiban* [My Life], in *Atmakatha* [Autobiographies], edited by N. Jana et al., vol. 1. Kolkata: Ananya Prakashan.

Dutta, Krishna, and Andrew Robinson (eds.). 1997. *Selected Letters of Rabindranath Tagore*. Cambridge: Cambridge University Press.

Jana, N., et al. (eds.).1981. *Atmakatha* [Autobiographies], vol. 1. Kolkata: Ananya Prakashan.

Pal, Prashanta Kumar 1990. *Rabijibani*, vol. 5: 1308–14. Kolkata: Ananda Publishers.

Rilke, Rainer Maria. 1968. *Duino Elegies*, edited and translated by J. B. Leishman and Stephen Spender. London: Hogarth Press.

Sarkar, Tanika. 1999. *Words to Win. The Making of* Amar Jiban: *A Modern Autobiography*. New Delhi: Kali for Women.

Tagore, Abanindranath. 2005. *Apan Katha* [My Story]. Kolkata: Ananda Publishers.

Tagore, Debendranath. 1981. '*Svarachita-Jibancharit*', in *Atmakatha,* edited by Naresh Jana et al. Kolkata: Ananya Prakashan.

Tagore, Rabindranath. 2006. *Relationships/Jogajog,* translated by Supriya Chaudhuri. New Delhi: Oxford University Press.

———. 2000. *Selected Short Stories*, edited by Sukanta Chaudhuri. New Delhi. Oxford University Press.

———. 1957. *Rabindra Rachanavali*, vol. 22. Kolkata: Visva-Bharati.

———. 1940. *Rabindra Rachanavali*, vol. 3. Kolkata: Visva-Bharati.

Vasudevan, Ravi. 2006. 'Nationhood, Authenticity and Realism in Indian Cinema: The Double-Take of Modernism in Ray', in Moinak Biswas, ed. *Apu and After: Revisiting Ray's Cinema*. London: Seagull Books.

CHAPTER 6

Tagore's Docile Daughters: Ambivalence in Family Life

Sanjukta Dasgupta

As a feminist critic there have been many occasions when I have referred to Tagore's fictional narratives, primarily the short stories, as unambiguous evidences of Tagore's understanding of women's exploitation and marginalization within the patriarchal family system and women's corresponding resistance—silent, vocal or rebellious. In fact, it would not be an over-statement to regard these narratives as some of the first male-authored Bengali feminist texts. Interestingly, Tagore's narratives seem so much more liberated and progressive than the contemporary regional/Bengali television soaps and serials that routinely churn out regressive stereotypes in the globalized twenty-first century. Yet when we think of the three daughters of Tagore, all *balika vadhus*, child brides, with no formal education in institutions one wonders about the social compulsions that made Tagore take these controversial decisions. Could it have been the possibility of the early demise of his wife, Mrinalini, and his long-term travelling schedules to distant lands that made him think that marriage of the daughters would liberate him from the role of guardianship of his daughters? Were there economic compulsions? Tagore's daughters do not seem to have been difficult daughters but in more likelihood were desirable daughters as Tagore's paternal care, concern and affection for them are undisputed facts. Yet though not abject, they were indeed docile daughters obedient to the wishes of their father, family and the patriarchal system that compelled urban, cultured and literate young girls in the nineteenth and early twentieth centuries to recognize marriage as compulsory, and also to realize that love between marital partners was accidental.

This element of docility iconized by the cultural construction of the self-effacing care giver domestic Goddess Lakshmi was integral to domestic peace and prosperity. If a woman deviated from the set norms of a Lakshmi in the house, repercussions in the form of punishment would inevitably follow due to the gross indiscipline that dared defy normative practices. As a result of rocking the patriarchal boat it was axiomatic that there was bound to be conflict and economic crisis within the family that would affect family members and also influence lack of progeny, birth of female infants, physically challenged children and illness. Despite their own very personal, liberated views as members of the Brahmo Samaj, in the pervading disciplining environment of the Hindu family system that internalized punishment at many levels for transgression, it is understandable that Tagore's young daughters obeyed their father's wishes and Tagore in turn was compelled to obey the systemic compulsions. Though the Hindu middle-class culture was significantly at variance with the social practices of the Brahmo Samaj, it had tangential effects on the Tagore family. Jorasanko Thakurbari, the Tagore mansion, was an island, but social relationships were dependent on negotiating with other families, and these were very different from the exclusivity that marked the Tagore family. Marriage was a social alliance with families who had their own value systems. The sons-in-law of the poet did reside at the Tagore mansion, and had converted to the Brahmo religion, but they could never become active participants in the Tagorean culture that was infecting urban Bengal, though they did try to conform in their own varying ways.

The riveting macro issues of the public domain, the threat of the partition of Bengal, the vibrant intellectual milieu of the Bengal Renaissance, setting up a school in Shantiniketan according to alternative educational ideals which was the poet's lifelong, all consuming dream, perhaps made Tagore think that the time-tested secure mode of liberation from the duties of a single parent of adolescent girl children in the early twentieth century was the marriage of the daughters. Tagore did select young men who had the potential of having promising careers, but in each instance, the three sons-in-law though successful in their own careers in varying degrees failed to sustain a relationship of understanding and friendship with their father-in-law.

As we know, Renuka and Madhurilata died early, while Mira had an unhappy marriage leading to an acrimonious divorce in the late 1920s. So in Tagore's own immediate family, his daughters' lives seemed a strange mix of home education personally supervised by their father, along with instructions from tutors, many of whom were British men and women. The fast consolidation of Tagorean culture, the culture of Jorasanko Thakurbari, widely imitated and of course criticized too—arranged marriage, dowry payments and bickering over dowry amounts, father-in-law paying for son-in-law's foreign education, death of his wife, Mrinalini, death from tuberculosis of two of his daughters, estrangement from husband and finally divorce of the youngest daughter, Mira, who survived her father, early death of his youngest son, Samindranath, and the widow remarriage of his eldest son Rathindranath—all indicate how challenging and extraordinary had been Tagore's personal life and his own immediate family. Quite unequivocally the poet's family stood alone in many respects, some even underscoring gender myopia.

Tagore himself took the initiative of negotiating the marriage between the widow Pratima Devi and his son Rathi and the marriage took place on 27 January 1910. In a letter to Mira, Tagore had stated that women at Shantiniketan who had found a particular case of widow re-marriage amusing and ridiculous proved their limited understanding of path-breaking initiatives. Tagore's irritation becomes obvious as he makes the following, somewhat essentialist observations,

> Women regard life in all its aspects very casually, their restricted outlook
> distorts all major aspects, all the great power that operates in the world,
> women lack awareness of all these, day and night they gossip and giggle, I
> have tried to protect all of you from becoming one of them. I hope my effort
> will not be futile, and you will not ruin your life's focus by unnecessary
> discussion of minor issues (Chattopadhyay 2000: 87; translation author's).

Interestingly, the factual data about the upbringing of Tagore's daughters in particular are quite contrary to the representations of women in Ashapurna Devi's trilogy, specifically the first two volumes, *Pratham Pratisruti* and *Subarnalata*. The late nineteenth-century and early twentieth-century rural, suburban and urban culture that defined the lives of women were extremely conservative, leading to domestic violence, verbal and psychological, if not always physical, which seemed to be the accepted way of life. In fact, Tagore's 'Streer Patra' (Wife's Letter) or even his social novels such as *Chokher Bali, Naukadubi* and *Jogajog* would seem to be closer to Ashapurna Devi's women in the trilogy, but Tagore's daughters in real life do not replicate the representations of Ashapurna's imagined women. Though there are overt coincidences in the historical timeline, socially and culturally the young Hindu women in Ashapurna's novels were in no way similar to the Brahmo women of Tagore's household, in this case, Tagore's own daughters, Madhurilata, Renuka and Mira. In the socio-political novel *Gora*, Sucharita was brought up in a Brahmo family (and in all respects converted to Brahmoism), but Anandamoyee was not a Brahmo. The juxtaposition of the semi-literate Hindu young woman and the well-educated Brahmo woman in *Naukadubi* can be an interesting study, but this foregrounds the real daughters of Tagore rather than his fictionalized imagined daughters. Marriage, marital partners, domesticity and illness played debilitating roles in the lives of Tagore's daughters, but his imagined daughters, mostly in his short stories such as Haimanti, Mrinal, Anila, Saudamini, Sohini, Kalyani have defined their roles as agents of resistance, not through flamboyant rebellion, but through subtle but steady resistance and rejection of gender injustice.

Societal practices and patriarchal norms seemed to have an implicit underpinning, in a far more complex form in the lives of Tagore's daughters, two of whom Madhurilata and Mira seemed to have had considerable talent, and all three were not just literate but were avid readers of both Bengali and English literary texts. Renuka died at the age of twelve, so one can just speculate that she would not have been different from her well-read, aware and talented sisters. Yet, all three daughters of Tagore seemed to have been regarded as primarily female bodies, and marriage was inevitable and compulsory for them. Frederick Engels, Virginia Woolf and Simone de Beauvoir have all interrogated the compulsory imposition of marriage on female bodies, and how the crucial issue of willingness or unwillingness was considered irrelevant.

In fact, as critiqued by Lois McNay (1992), while analysing the history of sexuality Foucault seemed to have a startlingly myopic outlook, for he defined women's roles and responsibilities as a social construct aimed towards the nurturance of the family system. Women, therefore, were trapped between the patriarchal regimen of discipline and control, passive objects instead of active agents, totally directed by their docile bodies, abject and sexualized. In *The History of Sexuality*, Foucault stated that the docile female body is placed, 'in organic communication with the social body (whose regulated fecundity it was supposed to ensure), the family space (of which it had to be a substantial and functional element) and the life of children' (Foucault 1978: 104). Also it is a proven fact that gender inequality and unequal power relations are scripted in the bodily differences between the male and female identities as argued by Lois McNay, 'The idea that women are inferior to men is naturalized and, thus, legitimized by reference to biology.'(McNay 1992: 17)

As a matter of fact, in his own life Tagore seemed to be much more conservative about roles women could play in terms of formal higher education, pursuit of professions and associated remunerative work. Rabindranath's elder brother Satyendranath seemed to be far more liberated in his views about women's liberation and women's formal education. Rabindranath arranged the marriages of his eldest daughter Madhurilata at fourteen years eight months, second daughter Renuka at ten years eight months, third daughter Mira at fourteen years six months and his son Rathindranath at twenty-one years and two months.

Interestingly, Satyendranath's only daughter Indira Devi was married when she was twenty-six to a person whom she had been courting for a while. Rabindranath did not admit his daughters to schools nor did he encourage their formal education though all three were literate, and the eldest Madhurilata showed considerable talent as evidenced from her surviving short stories, letters and other writings. The contrast becomes glaring as Indira Devi graduated from Calcutta University in 1892 with a honours degree in French while Madhurilata's marriage was arranged when she was not yet fifteen. Also, 'Tagore even paid dowry money to all the three sons-in-law besides sending them abroad for higher education at his expense' (Murshid 1983: 230). In fact, Saratkumar Chakravarty, husband of Madhurilata, went to England and returned as a barrister. Rabindranath even paid him 10,000 rupees as dowry, though initially Saratkumar's family had asked for 20,000 rupees. Tagore had to pay for the higher studies of his sons-in-law. Satyendranath Bhattacharjee, married to Renuka, was expected to go to America for a degree in homeopathy but stayed back in England for a considerable period while the third son-in-law Nagendranath Ganguly married to Mira, went to America and returned with a degree in agriculture (ibid.: 230).

Interestingly, long after the demise of his two daughters and an unhappy marriage of his youngest surviving daughter Mira, in the essay on the 'Indian Ideal of Marriage' that he wrote in 1925, in response to Count Keyserling's request to analyse Indian marriages, Tagore referred to eastern values and the traditional customs of a woman's life as a wife and mother as services to certain ideals. This essay titled 'The Indian Ideal of Marriage' was published in the *Visva-Bharati Quarterly* in 1925. Significantly however, Tagore ended the essay almost as any contemporary feminist critic would:

> The marriage system all over the world, from the earliest till now, is a barrier in the way of such true union. That is why woman's *Shakti*, in all existing societies, is so shamefully wasted and corrupted. That is why, in every country, marriage is still more or less of a prison-house for the confinement of woman, with all its guards wearing the badge of the dominant male... (Das 1996, 3: 537).

Yet, in his essay 'Woman and Home' included in *Creative Unity* (1922), Tagore had made certain ambivalent statements about women's liberation and agency. Tagore focuses on the peripheral role of women in a male-centred universe as he writes, 'She has been an inspiration to man, guiding most often unconsciously, his restless energy into an immense variety of creations in literature, art, music and religion. This is why in India woman has been described as the symbol of Shakti, the creative power (Das 1996, 2: 552). Furthermore, Tagore elaborates,

> Woman has to be ready to suffer... It is a religious responsibility for them to live the life which is their own. For their activity is not for money-making, or organizing power, or intellectually probing the mystery of existence, but for establishing and maintaining human relationships requiring the highest moral qualities. It is the consciousness of the spiritual character of their life's work, which lifts them above the utilitarian

standard of the immediate and the passing, surrounds them with the
dignity of the eternal, and transmutes their suffering and sorrow into a
crown of light (ibid.: 554).

It is this ambivalence that indicates a lifelong tension within the
poet's psyche, as his own life and responses along with his fictional
and non-fictional writings juggle with the issues about the need for
women's liberation, selective liberation and women's confinement
within the private/personal space and women's irrelevance as agents
in the public domain.

TAGORE'S DAUGHTERS

Madhurilata (1886–1918)

The Tagore life historian Chitra Deb clearly described the exceptional
care Tagore took in educating his eldest daughter, Madhurilata. Her
pet name was Bela, often the poet called her Beli, and she was as
radiant as the soft white tropical flower Beli which perhaps inspired
the naming of Tagore's first daughter. Deb wrote:

> Though she was a woman of the Tagore household, even then
> Madhurilata's upbringing was somewhat exclusive. Indeed remarkably
> exclusive. Unlike the daughters of Satyendra and Hemendra she did not
> study in the anglicized Loreto school. She hadn't studied in the more
> indigenous Bethune School either. She was educated at home. She stud-
> ied with three female English teachers, along with Mr. Lawrence and
> Hemchandra Bhattacharya. Apart from them, she studied with her father.
> He may not have sent her to school, but the poet did everything to edu-
> cate Madhurilata. He saw to it that she learnt both Indian and Western
> music and literature and even nursing (1981: 183, translation author's).

As the editor of the anthology of the women writers of the
Tagore family, Parthajit Gangopadhyay observed, 'When most of
the families in nineteenth-century society were mired in meaningless conservatism about women's education, in the Tagore household it was a very different environment, it was brightly lit with
liberated ideas' (2012: 2; translation author's). Gangopadhyay

further elaborated on the transformative impact that the women of the Tagore household had made on the women of Bengal: 'This transformation in the Tagore household, this endeavour to progress towards modernity was not restricted within the precincts of Jorasanko, it had an influence on the larger social life. Slowly Bengali women became enlightened. There is no doubt about the fact that the women folks of Jorasanko had been the guides in steering the women of Bengal towards modernity'(ibid.: 3; translation author's).

Yet, despite such progressive attitudes towards women's education Sunil Gangopadhyay observed in his classic historical narrative about Tagore agreeing to dowry payment for his eldest daughter, the talented Madhurilata, his favourite first-born:

> The fact that the payment of dowry in marriage was tantamount to the buying and selling of cows and goats, that it was necessary to get rid of this malpractice from society, Rabindranath had pondered about this many times. Debendranath too was firmly against this malpractice, yet Rabindranath suddenly became oblivious of all this. In order to secure Biharilal's son as his daughter's bridegroom he was willing to fulfil the dowry demand. Then began the haggling as in an animal fair. From twenty thousand the dowry demand was eventually lowered to ten thousand, and the groom's family were absolutely firm that this amount was non-negotiable. Ultimately, Tagore confirmed that he would pay the amount as dowry, then again the groom's family demanded payment of an additional two thousand rupees for the groom Sarat's train travel from Munger to Calcutta along with the train fare of those accompanying the groom. So the total demand was twelve thousand (2010: 825; translation author's).

Also, in the concluding section 53 of his novel *Pratham Alo,* Sunil Gangopadhyay made two significant if not explosive comments. In the first one Gangopadhyay stated,

> The real reason was about self-interest, this fact however no one will admit in public. Or else this idea was perhaps lying dormant in the unconscious of many others. Till the present, Debendranath had been bearing the expenses of all the marriages held in the Tagore family. The aging Debendranath was falling ill periodically, there was no way to speculate when he might pass away. On his death, the property would be divided between the brothers and so all expenses would have to be borne

by the brothers on their own. If marriages of sons and daughters could be arranged within Debendranath's lifetime then quite a few thousands could be saved (ibid.: 831; translation author's).

Gangopadhyay concluded in section 53 thus:

'Madhurilata was married on 1 Ashar (15 June) Renuka was married on 21 Sravan (4 August). Renuka was just ten and half years old. The poet who had written against child marriages once upon a time, now under such compulsions, became oblivious of his earlier stand. Not as a poet, but as a father of a marriageable daughter this time his arrangements were flawless and successful. But the poet had to pay a price for this. For the next two or three months he did not write a single poem, nor could he compose a single song. Just prose!' (ibid.: 831; translation author's)

This writer's block underscored the tensions and stress that the poet suffered as he encountered the relentlessness of exploitative social norms to which he had to succumb and surrender, however painfully, thus making compromises with his ideological beliefs and his overwhelming spirit of freedom which he enshrined as the required guiding star of human life.

Soon after Madhurilata's marriage, Tagore seemed to have written a letter of advice to his newly married daughter about her marital duties. This letter has remained untraced. However, in response to her father's letter, Madhurilata responded,

I shall try to follow all your advice to the best of my ability. I will always try to remember that my husband is superior to me in all respects and that I can never be his equal. I shall try to enhance the glory of his household. I will remember that as I belong to the Tagore family he will have hopes of my having many talents and I will try not to disappoint him at any-time' (Pal 1990, 5: 18, translation author's).

Madhurilata was neither Ashapurna Devi's Satyabati nor Subarnalata. As a very young teenager not unlike the Bronte sisters, who were chronologically much older than the daughters of Tagore, particularly like Charlotte Bronte who expressed her desire to be included in the discourse of the macro issues of life, Madhurilata petulantly wrote to her globe-trotting father about the claustrophobic environment and the myopic outlook of the women's world in which she was growing up, 'You don't feel lonely, because you can ponder over great issues, you can discuss these and spend your time doing so. We are very insignificant people, we sometimes desire to gossip and meet other folks. And when you are back and you decide to stay here, do share a little with us all those profound issues in which you engage.' (Deb 1981: 184; translation author's).

After marriage, when Madhurilata went to live with her husband in Muzzafarpur, she met the writer Anurupa Devi and together they set up a 'Ladies Committee' and also a school, 'Chapman Balika Vidyalaya'. In colonial Bihar, lives of young women were trapped in total ignorance and illiteracy. Women were subservient to all ferociously protective patriarchal laws that denigrated them in body and mind. Around the same time, in Bhagalpur in Bihar, interestingly Begum Rokeya (also known as Rokeya Sakhawat Hossain), a married Muslim woman set up a school for Muslim girls, a most revolutionary act at a time when Bihar had shrouded its young women in burkhas and hidden them behind purdahs (Deb 1981: 186–88).

But death stalked the poet's family with relentless determination and Madhurilata could not continue with her social work. Madhurilata contracted tuberculosis. The poet would visit his dying daughter every morning till the day of her death. In 1918, in his volume of narrative poems titled *Palataka*, the elusive one, the imminent death of Madhurilata is anticipated in the poem *Mukti* (Freedom), among others, and perhaps Renuka is also remembered in such a poem as *Hariye Jaoa* (Getting Lost). *Mukti* is a remarkably feminist narrative poem that reads like a dirge of despair of married Bengali women of the nineteenth century.[1]

Freedom *(Mukti)*

> ... I had come into this family as a nine-year-old girl.
> Since then I have been pacing the long corridor of this family,
> Living according to the desires of others...

> For twenty two years
> I felt imprisoned infinitely within your house
> Yet I was not sad about that....
> All my relatives
> Praise me as Lakshmi.

> In this life it seems this is my greatest glory-
> To be praised by others as I remain in a corner of the house!...
>
> At last it seems for the first time the strains
> Of a wedding flute is heard between the earth and sky...
> Open, open the door
> Let me drift away from the hopeless twenty-two years into the sea of
> infinity.
> —'*Daktarey ja bole boluk nako*', *Rabindra Rachanabali*,
> vol. 2, 1961: 531–33. Visva-Bharati.

Renuka (1891–1903)

After Madhurilata got married, within weeks Tagore seemed eager to arrange the marriage of his second daughter, Renuka. He wrote to his wife, Mrinalini, about the reason for the urgency, which was primarily about early adjustment and acculturation:

> If Rani too gets married and has to go far away it will be good for her. Of course the first two years she will stay with us—but soon after as she comes of age it will be good for her to be away from us. The education, culture, customs, conversation and ideas of our family are very different from all Bengali families—therefore after marriage the women of our family need to go somewhat far away from us... Rani's nature is such... if she is cut off from her parental home she will change herself—if she stays close to us her previous 'association' will linger (Pal 1990, 5: 22–23; translation author's).

The word 'association' is the only English word Tagore used in his letter written in Bengali. It seemed the poet's wish came true within weeks. Referring to Rani's marriage within weeks of the marriage of Madhurilata, Tagore wrote to his scientist friend, Jagadish Chandra Bose, 'Suddenly my second daughter got married. A doctor said, I'll marry her—I said all right. The day I gave my consent, just after the third day the marriage was held. Now the young man is getting ready to leave for America in order to gain a degree in homeopathy as he has a degree in allopathy already. He won't have to stay there for long. He is a good boy, humble, meritorious' (ibid.: 28, translation author's). Tagore's biographer Prashanta Kumar Pal remarked that at the time of marriage, Renuka was just ten and half years old, 'it's a matter of surprise that at one time Rabindranath had engaged in a war of words with Chandranath Bose against early marriage' (ibid., translation author's).

Getting Lost (*Hariye Jaoa*)

> ...I was on the terrace
> In a spring night with a sky full of stars,
> Suddenly hearing my daughter's cry
> I rushed to find out—
> As she was going down the dark stairs
> The wind had blown off the light of her lamp.
> I asked, 'What's the matter, Bami?'
> She cried out from below. 'I am lost'....
> —'*Palataka*', *Rabindra Rachanabali*, vol. 2, 1961: 569.

But the young man Satyendranath Bhattacharya returned from England, did not go to America for studying homeopathy as had been agreed, and became a resident at the Tagore mansion (ibid.: 88). Soon after Renuka fell ill and the poet followed all medical advice about taking her to Almora, exposing her to the sunlight and the breeze of the pine trees, but all efforts were in vain. On 15 September 1903 Renuka died at the age of twelve years and seven months (ibid.: 148). It must be noticed that tuberculosis emerges as the relentless killer disease of the nineteenth and early twentieth century, the emperor of all maladies during those times, as we find death from tuberculosis complications snatched away so many members of the Tagore family and it is axiomatic that the disease had killed thousands in colonial Bengal. Also remarkable is the fact that five years after Renuka's death, Tagore himself took the initiative of arranging a marriage for his widower son-in-law. The selected bride was a widow and a relative of the Tagore family.

Mira (1894–1969)

Having lost two daughters the poet became deeply attached to Mira (Atashilata). However, the same compelling reason that biographers identified as the primary root cause of the early marriages of his daughters, prevailed in the case of Mira as well. As in the case of his second son- in law, Satyendranath, the agreement this time too was that the bride's father would send the groom to America for higher studies. Tagore obliged. However, in a few years, Mira felt that her husband, Nagendranath Ganguly, had drifted away from her, though on his return from America, he lived for some time in Jorasanko. They had two children. A boy and a girl, Nitindra and Nandita, the latter was Tagore's favourite grandchild. Though Mira's husband became the most illustrious of the three sons-in-law, Tagore despaired at the bitterness of the marital relationship, which despite all efforts ended in a divorce.

Tagore built a house named Malancha for Mira, where she lived for the rest of her life. In fact, Mira lived for almost seventy-seven years and wrote many essays, paraphrased and translated from many western texts and a memoir *Smritikatha*, that were reminiscences of her days in the company of her father and in the Tagore family.

Tagore realized that in his eagerness to get his daughter married, which in a way liberated him of the responsibility of looking after a single unmarried daughter, he had made his youngest daughter unhappy and miserable, beyond redemption. Evidences of Nagendranath's contempt for the Tagore family and its selective adherence to the tenets of the Brahmo Samaj are replete in biographer Prashanta Kumar Pal, *Rabijibani* (vol. 5). Nagendranath was a staunch believer in the dogmatic anti-Hindu sentiments of the more extremist members of the Brahmo Samaj. But in order to fulfil his ambitions of pursuing higher studies in America, Nagendranath made the compromise with his ideological beliefs by marrying the daughter of Tagore, a compromise for which he could not forgive himself, it seems. Extremely aggrieved by the sufferings of his much loved youngest daughter Tagore wrote to his son Rathindranath, 'That I am responsible for Nagen—this is a fact that I'll never be able to forget.' Tagore referred to his daughter's sufferings and wrote in total despair about a fearful incident that took place on the wedding night, which could have been fatal for Mira, 'on the wedding night as Mira was entering the bathroom suddenly a cobra snake which was inside, raised its venomous hood—today I feel if the snake had bitten her that night she would have been saved from all her agony'. Pal commented that how much the poet must have suffered to have pronounced such a cruel fate for his beloved daughter (1990, 5: 365, translation author's). It must be noticed that though Tagore's docile daughters were obedient to their father's wishes regarding their marriage and marital partners, they were also surprisingly well educated and aware. This feature was uncommon among young women of nineteenth-century Bengal who were mostly denied formal or informal education. Yet sadly, the life-experiences of Tagore's good, obedient and dutiful daughters, their sense of identity trapped within their docile bodies, replicate the lives of many passive and abject Bengali women of those times, many of whom died from illnesses at an early age or experienced living death by having to experience the trauma of an unhappy marriage.

NOTE

1   Both poems cited are translated by Sanjukta Dasgupta.

REFERENCES

Chattopadhyay, Purnananda. 2000 (1406 B.S.). *Rabindranather Teen Kanya.* Kolkata: Mitra and Ghosh Publishers.

Das, Sisir (ed). 1996. *The English Writings of Rabindranath Tagore,* vols 1, 2 and 3. New Delhi: Sahitya Akademi.

Deb, Chitra. 1981 (1387 B.S.). *Thakurbarir Andarmahal.* Kolkata: Ananda Publishers.

Foucault, Michel. 1978. *The History of Sexuality: An Introduction,* translated by R. Hurley. Harmondworth: Penguin.

Gangopadhyay, Parthajit. 2012. *Thakurbarir Meyeder Lekha.* Kolkata: Gangchil.

Gangopadhyay, Sunil. 2010. *Pratham Alo.* Kolkata: Ananda Publishers.

McNay, Lois. 1992. *Foucault and Feminism.* Boston: Northwestern University Press.

Murshid, Ghulam. 1983. *Reluctant Debutante: Response of Bengali Women to Modernization (1905–1849).* Rajshahi: Sahitya Samsad Rajshahi University.

Pal, Prashanta Kumar. 1990. *Rabijibani* vol. 5. Kolkata: Ananda Publishers.

CHAPTER 7

Re-reading Rabindranath Tagore's 'Streer Patra' (The Wife's Letter, 1914) in the Light of Epistolary Culture in Colonial India

Nandini Bhattacharya

This essay examines letter writing as a cultural phenomenon at the turn of the century in Victorian England and British India; the reinvention of this traditional mode of communication in times of colonial modernity;[1] and the contouring of gender relations thereby.

It focuses on Rabindranath Tagore's letter-narratives (primarily short stories) while situating them amidst a cluster of epistolary narratives in Indian *bhasas* (languages; other than Bengali) engaging with the woman question. The essay also bounces off Tagore's epistolary narratives against his essays or polemical tracts, espousing the letter format and debating the woman question, and examines thereby means by which epistolary forms informed Tagore's writings, and shaped his approach to questions of conjugality.

I

In his 'The Confessions of a Young Bengal', the nineteenth-century Bengali novelist and ideologue, Bankimchandra Chattopadhayay, describes the colonial intervention in India, thus: 'The stamp of the Anglo-Saxon foreigner is upon our houses, our furniture, our carriages, our food, our drink, our dress, *our very familiar letters and conversation . . . We have exchanged the cumbrous forms of Bengali epistolary correspondence for those Cook's Universal Letter Writer...* (Chattopadhayay 1969: 137–38; emphasis mine).

The moment of rupture within an indigenous culture is examined in terms of certain 'arrivals'—the significant one in this instance being a novel mode of communication, the modern letter; its formalization as a genre with deference to (and in acknowledgement of) the British modular structure; and the attendant cultural shifts, as the 'arrival' proceeds to inform 'familiar...conversations' (Chatterjee 2009 [1986]). Unlike Partha Chatterjee who describes the intervention as necessitating a split of the *andar* (inner) and the *bahir* (outer) domains of the colonized subject, and of the colonized subject claiming the andar as both inviolate and imbued with agentative possibilities, Bankim suggests that the bahir (of the Anglo-Saxon letter writing form) produces the andar and renders what is 'familiar' and 'intimate'.[2]

The 'novelty' and 'modernity' of this communicative mode was materially produced through the reform and expansion of postal systems, and the advanced road/railway communication in the second half of the nineteenth-century India only enriched our understanding of how the modern letter informed affective structures and produced colonial modernity. It is comparable perhaps to the momentous impact of electronic texting, mailing and chatting on contemporary lives, and its role in the production of the cultural phenomenon of globalization.

The postal revolution in Victorian England (introducing pre-paid postage, affordable one-penny stamps affixed to envelope carrying letters, and abolishing of arbitrary franking rights) at the behest of reformers such as Rowland Hill and the active support of the youthful Queen Victoria, informed the Victorian civilizing project and a great deal of what was recognized as 'enlightened', 'ethical' and English.[3] Rowland Hill's words on the subject in his *Post Office Reform: Its Importance and Practicability* are enlightening:

> When it is considered how much the religious, moral, and intellectual progress of the people would be accelerated by the unobstructed circulation of letters and of the many cheap and excellent non-political publications of the present day, the Post Office assumes the new important character of a powerful engine of civilization (Hill 1837: 8).

In British India, postal systems were homogenized and reforms instituted in 1851 at the behest of the postal commissioners, Courtney, Forbes and Beadon; leading to the Postal Reforms Act of 1854. In their *Postal Reforms Manual*, Courtney, Forbes and Beadon describe the postal system in evangelical and civilizational terms rather than as information-gathering, surveillance and profit-making enterprises. They commend the postal system in India as 'annihilating distance and placing it within the power of every individual to communicate freely with all parts of the Empire . . . providing 'unrestricted means of diffusing knowledge, extending commerce and prompting in every way the social and intellectual improvement of the people' (Clarke 1921: 25).

However, it is to the pictorial depictions of Victorian letter sheets, and more specifically, Mulready's stationery, that we must turn to gauge the 'modern' postal system's ability to produce colonial subjectivity and contour gender relations. The Mulready design[4] (both feted and lampooned in its own times) indicates the British postal system's role in scrutinizing, controlling and homogenizing the far-flung, culturally disparate parts of the Empire; inscribing what is peculiarly 'British'. While the upper portions of the letter sheet depict colonial subjects of varied races/ethnicities receiving missives from the central figure of Britannia riding the lion, the bottom corners are devoted to the depiction of the 'angel in the house' (who reads a letter as she goes about her domestic duties), and the care-giver who reads a comforting letter to a bedridden patient. The Mulready sheet makes graphically evident thereby the role of British posts in the production of the disciplined, gendered subject.

Bankimchandra Chattopadhayay's reference to Reverend Thomas Cooke's *The Universal Letter Writer* (1788) as reforming Bengali-Indian affects directs our attention to the cult of epistolary manuals in Victorian England' their circulation in the colonies[5] and their importance in contouring and calibrating intimate affects such as 'romantic love', 'friendship' or 'sorrow on the occasion of bereavement'. The 'Preface' to Cooke's *The Universal Letter Writer or New Art of Polite Conversation* proclaims that 'letters are the life of trade—the fuel of love—the pleasure of friendship—the food of the politician—and the entertainment of the curious' (1857: vi). Cooke's manual that was popular in colonial Bengal and went on being printed for nearly a hundred years after its date of publication has a whole section devoted to 'Courtship and Marriage'.

While the impact of such 'civilizing epistolary missions' were felt in distinct ways in colonial margins like late nineteenth-century Bengal, as all 'arrivals' emanating from the master's culture, the Victorian Englishman considered the epistolary art as equally pivotal so far as societal progress and civility were concerned. Cooke underlines the civilizing dimensions of the 'letter' as he constructs a genealogy of epistle-writing; tracing such socially commendable practices from the time humans learnt to write to the Greeks and Romans (especially Cicero),[6] the French, and finally, the lately civilized British. Cooke's prioritizing of the written letter over verbal exchanges as constitutive of civility and his prescriptive stance that human society developed by 'drop[ing]' the 'verbal messenger'; committing the 'language of the heart' to written 'characters' that 'faithfully preserved it' and rendering, thereby 'social intercourse' more 'free and agreeable' is noteworthy, to say the least (Cooke, 'Preface' 1886). Note that Mrinal (the protesting wife) in Rabindranath's 'Streer Patra' (The Wife's Letter) creates a similar hierarchy between the spoken word and the written epistle and identifies her written letter to her husband (the first in their fifteen years of loveless conjugal existence) as the objective correlative of her emerging subjectivity.

While discovering more letter manuals in Indian languages in response to Cooke's manual is a worthy area of research, it is not entirely insignificant that Rabindranath's letter-essay, *Chithipatra* (Letters and Missives)[7] debates the correct form of letters writing in times of colonial modernity and changing modes of social behaviour as inscribed through such letters (*Chithi likhite arambho kariai tomake ki path likhibo ai bhabna mone uday hoe;* I worry about the correct form of letters, the moment I sit down to pen one; translation author's; 'Streer Patra': 862). This epistolary essay containing a dialogue/debate between grandfather Shashticharan (representing tradition, pre-modernity or *sekal*) and grandson Nabinkishore (representing modernity; these times, or *ekal*) is as prescriptive an exercise as Erasmus' *Libellus de Conscribendis Epistolis* (1521), or Hill's *The Young Secretary's Guide: Or a Speedy Help to Learning* (1696) or Thomas Cooke's *The Universal Letter Writer* (1857). That *Chithipatra* was written originally for *Balak* (the child)—a journal technically edited by Jnanadanandini Tagore (the wife of Rabindranath's elder brother Satyendranath Tagore) but chiefly structured by Rabindranath with

the express intent of recasting the child in times of colonial modernity is revealing, to say the least.

What is also worth attention at this juncture are ways in which
genres in India (such as the personal essay, polemical tracts, short
story and the novel), naturally veering towards the dialogic, were
being informed by the modern letter writing form during the first
two decades of the twentieth century. The close correspondence
between the epistolary form and women's issues (especially issues
of conjugality) is worth noting in Rentala Venkata Subba Rao's
Kamala's Letters to Her Husband penned originally in English in 1902
(and subsequently translated into Telugu). Significantly, 1902 also
marks the appearance of Tagore's lesser known epistolary short
story entitled 'Darpaharan' (Pride Demolished), engaging with
women's writing, the conjugal relationship, and the letter form in a
mock-serious manner. Kanuparthi Varalakhshamma, who edited a
women's journal entitled *Gruhalakshmi* (The Goddess of the Home)
around 1928 in Telugu, ran an entire column entitled *Sarada Lekhalu*
(Letters from Sarada) where the imaginary character Sarada and her
friend Kalpalata, exchange letters discussing the women question;
questions of conjugality; the Sarda Act (Child Marriage Restraint
Act of 1929) and divorce laws. The Kannada epistolary short stories
of Kodagina Gowramma (anthologized in *Jeevanapreethi: Kodagina
Gowramma bareda ella kathegalu*—Love for Life: A Complete
Collection of stories written by Kodagina Gowramma), are cases
in point.[8]

I also take this opportunity to bounce off Rabindranath's
'Streer Patra' against some actual letters written by Indian wives
to their husbands and women friends/mentors discussing women's
issues such as the age of consent, the role of the wife and duties of
the husband in these new times. I refer to Anandibai Joshi's (1865–
87) letters exchanged between her American mentor B. F. Carpenter
(15 December 1880; March 1881; 20 January 1881) as well as those
between her husband Gopal Rao Joshi (1884); as anthologized in
Kashibai Kanitkar's *Pa Va Sau: Dr. Anandibai Joshee Yancile Charitra
va Patre* (1912), and as translated into English by Meera Kosambi
in her essay 'Ananadibai Joshi: Retrieving a Fragmented Feminist
Image' (1991). Kosambi deploys these letters to explore the ambivalent approach of this remarkable Marathi woman-doctor towards

Hindu structures of conjugality and the asymmetry of power inherent in such structures. Remarkable is the tonal complexity of the letter where Anandi expresses her trauma at being repeatedly beaten up by her husband in the early years of their conjugal life but acknowledges that such harshness was instrumental in her becoming a doctor.[9] Kosambi notes that the letters (which Anandi wanted to be kept private but Gopal Joshi was intent on making current and public) express and constitute Anandi's emerging subjectivity albeit in a complex and circuitous manner. Rabindranath's letter-short story 'Streer Patra' can be understood much better when situated within these contexts.

I propose to examine the cultural impact of letter-writing on Rabindranath Tagore's writings in particular and gauge the centrality of the epistolary genre to his *oeuvre*. It is certainly not a chance that Tagore creatively deploys the letter format to shape practically every genre that he tries his hand at: poetry ('Chithi', in *Balak*, Phalgun BS1292/ mid-February–mid-March 1885: 137; *Patraduti*, Asharh BS1345/mid-June–mid-July 1938; *Rabindra Rachanabali*, vol. 12: 683, in reply to *Garthikani*, Asharh BS1345/mid-June–mid-July 1937, *Rabindra Rachanabali*, vol.12: 18; *Nasik hote khurar patra*, Bhadra–Ashwin BS1293/mid-August–mid-October 1886, *Rabindra Rachanabali*, vol.12: 35; *Adhunika* 1935; *Rabindra Rachanabali, vol.* 12: 7–10; 'Shillonger Chitthi', 25 Jaistha 1330 BS/mid-May–mid-June 1923: 102); travel writing (*Europe Pravasir Patra*, 1887, *Rabindra Rachanabali* vol. 1: 797–829; 'Java Jatrir Patra' July 1927–October 1927, *Rabindra Rachanabali*, vol. 10: 501–49; 'Russiar Chithi', September 1930–October 1930, *Rabindra Rachanabali*, vol. 10: 554–603); personal/informal essay ('Chithipatra', Chaitra 1292–Jaishtha 1292 BS/mid-April–mid-May 1885; *Rabindra Rachanabali*, vol. 1: 879); 'Barshar Chithi' in *Balak*, 1292 BS/1885: 335); *Chinnapatra* (1912); short story ('Streer Patra' 1914, *Galpaguccha*, vol. 3: 567–76 and 'Darpaharan' 1902, *Galpaguccha*, vol. 2: 412–27); and a novelette (*Dui Bon* or Two Sisters, in partially epistolary form, Agrahayan–Phalgun 1339 BS/mid-November–mid-March 1932, *Rabindra Rachanabali*, vol. 3: 427–39). It is certainly not a chance that he names one of his seminal plays, *Dakghar* or the Post Office (1318 BS /1911, *Rabindra Rachanabali*, vol. 6: 355–71). Tagore's letter narratives gaze self-reflexively at this new 'text' of communication; and explore the generic form of the letter, as not simply a site of cultural negotiations but as producing those cultural shifts.

II

'STREER PATRA', 1914: The 'Woman-Handled' Letter

'Streer Patra' (The Wife's Letter), a short story in an epistolary form, originally published in the Pramatha Chaudhuri edited Bengali journal *Sabuj Patra*[10] in Sravan 1321 BS/mid-July–mid-August (1914) and subsequently anthologized in the third volume of Rabindranath's *Galpaguccha* (*GG*; bunch of short stories), narrates the life of Mrinal, the *mejobou* (the wife of the second brother) of a well-to-do-Kolkata family, enduring a loveless conjugal life within the confines of her marital home in colonial Kolkata. Her residential address—number 27 Makhan Baral Street—is indicative of the mundane, soulless and constrictive nature of her marital existence. Mrinal's giving birth to a still-born baby girl and the entry of a plain-looking destitute, adolescent girl, Bindu, in the family precipitates the crisis. They expose once and for all to the spirited Mrinal, the true position of women within the Bengali family. Bindu is made to feel her dependant status at each step and coerced into marrying a mentally challenged man so that the family need no longer support her. After repeated attempts to escape the traumatic situation, she finds freedom in suicide. Bindu's fate provokes Mrinal to leave her husband's Makhan Baral street residence finally, and write a letter from the ocean-swept beaches of Srikhetra (Puri) relinquishing the role of a 'wife'. Inspired in all probability by the Snehalata incident where a young Bengali girl in Kolkata committed suicide by setting herself to fire to save her family from the compulsion of paying a heavy dowry and consequent financial ruin,[11] 'Streer Patra' marks a new chapter in Rabindranath's engagement with, and strident critique of Hindu conjugality. The story touched a raw nerve so far as Hindu nationalists were concerned, and evinced several epistolary narratives' responses ranging from the nationalist ideologue Bipin Chandra Pal's 'Mrinaler Katha' (Mrinal's Narrative) where the penitent Mrinal returns to her husband's home, and signs her letter as 'Mrinal, forever within the shelter of your feet' (*Narayan,* Sravan, 1324 BS /mid-July–mid-August 1917); to Lalit Kumar Bandopadhayay's 'Swamir Patra' (The Husband's Letter) in the same volume of *Narayan* critiquing, in a not so oblique fashion, Rabindranath's transgressive (especially within the Hindu context) views on conjugality; and an unnamed literary parody entitled 'Mrinalini Devi: Streer Prakrita Patra' (The genuine letter of the wife) published in the journal *Aryavarta* in Ashwin 1321BS/mid-September–mid-October 1915.[12] Rabindranath also penned an epistolary reply to an actual letter written by a woman reader, questioning the 'genuineness' of his portrayal of an adulterous Hindu wife in his 1915 novel *Ghare-Baire*; and insinuating that such things actually happen only within the context of westernized and fashionably elite communities such as Brahmos, and never in 'regular' Hindu Bengali homes. Tagore's answer is illuminating in so far as 'Streer Patra' is concerned: 'Does that mean,' he responded 'that in an orthodox Hindu family, man always follows the commandments of Manu and never goes astray or bids for freedom?' (cited in J. Chattopadhayay 2003: 191–2).

In 'Streer Patra', the letter is not merely a convention of narrative, but shaping what it desires to communicate. The narrative directs its self-reflexive gaze, at the very act of writing a letter, with forms of address, and signing off.[13] Sumit Sarkar in *'Ghare Baire* in Its Times' and Tanika Sarkar in 'Many Faces of Love: Country, Woman and God in *The Home and the World'* point to Rabindranath's critical engagement with the woman's voice, in and around 1914–15 and its expression in a cluster of proto-feminist short stories published in *Sabuj Patra*. They also note that this voice is textually constituted through the deployment of *chalit bhasha* in his short stories and novels, and through a self-reflexive look at *ecriture feminine* as constitutive of female subjectivity.[14]

I would like to complicate this position somewhat by noting that such constitution of female subjectivity (necessarily fractured, compromised and incomplete)[15] is rendered more possible through the act of writing letters. The epistle's paradoxical possibilities of confidentiality and communication, enables inscription of female subjectivity. The letter (written in privacy but intending to communicate) metonymically encodes the Indian woman situated within that inviolate 'andar' but tentatively stepping out into that colonized 'bahir'.[16]

Mrinalini's letter is the first one written by the wife to the husband as their conjugal relation (dulled by its location within constricting urban confines, habitual proximity and the spoken word) had never required the illumination of the written epistle ('*Aj ponero bocchor amader bibaha hoeche, aj parjanta tomake chithi likhi ni. Chiradin kachei pode acchi-mukher katha onek shunecchi, chithi lekhar phank tuku paoa jaye ni*'; We have been married for fifteen years, but I have never written you a letter, till this instance. I had to make do with plenty of spoken exchanges, as I was in perpetual proximity. There was never the space for exchanging of letters; translation author's; 'Streer Patra': 567). Note that Mrinal, like Reverend Cooke prioritizes the letter over the spoken word. The very act of writing a letter is an act of discovering and inscribing self, of discovering the true nature of the conjugal relation; of freeing the self from socially imposed shackles. It is not Mrinal's situatedness on the vast; wave-washed and wind-swept beaches of Srikhetra[17] which emancipates her but her ability to free herself from meaningless verbal exchanges and discover the space to write a letter.

Rabindranath considered the letter to be one of the more intimate and lyrical of creative spaces and found in its writing, the coming together of natural beauty, freedom from social restrictions and discovery of self. It is not entirely coincidental that some of his most beautiful letters were written to his niece Indira Tagore (fondly referred to as Bibi) from the natural retreat of Selidaha, describing the beauty as well as poverty of rural Bengal. These letters published in 1912 as *Chinnapatra* (Epistolary Fragments) were described by the poet as 'cover[ing] those very years which were most productive for me and therefore . . . act[ing] like a footpath in my life history, unconsciously laid by treading of my thoughts' (cited in Dutt and Robinson 2009: 111). The writing/posting of letters, the freedom they presuppose, the creative energies they tap, and the simplicity of nature they are divested in, come epiphanically together in the figure of Gagan *harkara*, a village post-boy, who did not survive his teens and who penned the original lyrics of Tagore's hauntingly beautiful and spiritually radiant song: '*Ami kothaye pabo tare, amar moner manush je re*' (Where will I find the person who is there in my heart; translation author's). Published in 1322 BS (1915), a few months after his writing of 'Streer Patra' in the Bengali journal *Prabashi*, the song illuminating the figure of the village post-boy, in eternal quest; unbounded by shackles; definitively evokes the infinite and freedom-granting possibilities of the letter.

That the writing of letters is also the availing of freedom from social shackles as well as city-ties[18] is nowhere more apparent than in Rabindranath's coded address to his wife Mrinalini as '*bhai chuti*', in a series of letters.[19] *Chuti* connoting emancipation, freedom or holiday, is in this context also an endearing form of *choto* (small, intimate). Tagore also wrote a series of intimate letters to Mrinalini from his European *prabash* referring to her as '*Bhai choto bou*', My little wife).[20]

Mrinal's inscripted letter is flanked by two letters—one that was not written and one that did not reach its intended destination. The opening lines of the wife's letter, acknowledge a letter that was not written and freedom that was not availed. The application of leave that Mrinal's husband refuses to write to his superior in office, to accompany Mrinal to Srikhetra, is what denies him his 'freedom' and opportunity to discover his self.[21] The British office with its European boss was possibly the most unfree of spaces for the colonial subject and nothing exposed the bondage or humiliation of 'service' than it's opposite, that is, the format of the letter begging grant of leave! Mahim, Gora's elder brother (in Tagore's eponymous novel), refers to the demeaning attitude of British bosses towards their 'native' clerks, (distorting the generic name of clerks in colonial lingo, that is, '*babu*' to 'baboon'); refusing leave from office at every instance, and fining them continually for every absence (Tagore 1909: 392). Mrinal recognizes her husband's servility/bondage to the colonial office, to the colonial city, and its meaningless but ruthlessly constricting customs most clearly when she recognizes her own restrictions and is able to unshackle herself through the writing of the letter:

Aj ami eshechi tirtha karte Srikhetre, tumi accho tomar opisher kaaje. Shamuker shange kholosher je sambandha kolkatar shange tomar tai, she tomar deha mone ete gieche. Tai tumi opishe chutir darkhashta karle na. Bidhatar tai abhipraye chilo; tini amar chutir darkhashta manjur karechen.

(Today I am in Srikhetra on a pilgrimage, and you remain in Kolkata enmeshed in your office work. Your relation to Kolkata is comparable to

the crustacean's relation to its shell; they are fused and inseparable. It is
fitting therefore that you could not apply for leave from your office. It was
also so ordained by God. He, however, has granted me leave of absence
[Tagore 1914: 567]).

While Mrinal is finally enabled to write the letter which her husband
presumably reads to complete the communicative circle, there are
other subalterns who cannot write; or even when they do, unable
to ensure its posting, or it being read or ensuring the completion of
the communicative circle. Mrinal rightly suspects that Bindu's letters
documenting her anguish/trauma in her marital home will never be
written or if at all, never reach the greater world. Her marital family
will employ every means to silence and erase Bindu's protests ('*Bindu
chithi likhte shahosh karbe na, likhleo ami pabo na*'—Bindu will not dare
write a letter, or even if she does, it will never reach me; translation author's; ibid.: 574). She, therefore, enjoins her non-conformist
brother Sarat to act as the channel of communication, and bring
news of Bindu. Sarat finally communicates that Bindu, before committing suicide (which, in any case, was an inevitability), had written
a letter to Mrinal but it was destroyed by her in-laws (*Tomar name she
ekta chithi rekhe giechilo, kintu she chithi ora noshto koreche.* She had left
behind a letter that was addressed to you, but they have destroyed
it; translation author's; ibid.: 575). Mrinal's freedom and agency as
inscribed through the writing and posting of the letter is informed by
impotence of two kinds, the woman subjugated by patriarchal shackles, and a man subjugated by colonial chains, both unable to write.

On a lighter note, Rabindranath in his *Jibansmriti* (Memories
of Life, 1319/July 1912) has referred to the inherent precariousness
of the communicative act, when he referred to the first letter that he
wrote at his mother's behest to his father, conveying his mother's
anxiety regarding an imminent threat of a Russian attack. The letter
had to be routed through the elderly *munshi* (writer of official letters) in his father's *daftarkhana* (office) and while this first letter was
posted, read and answered, the subsequent letters (that the child
penned in his unbounded enthusiasm) never reached their destination as the munshi was far more sensitive to the 'costs' involved in
posting such letters, and wont to circumscribe the child's desire to
communicate endlessly.

When I revisit 'Streer Patra'—a short story written in the form of a letter—I pay the greatest attention to the very form of the epistle, in this case, to the distinct form in which the wife/subservient addresses and signs off a letter that is directed towards a husband/superior. Such 'salutations' are culturally coded and provide vital clues to the understanding of the narrative. The advent of the 'Anglo-Saxon foreigner' led to an intense scrutiny/questioning traditional relational hierarchies encoded through epistolary salutations. The first definitive history of British postal system of India by an Englishman, Geoffrey Clarke, defines such 'cumbersome forms', 'mixed up with invocations to the Deity and many other high-sounding phrases' as definitive of the 'contra-enlightened essence' of Indian subjects (Clarke 1921: 6–7).

That Rabindranath was fascinated with the bicultural nature of the modern letter, intimate yet alien; encoding and refusing to encode the colonized Indian's social intentions is best expressed through his creative recasting of English and alien 'salutations' such as 'dear' and 'yours faithfully' as *bhai* or *priyo*, and *anugoto*, respectively (Dutt and Robinson 1997: 'Salutations': xxix).

In 'Streer Patra', the letter narrative (inscripted by the wife who is suggestively named Mrinal or the lotus) is addressed to the husband in the socially accepted and reverential form of *sricharankamaleshu* (directed to your revered lotus-like feet). Note that the word *swami* connotes 'master' and 'deity', and the address to the lotus-feet is a cultural encoding of relational hierarchies within the Hindu conjugal unit.

In the fascinating *Chithipatra*, the grandfather Shashticharan Debsharmana reproves his *ekaler nati* (grandson belonging to these times, and by association, enlightened young people attacking traditional customs) Nabinkishore, for not just using culturally dissonant epistolary addresses such as 'my dear' but for debunking the indigenous forms of salutation (such as sricharankamaleshu) as *ashabhya* or uncivilized (Tagore 1885: 862). Shashticharan rightly notes that salutations such as 'my dear' are as much of conventions (and thus as 'unrealistic' or 'uncivilized') as sricharankamaleshu, as every person addressed in a letter cannot really be dear to oneself (ibid.)!

Each age and society devises behavioural modes conveying 'respect' or 'derision'. Indian Hindus have devised the behavioural mode of touching feet in outward (bodily) show of respect and textually encoded such respect by addressing epistles to the revered person's feet. Had the clapping of hands thrice (for example) been the way of showing respect among Indian Hindus, then the touching of feet and framing of addresses such as sricharankamaleshu would be meaningless or may be even insulting (ibid.: 863). Salutations in letters are, therefore, a reflection and encoding of cultural norms and are not interchangeable. Shashticharan argues for the untranslatability of epistolary salutations. Krishna Dutta and Andrew Robinson (editors, translators of Tagore's letters) many decades later, conclude in a similar vein: 'translations of beginnings and end of letters is difficult because they have a customary meaning different from their literal meaning, which also alters over time' (*Selected Letters of Rabindranath Tagore* 'Editorial Note': xxix). *Chiranjeebeshu* (addressed to one who will live forever); and sricharankamaleshu (addressed to one's revered lotus-like feet) then embody the relational hierarchies within Hindu families, and affective structures that illuminate them. Genres are not transportable categories, and specifically genres (such as letters and emails) that are intended to communicate in a practical way are particularly contoured by cultural exigencies.[22]

However, when the wife addresses her husband's *sri charan* (revered feet) and accepts him as the superior, this 'superiority/ inferiority' binary is mediated through the ameliorating filter of bhakti, or loving reverence/worship. It is this bhakti that the devotee directs towards the deity, (and by association) the wife towards the husband, unbidden and unprompted. Grandfather Shashticharan's prescriptive stance regarding the wife's address to the husband in nineteenth-century Indian Hindu society in *Chithipatra* is revealing:

> *Amader deshe je swamipriti ba swamibhakti chilo (ekhono hoeto acche) taha ki? Taha kebalmatra byaktibishesher prati priti ba bhakti noe taha byaktibisheshke atikram karia bartaman, taha swami namak bhabgata astitvar prati bhakti.* (What exactly is the stuff named 'husband-love' or 'husband-devotion', that prevailed in our country, and possibly still prevails? It is not merely love or reverence for a particular individual but that devotion which

subsumes the individual, and is directed towards the idea, and ideal of a husband; ('Streer Patra': 879; translation author's).

Note that it is this unprompted, unmediated devotion that Bimala aspires for in her conjugal relation, and nostalgically discovers as located in her mother (and those pristine, pre-modern times), but realizes that it is something that will perennially elude her grasp.[23] Bimala, in *Ghare-Baire* (a text that was written almost at the same time when 'Streer Patra' was inscripted) makes the telling comment:

> My husband used to say that man and wife are equal in love because of their equal claim on each other... but my heart said that devotion never stands in the way of equality... My beloved, it was worthy of you that you never expected worship from me. But if you had accepted it, it would have done me a real service... (Tagore 1921: 5)

Mrinal's address to the husband's *sricharankamal*, which is an implicit cultural expression of bhakti, and submission to his protection is important for an understanding of the letter narrative. Note that Mrinal mentions another letter in the very first paragraph of her epistle, a letter which her husband did not write to his superior in office asking for leave. At one stroke then, the epistle writer points towards two kinds of hierarchies—one of the bahir and the other of the andar—one in which submission is unbidden and forthcoming and the other where it is forced and unnatural. Or is it so?

In a reversal of categories, the sricharankamal that Mrinal actually directs her letter to is not the man she was married to, nor that societal ideal of the husband (as suggested by Shashticharan) but a *jagadiswar* (the owner of the world), a god, which is also her newly discovered self. The *jagat* (world) of no. 20 Makhnan Baral Street and its lord (her husband) is posited against the limitless universe of the jagadiswar, unframed as it were by the open skies and the unbounded oceans, but also informed by Mrinal's emerging subjectivity. Significantly, this first letter that she pens in her *prabash* (exile, homeless state) in Srikhetra facing the limitless oceans (as this is the first time in fifteen years of her conjugal life that her physical separation from her husband and his prison-like Kolkata house necessitates an inscripted missive) is to rethink her relationship with the world, its maker and every man-made hierarchy, and question them. To write the letter is to become human and not just a wife.

In what I would call in translation theory terminology a deft bit of 'woman-handling',[24] the generic form of a letter from the servant/devotee/service holder/wife's to her master/deity/boss/husband is radically destabilized.[25] Mrinal signs off her letter as someone who has been torn away from the shelter of the husband's feet (*charanashrayatalachinna*). The ironic pairing of the devotional salutation—sricharankamaleshu and the irreverent signing—*charanasharaytalachinna*, Mrinal fractures the rhetorical form of the wife's letter to the husband and the relational hierarchies encoded through it from within, leaving the reader with no firm generic (or relational) grounds to stand upon.

NOTES

1   Refer to Chapter Two ('The Origin of Post Office') of Geoffrey Clarke's (1921) for more on the pre-British Indian mode of postal communications. Clarke quotes the historian Ibn Batuta to record the existence of an organized network of foot and horse-riding couriers during the reign of Mohammad Bin Tughlaq. Colonel Wilks' *Historical Sketches of the South of India* records measures taken by the Raja Chick Deo Raj (1672) of Mysore in establishing a postal network. This system which was also a means of spying over subjects and meant to sustain 'despotic' rule according to Clarke was further developed by Hyder Ali. The first important initiative to establish a 'regular' postal system was taken by Lord Clive in 1766. However, most of the early governor generals such as Warren Hastings depended a great deal on Indian landowners to provide for postal services in their respective areas. A general and uniform postal system under a British Post Master General came to be operative in India only after 1837, and a postal reform, regularizing/homogenizing the postal rates became effective from 1851, that is within ten years of such a reform being effected in Victorian England. See Clarke (1921: 10–17).

2   Refer to Chatterjee (2009 [1986]).

3   Refer to Rowland Hill and George Birbeck Hill (1880) for more on this. Also refer to Golden (2009) for a contemporary recounting of the penny postage revolution in Victorian England and its impact on modern lives.

4   The Mulready letter sheet was developed by the British painter/artist, William Mulready (1886–83).

5   On 18 July 1879, *The Amrita Bazar Patrika*, a well-circulated contemporary newspaper, testifies to the popularity of the British postal system as providing new material conditions of epistolary communication in colonial India, even while poking fun at the 'unenlightened native's' mishandling of such modern facilities. While, 'postal cards are now a rage all over India' there are some ignorant Indians 'who write their thoughts on postcards and enclose them in an envelope, and attach a half-anna stamp before posting' and it is with the greatest of difficulty that one can 'teach the people' living 'under the enlightened rule of the British' 'on which side of the card the address is to be written' (cited in Clarke 1921: 8).

6   *Ars dictaminis* or the art of letter writing had a long and respectable history in Western aesthetics and was considered pivotal to rhetoric studies. The eighteenth and nineteenth-century British writers of letter manuals who informed manners while they taught letter-writing forms were following Erasmus' example as laid down in *Libellus de conscribendis Epistolis* (1521) offering advice regarding socially correct behaviour. Letter manuals (teaching socially acceptable behaviour and thereby producing it) can be traced back to William Fullwood's *The Enemie of Idleness* (1568); Angel Day's *The English Secretorie;* Thomas Blount's *The Academie of Eloquence* (1653); Nicholas Breton's *A Post with a Packet of Mad Letters* (1602); Charles Hoole's *A Century of Epistles English and Latin* (1660); John Hill's *The Young Secretary's Guide* (1696); Hannah Woolie's *The Gentlewoman's Companion or a Guide to Female Sex* (1672); William Mather's *Young Man's Companion* (1681); Charles Halifax's *Familiare Letters on Various Subjects of Business and Amusement... for the Service of the Younger part of both Sexes* (1754); Thomas Cooke's *The Universal Letter Writer; or the New Art of Polite Correspondence* (1771); Dorethea Du Bois *The Lady's Polite Secretary* (1771).

7   *Chithipatra* was originally inscribed as four sets of letters (with one unanswered fifth stand-alone epistle) exchanged between grandfather Shashticharan, and grandson Nabinkishore (literally, the new youth) and published in the children's journal *Balak* as Chiranjeebeshu (addressed to one who will live forever) and Sreechareneshu (addressed to one's revered feet). These traditional Hindu salutations in letters are also the subject of the debate within these letter-narratives.

8 I am indebted to Professors Alladi Uma and P. Sridhar (formerly of the Department of English, University of Hyderabad, now independent scholars) for inputs regarding Telugu epistolary narratives; to Dr. Sowmya Decchamma (Centre for Comparative Literature, University of Hyderabad) for information regarding the Kannada epistolary narratives of Gowramma; and the late Dr. Meera Kosambi (formerly affiliated to SNDT University Mumbai) for her extremely valuable translation of Anandibai Joshi's letters to her husband; and use of the same to explore the problematic interstitial spaces within Hindu conjugal structures.

9 Note the tonal ambiguities of Anandibai's letter 1884 letter to her husband Gopal Rao Joshi from America, rememorating and examining Hindu conjugal relations with the advantage of perspectival distance: 'It is not all my intention,' she writes 'to distress your dear heart or cause a rift in our love by raking up old memories... It is very difficult to decide whether your treatment of me was good or bad. If you ask me, I would answer that it was both. It seems to have been right in view of its ultimate goal [educating Anandi and enabling her to become a doctor]; but in all fairness, one is compelled to admit that it was wrong, [submitting her to intense physical and mental torture] considering its possible effects on a child's mind.... A Hindu woman has no right to utter a word or advise her husband.... Every Hindu husband can, with advantage learn patience from his wife' (cited in Kosambi 1996: 3192).

10 See Introduction, Note 4.

11 I am indebted to Sumit Sarkar's '*Ghare Baire* in Its Times' for this idea. I quote Sarkar's note number 40 in the same essay; 'Several other similar cases of dowry immolation were in fact reported in the wake of the Snehalata case.... Girija Shankar Bhattacharya and four other teachers of Beherampur College mentioned the immolation of Nibhanani soon after Snehalata, in a long joint letter entitled "The Dowry system: Its Effect and Cure"' (*Modern Review*, April 1914). In 1917, an article in *Bharati,* a monthly associated with the Tagore family, pointed out that the suicide rate among women in Calcutta was four times that among men.... A *Modern Review* article of February 1920 was referring to an 'increasing suicide mania among Bengali young girls' (Sarkar 2003: 172). Refer to Rochona Mazumdar (2009) for more on this.

12 Refer to Ashok Kumar Sarkar (1994).

13 Dutt and Robinson define both these devices, the 'address' and the 'signing off' as 'salutations' in their *Selected Letters of Rabindranath*

Tagore. I, however, feel that they need to be distinguished as they serve different functions. In 'Streer Patra' the very meaning of the narrative is determined through the dissociation of these 'salutations'.

14 Tanika Sarkar notes: 'It was this new presence of women's writing in the public sphere that enabled Tagore to develop a fresh expressive form at this time. With 'Streer Patra' in 1914, he began to use the persona of a female narrator or writer who writes her own life in first person within his narrative' 2003: 31). Sumit Sarkar writes: 'This critical attitude to Hindu nationalist notions of femininity deepened between 1914 and 1917 in a spate of short stories, published... in *Sabuj Patra*, itself an experimental, in some ways deeply iconoclastic monthly.... 'Streer Patra' and *Ghare-Baire* were the first works of Tagore written in the *chalit* (colloquial) Bengali prose. As contrasted with the prevalent, more Sanskritized *sadhubhasha*, this must have been intended as a democratising move' (2003: 146).

15 Refer to Supriya Chaudhuri (2003: 45–65) for more on the impossibilities of such subject-formation, so far as Tagore's female protagonists were concerned; see also Chapter 5, this volume.

16 Amartya Sen in the 'Foreword' to Dutta and Robinson (eds, 1997) comments on the inherent duality of the letter genre, intending to communicate but also meaning to conceal: '... despite the eventual possibility of sharing, the form of a letter can give its contents an immediacy and directness that would seem inappropriate meant directly for "all"' (1997: xvii).

17 The idea of the inspiration inducing/authentic country as informing female writing and subjectivity vis à vis the stifling/inauthentic/male city runs through Rabindranath's works. Refer to the short story in an epistolary form, 'Darpaharan', where the husband's 'inauthentic' plot borrowings from western novels to frame his own narrative, loses out to the wife's intimate and authentic story about her country relatives, and their simple lives. A more well-known example is found in *Nashtanir* (The Broken Nest) where Charulata's simple tale of her village and its customs find commendation while the learned and 'experienced' Amal's artificial and convoluted style and content are rejected.

18 Note Mrinal's 'natural' affinity to cows in her constricted city home and her empathy towards these neglected, underfed, alienated bovine creatures in the heartless brick and mortar city. Her in-laws compare her derisively to these 'lower creatures', witnessing her affinity towards them. The city/country binary is also emphasized at the beginning of the narrative as Mrinal, a country girl, is doubly marginalized and

must await (in trepidation) the approval of city males (city gods as they
are described in the story) for survival (in this case, marriage).

19   Refer to Dutta and Robinson (1997) who note in their introduction that
      Tagore's 'finest letters were written during the 1890s to his niece Indira'
      and cite Nirad Chaudhuri's comment that the estate letters to Indira
      were among his great works of literature, revealing Tagore's character
      and personality with unadorned truth to authenticate their claim.

20   Annotating (no. 4) the letter, Rabindranath wrote to Mrinalini address-
      ing her as *bhai chuti* (1997: 46–49), Dutt and Robinson write 'This
      greeting is untranslatable. It means, literally "brother holiday"; *chuti*
      recalls *chota bou* (Little Wife) RT's earlier greeting to his wife' (ibid.:
      48). This letter was originally published in *Chinnapatra* and written
      from Selidaha in June 1898 to his wife Mrinalini. Rabindranath's letter
      addressing Mrinalini as *choto bou* is anthologized and translated in
      English, in Dutta and Robinson's book (1997: 19).

21   Supriya Chaudhuri in her essay 'A Sentimental Education: Love and
      Marriage in the *Home and the World*' notes that when compared to
      Ghare Baire's Bimala, Mrinal the wife's point of view in respect to con-
      jugality is 'far less equivocal' and that the 'story grants' the husband
      no 'personal space' (2003: 50). I beg to disagree because I feel Mrinal
      is as acutely aware of her husband's impotence as she is about Bindu's
      helplessness within the given social context. Both lack agency in life,
      though Bindu does achieve the same through death.

22   In Rabindranath's novel *Chaturanga* (The Four Quartets), the protago-
      nist Shachish's *jyathamoshai* (uncle) the agnostic Jagamohan, displays
      his iconoclastic mindset by irreverently rejecting such 'hypocritical'
      and 'unrealistic' display of reverence in Hindu letter-salutations.
      Jagamohan does not take into account the third or mythic level of
      signification within the communicative act, as spelt out by Roland
      Barthes in his *The Fashion System*. Barthes notes that symbols such as
      'feet' acquire mythic connotation within a given culture as they pro-
      ceed to move beyond the primary level of connotation as signifying
      merely specific parts of the body, to the tertiary level of denotation
      (the mythic level) signifying 'servitude', 'humility', 'low-status' and
      so forth. While Jagamohan in *Chaturanga* apprehends the epistolary
      address *sricharaneshu* literally (and therefore ridicules it), Grandfather,
      Shashticharan (in *Chithipatra*) is quick to apprehend this 'mythic' level
      of signification, and point out that such significations are culturally
      constituted and maintained.

23 I am indebted to Supriya Chaudhuri's 'A Sentimental Education: Love and Marriage in *Home and the World'* (2003) for this idea.
24 This term was first used by translation scholar Barbara Godard to suggest ways in which the text could be actively rewritten to suggest the woman's point of view and expose the phallogocentrism inherent to language used in society.
25 For a taste of British conventions of epistolary servitude, refer to a model letter 'A Letter from a Servant in London to his Master in the Country' that is addressed as 'Respected Sir' and duly signed off as 'Your most obedient and trusted servant, Sam Trusty' (Bannet 2005: 21 and Cooke who has an entire chapter entitled 'Suitable Direction for Addressing People of All Ranks both in Writing and Discourse', 1857: 211–15).

REFERENCES

Barthes, Roland. (1967) 1990. *The Fashion System*, translated by Mathew Ward and Richard Howard. Berkeley: University of California Press.

Bannet, Tavor, Eve. 2005. *Empire of Letters: Letter Manuals and Transatlantic Correspondence 1680–1820.* Cambridge: Cambridge University Press.

Chatterjee, Partha. 2009 [1986]. *Nationalist Thought and the Colonial World: A Derivative Discourse? Partha Chatterjee Omnibus.* New Delhi: Oxford University Press.

Chattopadhayay, Bankimchandra. 1969. 'Confessions of a Young Bengal', in *Bankim Rachana Samagra*, edited by J.C. Bagal. vol. 3. Kolkata: Sahitya Samsad: 137–48.

Chattopadhayay, Jayanti. 2003. 'Ghare Baire and Its Readings', in *Rabindranath Tagore's* The Home and the World: *A Critical Companion*, edited by P. K. Dutta. New Delhi: Permanent Black: 187–204.

Chaudhuri, Supriya. 2003. 'A Sentimental Education: Love and Marriage in *The Home and the World*', in *Rabindranath Tagore's* The Home and the World: *A Critical Companion*, edited by P.K. Dutta. New Delhi: Permanent Black: 45–65.

Clarke, Geoffrey. 1921. *The Post Office of India and Its Story.* London: John Lane and Bodley Head. New York: John Lane and Co.

Cooke, Thomas. 1886. *The New Universal Letter Writer. Containing Letters on Duty, Amusement, Love Courtship, Marriage, Friendship, Trade, Religion and Other Useful Subjects.* Montpelier Vt.: Q.C. Bowles.

Cooke, Thomas. 1857. *Universal Letter Writer: Or the New Art of Polite Conversation Containing a Course of Interesting Original Letters.* London: Milner and Sowerby.

Dutta, Krishna and Andrew Robinson. 2009. *Rabindranath Tagore: The Myriad Minded Man.* London: I.B. Tauris.

———. (eds.). 1997. *Selected Letters of Rabindranath Tagore.* Cambridge: Cambridge University Press.

Ellis, Robert, F.L.S. (ed.). *Great Exhibition of the Works of Industry of All Nations 1851: Official Descriptive and Illustrated Catalogue of the Great Exhibition of 1851.* vol. 1. London: Spicer Brothers; W. Clowes and Sons, Printers.

Gangopadhaya, Parthajit (ed.). 2010. *Balak.* Kolkata: Parul Prakashani.

Godard, Barbara. 1992. 'Theorizing Feminist Discourse/Translation', in *Translation/ History/ Culture: A Sourcebook*, edited by Susan Bassnett and Henri Lefevre. London: Routledge: 87–94.

Golden, Catherine J. 2009. *Posting It: Victorian Revolution in Letter Writing.* Florida: University Press of Florida.

Hill, Rowland. 1837. *Post Office Reform and Its Practicability.* London: Charles Knight.

Hill, Rowland, and Hill, George Birbeck. 1880. *The Life of Sir Rowland Hill and the History of Penny Postage.* 2 vols. London: Thos. De la Rue and Co.

Kipling, Rudyard. 2007. 1886. 'The Overland Mail', in *Departmental Ditties and Ballads and Barrack Room Ballads.* Middlesex: The Echo Library, Verse 226: 29–30.

Kosambi, Meera. 1991. 'Anandibai Joshee*: Retrieving a Fragmented Feminist Image*', *Economic and Political Weekly* (7 December): 3189–97.

Mazumdar, Rochona. 2009. 'Snehalata's Death: Questions of Dowry', in *Marriage and Modernity: Family Values in Colonial Bengal.* Durham, NC: Duke University Press: 24–54.

Rentala Venkata Subba Rau (ed.). 1902. *Kamala's Letters to Her Husband.* Madras: English Publishing House.

Sarkar, Ashok Kumar. 1994. *Sabuj Patra o Bangla Sahitya.* Calcutta: Pustak Bipani: 56–57.

Sarkar, Sumit. 2003. '*Ghare Baire*: in Its Times', in *Rabindranath Tagore's* The Home and the World*: A Critical Companion*, edited by Pradip Dutta. New Delhi: Permanent Black: 143–73.

Sarkar, Tanika. 2003. 'Many Faces of Love: Country, Woman and God in *The Home and the World*', in *Rabindranath Tagore's* The Home and the World: *A Critical Companion*, edited by Pradip Dutta. New Delhi: Permanent Black: 27–44.

————. 2000. '*Mrinal: Anya Itihasher Shakhshar*', *Desh*, 5 August.

Sen, Amartya. 1997. *Selected Letters of Rabindranath Tagore*, edited by Krishna Dutta and Andrew Robinson. Cambridge: Cambridge University Press.

Tagore, Rabindranath. 1921. *The Home and the World*, translated by Surendranath Tagore and Rabindranath Tagore. London: Macmillan and Co.

————. 1915. *Ghare-Baire*, *Rabindrarachanabali* (1986), vol. 4. Kolkata: Visva-Bharati: 469–593.

————. 1914. *Chaturanga*, in *Rabindrarachanabali* (1986), vol. 4. Kolkata: Visva-Bharati: 423–67.

————. 1914. 'Streer Patra', in *Galpaguccha* (1927), vol. 3. Visva-Bharati Sanshkaran; Kolkata: Visva-Bharati Granthana-Vibhaga: 567–76.

————. 1912. *Jibansmriti*, in *Rabindrarachanabali* (1986), vol. 9. Kolkata: Visva-Bharati: 409–514.

————. 1909. *Gora*, in *Rabindrarachanabali* (1986), vol. 3. Kolkata: Visva-Bharati: 375–65.

————. 1902. 'Darpaharan', in *Galpaguccha* (1927), vol. 2. Kolkata: Visva-Bharati: 421–27.

————. 1891. 'Postmaster', in *Galpaguccha* (1927), vol. 1. Kolkata: Visva-Bharati: 16–26.

————. 1885. *Chithipatra* (originally published as 'Chiranjeebeshu' and 'Sricharankamaleshu' in *Balak*: 279; 306); *Rabindrarachanabali*, vol. 1: 859–84.

PART IV

SELFHOOD AND AGENCY

CHAPTER 8

How to Fool Women: Tagore's Tales of Seduction

Tirthankar Bose

Women deceived in love have been a perennial subject of narratives in world literature, the tragic tone of the genre deepening in the nineteenth century with its growing emphasis on female chastity. In the ethos of middle-class gentility of the era, the genre assumes women to be frail creatures utterly incapable either of seeing through designing males or of recapturing their self-esteem after falling victim to the snares of romantic attachment. This conventional wisdom is undercut in Tagore's fiction as also in late Victorian narratives of the New Woman, a frequently cited example being Olive Schreiner's *The Story of An African Farm*.[1] Even though Tagore's milieu was only partly affiliated with the western ideology of gender, he found the theme of women's disastrous love relevant both to contemporary social reality and to his own lifelong effort to understand women. This chapter will offer a close study of two of his narratives, *Ghare-Baire* (1916) and *Sesher Kavita* (1929), both in my view dealing with seduction but one brutally obvious and the other deviously indirect, and both concluding with the female protagonist's victory. Victory comes at a great cost but Tagore demonstrates that the achievement of a selfhood invulnerable to social mutability is worth the cost.

Ever since the invention of gender, men and women have been playing games of domination with one another, the batting average so far standing decisively higher for men. In these encounters, the relationship called love is a potent instrument although its weapon-grade functionality is hardly ever recognized in social communication or in the vast literature it has spawned. As a profound observer of all that is human, Tagore put love to the keenest scrutiny, using love as the touchstone for human motives that range from the noblest to the basest. The latter, regrettably, is only too common a feature of love, as Tagore acknowledges in some of the legends of love he created, investing his understanding of relationships between men and women with an ever-present ambiguity. Taking two works of fiction, *Ghare-Baire* (1916) and *Sesher Kavita* (1929), the first an exercise in exploitive duplicity, the second in persuasive self-deception, I argue that while Tagore never failed to assert that moral wisdom eventually overcomes greed and folly in emotional transactions, he also recognized deception as an occupational hazard of love.

The literature of love is mainly a celebratory tradition that assigns such selfless mutuality to lovers, and exalts love so uncritically as total surrender that it has turned love into the dominant metaphor for the human–divine relationship. That is the tradition within which Tagore wrote about love. But, as I shall try to show, he did so not entirely without reservations. He did subscribe in general to the valorization of love as a self-effacing and ennobling attachment. But I believe he also recognized that the relationship is not without expectation of return, even if the specifics of exchange are implied rather than stated, which leaves it as an undefined contract. In my view that is the loophole in the game which Tagore detected and identified accordingly to protect the integrity of the conception of love as a noble condition of humanity. Let us also bear in mind that, ironically, it is the very lack of definition that romantic idealists, Tagore included, employ to idealize love as an unconditional commitment. It may be worth noting too that a commonplace of Tagore criticism is that virtually all of the songs in his *Gitabitan* placed in the section called *Prem* (songs of love) can be moved under the section *Puja* (songs of devotion).

Not every lover, however, is selfless or trusting, and many have attempted to nail down the terms of exchange. Christopher Marlowe's Passionate Shepherd tried out what he thought was a fair deal by offering his nymph coral clasps and amber studs, exhorting her, 'If these delights thy mind may move/Come live with me and be my love'.[2] But this businesslike 'if-then' stipulation ignores practical details, as Walter Raleigh's nymph points out in her level-headed if ungracious reply to the shepherd, noting that all worldly goods and all good intentions 'Soon break, soon wither, soon forgotten/In folly ripe, in reason rotten' ('The Nymph's Reply to the Shepherd').

The literature of love is full of male advice on the technology of love, from Vatsayana's *Kamasutra* (400 BCE–200 CE) to Ovid's *Ars Amatoria* (200 CE) to Damodaragupta's *Kuttanimatam* (8 CE), all trying to put love on a business basis. Whether love as commerce does indeed lead to bad bargains is not always certain but its inherent consumerism is anathema to the romantic tradition in the arts and ethics, all of which take love rather as the repudiation of self-interest and elevate the lover's surrender to mystic heights. True to that tradition, Tagore commonly treats love as a religion in which complete surrender to the beloved is the highest ideal.

The truth is that Tagore was a man of the world and recognized the abundance of perfidy in human relations. He recognized equally well that love is a high-risk business which, as a private matter, leaves each party entirely at his or her own devices in dealing with the other in a state of social alienation that fosters huge opportunities as much for high affective returns as for emotional embezzlement. While the course of love runs straight and true in countless poems and stories in which Tagore takes for his subject the ecstasy of mutuality that unites two individuals, he also shows in many of his works how somebody, a man in particular, can wield the signifiers of love to exploit, control and possess another. These expositions of conquest are virtually cautionary tales for the unwary, detailing as they do how women can be deceived. Not every woman is fooled, at least not all the time, as we shall see. But I suspect that the lessons inherent in these stories can be and indeed have been used to great effect as manuals for the love predator.

Of several possible strategies of love conquest, Rabindranath mainly deals with two, one that I call the hammer and sword invasion, the other the butter and honey insinuation. The prime example of the first is of course *Ghare-Baire* which springs to mind particularly after Soumitra Chatterjee's bravura film performance as Sandip. In Satyajit Ray's film (National Film Development Corporation of India, 1984) as in Tagore's text, Sandip stands out as a ruthlessly power-hungry egoist who compulsively consumes every object of value in his view, whether it is the nation he pretends to serve or women. The two in fact become entwined in his eyes, formulating a perverse equation that he uses to entice Bimala by its grandeur, as has been noted by Indrani Mitra in a 1995 essay. Conceiving Sandip as

a predator, Tagore lays out his hunting technique step by step as
a case study in deception in the name of love which is so effective that his prey Bimala finds herself falling into his trap even as
she sees through his game. His strategy of seduction is two-fold:
on the one hand, he tries to sweep her away by the sheer force of
his desire; the other technique is more complex, for it is a heady
mix of flattery and idealism. Not only does he dangle before her, as
before his young followers, that most powerful of all temptations,
the temptation of high ideals, but also declares her to be the only
human being capable of arousing and directing the energy of India's
multitudes towards the goal of freedom. His power of persuasion is
as great as his personal magnetism. Bimala begins with distrust of
his palpable self-seeking and his exploitation of her husband, and
yet the moment she sees and hears him declaim on the need for
self-sacrifice to the motherland, she gets drawn into his orbit, convinced of his saviour status (*Ghare-Baire*: 857–58).[3] She suspects his
motives, detecting in his photograph 'something that is not pure' in
his eyes and lips. But when he begins to speak at a meeting he seems
to her 'an immortal', the hero of Bengal whose speech is a fire that
burns brighter and brighter as he casts his eyes on her face. Even
when he preaches the necessity for doing wrong for the right end,
Bimala aligns herself with him against her husband's moral balance,
seduced by his doctrine of expedient violence that offers her the spe-
cious justification that only women can be 'truly cruel', that 'women
can storm into wrong-doing', and that 'our' poet—unnamed—has
invoked sin as an intoxicating woman: [*eso paap, eso sundari!/taba
chumbana-agni-madira rakte/phiruk sanchari.*] Come Sin, come my
beauty,/Send the fiery wine of your kisses/Coursing through my
veins (*Ghare-Baire*: 862).

With this bit of *fin-de-siécle* posturing, Sandip projects an ideal
of womanhood based on his unceasing worship of brute force,
which makes his ideal woman the centrepiece of a cult of violence
that parodies the mystique of Kali. It is worth noting that Sandip
does invoke '*ma prakrti, ma shakti, ma mahamaya*' (Mother Nature,
Mother Shakti, Mother Mahamaya) to legitimize his lust for life
(*Ghare-Baire*: 891). The ideal he thus erects is exactly the opposite of
the ideal femininity Tagore habitually proposes, an ideal consisting
of conservation, nurturing and self-sacrifice.[4] I may note in passing

that Tagore's own disposition to essentialize women ceases to be a fallacy in *Ghare-Baire* because here Nikhilesh is, in fact, the embodiment of his feminine ideal, an act of gender levelling, which takes its force from Tagore's belief that there is a 'woman within our inner self'.[5]

Admittedly, the gentle course of action taken by Tagore's ideal man and woman is tame and seems altogether anaemic. In contrast, Sandip's cult of violence promises drama, excitement and the thrill of mindless action. Like Ravana, Sandip unleashes a blitzkrieg. A potent technique indeed, and for Bimala, it is a literally hair-raising onslaught: *'amar samasta sharire kanta diye uthlo'* (the hair prickled over my entire body) (*Ghare-Baire*: 863), and she is on the brink of swallowing his lure. But in a move typical of Tagore's art of correlating opposites, he arms Bimala with a sceptical response when Sandip overreaches himself by his call, 'You are the goddess of the fire that burns the home, burns the world, . . . come, transform our iniquity into beauty.' In a flash of independence, she wonders to herself, 'Can it be that this is a display of histrionics honed by long practice at capturing the mind of the masses?' (ibid.).

Sandip's technique of seduction in this first encounter with Bimala is his calculated self-projection as a man bound by no rules. He is the stereotypical man's man who stands for adventure, danger and violence. As he later tells himself, whatever he can grasp by force is rightfully his, for the truly anointed son of nature is he who 'leaps over walls, kicks doors open, and takes by force what he wants, for nature surrenders only to the brigand' (ibid.: 868). Most significantly, where Bimala is concerned, he goes on to the further confession, a few lines later in his self-revelation, *'ami je chale chali tate meyeder hriday jay karte deri hoi na'* (My way is such that it takes no time for me to win the hearts of women), and *'bar bar dekhlum amar sei icchar kache meyera apnake bhasiye bhasiye diyeche'* (I have seen again and again that women have let themselves be swept away before this will of mine) (ibid.: 869). Women are to be consumed and discarded, as we learn from his self-congratulatory reminiscence about 'Kusum, the widow who surrendered to me, trembling and fearful though she was,' and 'that Firangi girl . . . who drove me out only to fall at my feet when I left' (ibid.: 879). It proves its power with Bimala as well, though not to the point of her total surrender, when we hear her admit, 'So terrible is the power of his will—as though he wants to drag me away by my hair like a cruel bandit' (ibid.: 883).

But this readiness to ravish is not Sandip's only weapon and, in fact, he upgrades his tactics when he realizes that Bimala is a woman of stronger character and cannot be bent to his will by a show of dominance. Instead of a direct assault, he uses flattery of the most transparent variety but effective nevertheless. It takes her little time to be convinced that 'whatever was going on in the land was rooted in Sandip's efforts, underlying which was this very ordinary woman's common sense' (ibid.: 871). The irony here is that *sahaj buddhi* or common sense is precisely what she has lost. Under flattery even her idiom alters to take on the flavour of Sandip's nationalism. As Ranajit Guha has remarked, 'The very first language in which the dominated learn to speak of power is that of the dominant' (1997: 101).[6] Abandoning his Ravana persona, Sandip puts on the mantle of an adoring bard panegyrizing Bimala as the soul of the nation, building her up as the only source of his inspiration, the spirit of the land, 'a flame that I have never found within a man . . . our Queen Bee . . . receive our homage' (*Ghare-Baire*: 867). Fire and flame are characteristically common images in Sandip's rhetoric, reflecting his own volatile temperament. Given that Sandip and Bimala are culturally determined to think of fire as a symbol of purifying energy, his invention of Bimala as the fire at the heart of India's redemption blinds her to the reality of fire as the destroyer. One of Tagore's sharpest ironies in the novel is that Sandip's romantic fire turns out to be the material fire of communal conflict, which too he himself lights. The flame he claims to discover within Bimala is equally destructive but not similarly, for it is not a social instrument of transformation but part of the romantic text into which he turns Bimala. She can see through his self-seeking but not through his poetry. She says, 'I do not respect him—in fact, I hold him in contempt,' and yet in the same breath she confesses, 'this *vina* made up of my body and soul—it sings in his hands' (*Ghare-Baire*: 883). Art is indeed satanic.

Why then does Sandip's art of seduction fail? It fails because it is a fabric of style, not of substance and ultimately proves ineffective against Bimala's ability both to analyse herself and to dispel the illusions of Sandip's smoke and mirror game. Perhaps Tagore's most powerful insight into the art of seduction is that it often catches the seducer himself in the web of his own rhetoric. Sandip is revealed both as hunter and prey when he confesses that she has made him feeble: 'I find no strength in myself to let go of Bimala' (ibid.: 893). He is no less subject to infatuation than Bimala but while she rises above it to regain her dignity and self-confidence, he descends into jealousy and petty recrimination. Her eyes wiped clean by his greed for the money he wheedles out of her, she realizes: 'Now at last Sandip understands that he is weaker than me. . . . He has realized that I have such strength that his tyranny will not work on me, that with one glance I can tear down the walls of his fortress. . . . At last I stand above him' (ibid.: 937). Significantly, this inversion of domination follows Sandip's exchange of the woman for her wealth; women and wealth being interchangeable commodities in a patriarchal ethos. The contrary ethos of romanticism that underpins *Ghare-Baire* marks that exchange as the milestone at which the invader turns back in defeat.

Win and loss are much less clear in my second example, the shorter novel *Sesher Kavita*. Ambiguity is most subtly crafted by Tagore here and at first sight the love relationship here seems unadulterated by any conscious thought of exploitation or even perhaps of conquest. Amit is the quintessential nice guy, in no way the playboy a father might have warned a daughter against. His wealth, his social standing, his cultural breadth—all speak of an absolute and unthinking assumption of entitlement that needs no demonstration. What also remains undemonstrated is any sign of personal attachment, whether to his airhead sisters or their shallow cohorts. Tagore underscores Amit's own shallowness explicitly when he remarks that Amit's sole addiction is to style (*Sesher Kavita*: 1106). Is there substance beneath the style? His clothes stand out in a studied attempt at constructing a personal fashion that Tagore calls 'a kind of elevated laughter' (ibid.) against the conventional fashionableness that rules his circle. But this rejectionist response is not so much creative as reactive. Dressing to be different is an iterative signal of his need to achieve difference in everything; in Shillong he puts on 'heavy highlander stockings of felt, thick-soled, stout leather boots, a khaki Norfolk jacket, knee-length shorts, and a sola topee'. Tagore's comment on this recognizes the deliberate anti-romanticism inherent in it when he says, 'not like Abani Thakur's *yaksa*—this could be the District Engineer on his road repair rounds' (ibid.: 1144). One can hardly miss Amit's sartorial alliance with the dominant British culture of his age, detailed by Tagore with perhaps more than a little irony. Gestures are vital to Amit's self-legitimation: he does not take novels for his holiday reading because that is 'common practice' but studies Suniti Chatterjee's Bengali linguistics in the expectation of finding fault with the author. As he sets out for the hills, in the garb of British officialdom, what he carries in his pockets are half a dozen thin editions of poetry in different languages. All these— clothes, books—comprise the manner that make Amit the Man.

Style is indeed all. Very early on in what Tagore calls 'just one of many examples' of Amit's dealings with women, we see how adept he is at speaking words without content, the phrases fashioned for their poetic balance and sparkle rather than their intellectual or emotional substance. Tagore makes rhetoric an essential signifier of Amit's stamp upon his world in the early episode between him and Lily Ganguly as they sit on the banks of the Ganges and watch the moon rise above the 'massed silence' on the other side (ibid.: 1107). The series of conceits he presents qualifies as the preamble to a declaration of love but leads to no actual commitment. Lily is moved for a second but like Cleopatra she knows that he only 'words' her and that the only thing true about them is their manner. Later, in a moment of rare perspicacity, Amit's sister Sissy tells him, 'Ami, all that you will spend your life with will be images in a mirror' (ibid.: 1113).

Wedded as he is to style and an expert at it, Amit knows that his social world lacks women who are authentic individuals. As he tells his sisters, 'I look without hope for one who is known for just what she is, who has no second in the world' (ibid.: 1108). His superficiality is jolted when he collides—literally and symbolically—with Labanya, a woman entirely outside his experience, whom he recognizes as a person of palpable moral, emotional and intellectual substance. This at last is a woman fit for his devotion. But gestures are so essential a part of his identity that in approaching her and recognizing his own feelings he defines his response exclusively through the artifice of poetry. He seems incapable of grasping experience except in metaphoric terms, which he records in extravagant prose and overdrawn conceits. It is not that this imaginative confectionery aims merely at conquest and consumption as Sandip's does. But Amit's welter of words makes it impossible to know with any certainty whether they indicate love for Labanya as a real person or for an idealized figure. Or, can it be that poetry is an end in itself, valorized only in terms of the aesthetics of stylized language?

If it is, then it works powerfully indeed on Labanya in securing her love. Drawn to him by his unconventional manner, which is in itself a fine net to catch attention, she is pulled in more firmly by his relentless poetizing. The transformative act that begins the process of her surrender is an act of language, not of personal magnetism as in Sandip's tactics. The key moment comes when Amit quotes Donne, typically moving Labanya by words and borrowed words at that. His approach becomes even more explicitly centred in language, proposing the legitimation of private mutuality by the invention of a private language 'like birdsong, like poetry' (ibid.: 1126). A private language? Just for you and me? Could any temptation be greater for the cultivated woman that Labanya is? Confident in the potency of this proposition, Amit's language demands the surrender of what is as yet beyond his reach:

> *Hey achena, mor mushti charabi ki kore,*
> *jatakshan chini nai tore?*
> (Stranger, how will you flee my grasp
> Until I have known you?)
> *…tor sathe chena*
> *sahaje habe na—*
> *kane kane mridukanthe nay…*
> (Knowing you
> Will not be easy—
> Never in faint whispers at your ears.
> I will conquer
> Your timid tones,
> Pull you with proud might
> From fear, shame, conflict, uncertainty
> Into a pitiless light.)

Amit's annotation on these lines is striking: 'Totally determined. How forceful! See the manliness of the composition?' (ibid.: 1127). The machismo inherent in his character must not be ignored just because it masquerades as art. Amit's alter ego Nibaran Chakrabarty's poems are 'like arrows, spears, thorns' that capture the reader by force 'as

Ravana captured Sita' (ibid.: 1109). This may not be Sandip's paean to violence but Amit's phrasing unquestionably attests to the not uncommon male thesis that women wilt before force. Indeed, Amit carries on, Sandip-like, 'This is like a firestorm in the solar system. Not merely a lyric, this is the cruel truth of life,' and concludes with a familiar image of fire and self-immolation:

> Let the flame of knowing you rise bright and high,
>> Let me offer my life to it as homage.
>> (*Tomar chenar agni deepshikha uthook ujvali,*
>> *Dibo tahe jiban anjali.*) (ibid.: 1128)

As the recitation ends, Amit grasps Labanya's hand. Labanya does not pull away. The conquest is complete.

Seduction by poetry clearly works, just as in Bimala's case seduction by the similar act of abstraction works, of patriotism in that case, and both I suspect have been favourite ploys of men, effective as they are in their implicit ascription of high qualities of mind and heart. Amit possesses none of Sandip's sheer animal magnetism, nor does he seem to signal sexual invitation as Sandip does. Amit is an aesthete and for him form trumps matter to the extent that he tries to turn even the material conditions of life into fiction. His vision of wedded life with Labanya is breathtaking in its romantic fancy, which prescribes separate dwellings by the Ganges on either side of a narrow channel, each with lamps on top, red to signal nights of union (shades of red-light districts!) and blue to indicate separation, a lotus-filled tank in which Labanya bathes as she readies herself for Amit, sitting on a carpet with jasmine garlands on silver platters, bowls filled with sandalwood paste and a lamp in one corner. Failing this idyllic arrangement, he is ready to live in a tiny flat but with the same separation, though in this case more symbolic than spatial (ibid.: 1143–46).

How well Amit's technique works never becomes quite clear from the story. That he loses Labanya to Shobhanlal is not the issue, for the valedictory poem from which *Sesher Kavita* derives its name might be read as a statement of undying love, though only notionally. This is not quite the idyllic end that Amit had imagined and there is considerable irony in the fact that he receives his coup de grâce in a poem. Why does he fail? It would seem that even the most determined tracker underestimates his quarry's power of self-preservation. As with Bimala, so with Labanya, their men overreach themselves, one by his naked aggression, the other by his conversion of life into art. Tagore posits an uncompromising clarity of under-standing on the part of both women, which gives them the power to see declarations of faith as illusions, when such declarations are driven by self-interest as in Sandip's case, or by the intoxication of aestheticism, as in Amit's. Vastly different as the two men are, they are similar in making the real object of desire not the women they pursue but themselves. Women can certainly be fooled but not every woman, nor all the time.

NOTES

1   London: Chapman and Hall (1873).
2   'The Passionate Shepherd to His Love'. Published in 1599, after Marlowe's death, the poem was very likely composed in 1588; see Forsythe (1925): 697–700. Raleigh's undated riposte came soon after.
3   All textual references to Tagore's novels are to those in the collected edition, *Rabindra Upanyas Samgraha* (1990). All translations are the author's.
4   'Woman', in *Personality*, Das (1996) 2: 411–16.
5   '*Prarthana*', *Rabindra Rachanavali*, 13: 475.
6   But Shakespeare anticipated Guha. One might recall Caliban's riposte to Prospero: 'You taught me language, and my profit on't/Is, I know how to curse' (*The Tempest* 1, 2: 362–3).

REFERENCES

Das, Sisir Kumar (ed.). 1996. *The English Writings of Rabindranath Tagore*, vol. 2. New Delhi: Sahitya Akademi.

Forsythe, R.S. 1925. 'The Passionate Shepherd and English Poetry', *PMLA* 40 (3) September.

Guha, Ranajit. 1997. *Dominance without Hegemony: History and Power in Colonial India*. Cambridge, Mass.: Harvard University Press.

Mitra, Indrani. 1995. '"I Will Make Bimala One with my Country": Gender and Nationalism in Tagore's *The Home and the World*', *Modern Fiction Studies* 41 (2) (Summer): 243–64.

Shakespeare, William. [1611]. *The Tempest*, edited by Stephen Orgel [1987]. Oxford: Oxford University Press.

Tagore, Rabindranath. 1990. *Rabindra Upanyas Samgraha*. Calcutta: Visva-Bharati.

———. 1966. *Rabindra Rachanavali*, vol. 13. Calcutta: Visva-Bharati.

CHAPTER 9

The Dichotomies of Body and Mind Spaces: The Widows in *Chokher Bali* and *Chaturanga*

Chandrava Chakravarty

I

The short story 'Jibita-o-Mrita' ends with the authorial comment: *Kadambini moria proman korilo, se more nai* [Kadambini proved, by killing herself, that she was alive.] (*Rabindra- Rachanavali* 9: 328).[1] Tagore here recounts the horrifying story of a young widow in nineteenth-century Bengal, who is taken to be dead by her in-laws after she suffers a sudden cardiac arrest and her body is sent for cremation. When Kadambini begins to recover, her companions think that her body is possessed by the devil and flee in terror. They, however, spread the news that Kadambini's dead body has been properly cremated. Thus begins a new phase in Kadambini's life when she becomes her own ghost, a living entity who now occupies an indeterminate space between life and death. The story could be read as a covert metaphor for the abject life of young widows in colonial Bengal, who became a dangerous site of border-crossing between the normative and the deviant:[2] 'Is she ever a material, corporeal presence, or is she a spectral being, actualized by death alone?' What is noteworthy is that anxiety with the widows sprung from a concern over their bodies. This essay will explore Tagore's portrayal of two very dynamic widows in contemporary literature—Binodini in *Chokher Bali* and Damini in *Chaturanga*—to highlight how Tagore grapples with the dichotomy between their experiential bodies and the discursive construction of widowhood in the context of colonial Bengal.

Fixed gender pathologies reflected the Indian nationalist anxiety with colonialism. The glorification of bodily chastity in the colonial and nationalist phase had distinct significance for women. The female body was deemed not only as a discursive site for adumbrating the nation in varied and contested forms, but also as a site of patriarchal restrictions and violence. As the twin processes of 'hegemonisation and homogenisation' (Uberoi 1990: 43) confined woman within fixed categories, all female identities outside the social stereotypes were erased. As Thapan notes, woman '...becomes an instrument and a symbol for the community's expression of caste, class and communal honour. Chastity, virtue and above all, purity are extolled as great feminine virtues embodying the honour of the family, community and the nation (1997: 6). In the poem 'Sabala' (A Strong Woman) Tagore posits rhetorical questions to protest against pervasive denial of woman's agency: *Nari ke apon bhagya joy koribar/Keho nahi dibe adhikar/Hey Bidhata.* [O Lord, why will you not allow woman the right to win over her own destiny?]. The last stanza of the poem voices a strong appeal: *Hey Bidhata, amare rek-hona bakyaheena/Rakte mor jage rudra beena* [O Lord, Do not let me be without a voice/ My blood resonates with a tumultuous melody] (*Rabindra Rachanavali* 8: 34). At this point, it needs to be questioned who is Sabala? Is she the same woman who suffers societal discriminations and subjection under colonial patriarchal economy in *Jibita-o-Mrita, Chokher Bali, Naukadubi,* 'Streer Patra' or *Chaturanga*? Tagore's Sabala is a rebellious force who rejects prescriptive norms and the confines of the domesticity: *Jabo na bashar kokshe badhu beshe* [I shall not enter the nuptial chamber as a bride; instead, she will break all shackles to meet her beloved on the shore of the wrathful ocean: *Dekha hobe khubdha sindhu teere.* She is an uncontrollable power, an embodiment of a boundless life-force that transcends the limits of the temporal world to merge with infinite cosmic energy. Tagore's poetry has been replete with such idealistic conceptualization of woman as a signifier of an elemental, primeval force; or as the very embodiment of a spiritual quest—the eternal lover craving for the beloved. 'Sabala' seems to encapsulate both the notions in its depiction of a self-assertive female lover. However, the 'sabalas' in Tagore's novels, especially the widows, cannot be situated in any mystic domain; they are fraught sites of various discursive struggles.

Their material bodies become the repositories of contradictory possibilities and their agency emerges as highly problematic. When a body transgresses social/cultural dictates, it behaves like some 'other' body—a queer body in the light of the social structuring of the body. Even if it cannot fully demolish the power and intractability of the formidable structure of social relations, the body challenges and betrays the vulnerability of this structure through various acts of transgression. It points, in the words of Nancy Fraser, to other 'subaltern counter publics' (1997: 71) beyond the bourgeois public sphere which opens up new spaces of contestation. The treatment of Binodini and Damini posits Tagore in an ambivalent relation to female sexuality. With a creative, humane appreciation of their strength, intelligence and vivacity, Tagore betrays a simultaneous discomfort with their sexuality.

II

Critical forays into the constructions/representations of the widow takes us into the tension between the 'body' as a site of embodiment (meanings/significations) which are historically, discursively imprinted and culturally practised, and the notion of an experiential material body as site of counter-hegemonic resistance. Inspired by Butler's idea of gender performativity, Irene Gedalof (1999) uses the term 'body work' to refer to that ideological frame within which the female body performs its communal, social and national identities. While selfhood/subjectivity is discursively constructed, the materiality of the body cannot be erased or said to be determined solely by discourse. Can the body be reduced to mere signs or symbols of gendered identities? Gender, after all, is a social practice that constantly refers to bodies and how the body performs to determine social practices. Yet bodies, in its material functions, propensities, libidos and enactments acquire an agency beyond the constraints of discursive practices and cultural formulations. A tension between prescriptive, normative femininity and human individuality creates a fraught space for reconstituting woman's subjectivity.[3] Nevertheless, to ascertain the working of heterosexual hegemony, bodies are brought under regulations. In the words of Judith Butler, the regulatory norms are strengthened and fortified by the production of a domain of abjected bodies which fail to qualify as fully human. In other words, the abjected realm creates pressure on the heteroerotic hegemony to articulate 'what qualifies as bodies that matter, ways of living that count as "life", lives worth protecting, lives worth saving, lives worth grieving' (1993: 16).

The body of the widow in colonial Bengal does not 'matter' in the sense that it does not qualify as a viable body, yet it matters immensely as a site of subversive possibilities which demands relentless surveillance and regulation. Whether the issue was *satidaha*, the legalization of widow remarriage, or the raising of the age of cohabitation, a nagging anxiety pervaded public concern over woman's sexuality. As it has been widely discussed, the Bengali intelligentsia relegated the inner domain of the spirit above gross materiality of the outer world, and projected woman as its sole guardian. The honour of a Hindu nation was made to rest on the symbolic purity of the Hindu woman as her chaste body turned into a transcendental signifier of the nation's virtue.[4]

Against the backdrop of a pervasive cultural tension over the constructed and experiential body of women, the widow's body deserves special attention. Colonial anxiety with widowhood is rooted in the perception of the widow's body as a dangerous, 'unaccommodable' entity—an erstwhile wife, located within the sanctions of domesticity and chaste conjugality, is suddenly dislocated from her position and made to occupy a 'queer' space. The widow becomes a 'queer' being because, in spite of the difficulty of accommodating her within the heteronormative domain, she cannot be dismissed like a prostitute.[5] However, her relation to heteronormativity remains curiously ambivalent. The widow thus occupies an in-between position, placed uncomfortably between the socially deviant and the normative. A woman, with all normal bodily cravings for pleasures, needs unrelenting disciplining so that she is mentally reconciled to her desexualized, subhuman status. The advocate of sati in Rammohan's tract opines that the true reason for supporting burning of widows is because 'women are by nature of inferior understanding, without resolution, unworthy of trust, subject to passion, and void of virtuous knowledge; hence it is evident, that death to these unfortunate widows is preferable to existence…' (Roy 1999: 143). In the first anti-sati tract Raja Rammohan Roy refers to

Manu's dictates to widows to establish his claim that widows should live long to demonstrate to the world the virtues of ascetic life:

> Let her emaciate her body, by living voluntarily on pure flowers, roots, and fruits, but let her not, when her lord is deceased, even pronounce the name of another man. Let her continue till death forgiving all injuries, performing harsh duties, avoiding every sensual pleasure, and cheerfully practicing the incomparable rules of virtue which have been followed by such women as were devoted to one only husband [*sic*] (1999: 115).

The opponent strongly asserts: 'The Ved especially declares, "by living in the practice of regular and occasional duties the mind may be purified..... Thereafter by hearing, reflecting, and constantly meditating on the Supreme Being, absorption in Bruhmu may be attained"' (ibid.). The rhetoric clearly searches means of accommodating a liminal being within the fold of social life, and thrusting upon the widow a life of severe penance and asceticism seems to be the only viable means of doing so. As the opponent of the custom of satidaha explicates, widowhood is the cursed state suffered by a woman who is held responsible for 'devouring'[6] her husband, and whose long life should ensure exemplary penance resulting in the expiation of her sin. The focus is neither on the suffering of the widows nor on the violation of human rights in the name of tradition. While masculine asceticism in colonial India became a means of resisting the imputation of effeminacy of Indian men and of highlighting their virility, the emphasis on female asceticism, mostly related to ascetic widowhood, bring to the fore a different sexual politics. Tradition, as sign of the nation's' cultural worth, is validated through acts of violence perpetrated on the body of the widows.[7]

A notable change in Rammohan's rhetoric on the issue of satidaha occurs in the second tract of his anti-sati writings. In this tract, we hear an impassioned appeal for sympathizing with the victims of male violence as the reformer articulates a new politics of looking. The focus is not on the transcendence of the widow's mind above gross corporeality, but on the transformation of her living body into a mutilated, charred mass of flesh: 'What I lament is that seeing the woman thus dependent and exposed to every misery, you feel for her no compassion that might exempt them from being tied down and burnt to death...' (ibid.: 145). Rammohan decries the practice of widow immolation as non-shastric, a heinous criminal act of homicide: 'But those, who, in direct defiance of the authority of the Shastrus, act the part of woman-murderers, in tying down the widow to the pile, and, subsequently applying the flame, burn her to death, can never exculpate themselves from the sin of woman-murder' (ibid.: 138). Rammohan thus constituted a new male gaze that legitimized the widow's status as sentient, living human entities, whose murder resulted in a horrifying violation of human rights. This enabled her redefinition as a perpetual victim of male tyranny.[8] Thus, as we move from the argument of the first to the second tract of Rammohan's anti-sati writings, a notable shift in his address of the widow's question is evident: the thrust is now shifted from her cultural importance as symbol of Hindu tradition to her recognition as a human entity. Such a re-description of the widow involved a recognition of her experiential, material body, its pleasures and pains.

The recognition of the widow's body and its natural propensities engendered a serious concern over disciplining it. Veering our gaze on the troublesome connection between the body and its embodiment, we look into, what Foucault calls, the 'technology of the self' implying training, practices, modifications, making people transform 'their own bodies and souls, thoughts, conduct, and way of being' (1997: 225). Widowhood in colonial upper-class Bengali society was deeply entrenched in various kinds of prescriptions, rigid religious observances and life-long privation. Manu, the ancient authority, who denied autonomy to women, prescribed a strict regime of self-flagellation and masochism for the widows to discipline their bodies.[9] Even while the widow remained the *ardhangini* (the half body of her husband) after her husband's death, she still posed a danger to social order by being out of the direct control of either her father or her husband. As child marriage was rampant among all the Hindu castes, a large number of widows were young, nubile girls moving into the experience of puberty and adulthood. Instances of clandestine liaisons between young widows and other men, elopement, accidental pregnancies and abortions were not rare. They were also the very objects of male desire within the domestic sphere providing the pleasures of consensual love and extra-marital sex for the male members.[10] In his appeal for legalizing Hindu widow marriage, Vidyasagar points to the dangers of imposing celibacy on young widows:

> Young girls whom misfortune turns to widows suffer unbearably through-
> out their lives..... How many hundreds of widows turn to the evil of pros-
> titution and commit the sin of abortion, bringing shame on the families
> of their husbands, fathers, and mothers, all because they are unable to live
> a life of chastity? Were the customs of widow marriage to be promoted,
> it would put an end to the suffering of widows, to the evil of prostitution,
> and to the sin of abortion.... As long as this beneficial custom is not pro-
> moted, the torrent of prostitution, abortion, and family shame will grow
> stronger, as will the torment of widows (2012: 68).

What is interesting about Vidyasagar's observation is that it reflects a candid acknowledgment of the widow's sexuality. What had long been a social anathema, was projected as subject of sympathetic consideration and judgement. Tanika Sarkar pertinently locates a discursive tension between the hegemonic projection of widows as dehumanized, sexless beings and a recognition of their material body with its libidinal impulses:

> The imposed and ceaseless flagellation shows that the prescribed codes
> did not really expect that bereavement would by itself cause the drying
> up of the widow's sexual life.... There was, thus, a constitutive tension
> or paradox within the widowhood regime: on the one hand an authorita-
> tive order that claimed perfect hegemony by grounding itself in the will
> of the subaltern—by being interpellated within her self-understanding;
> on the other hand coercion and a penal regime coexisting with that...
> 2007: 101).

Despite all efforts to discipline the widow's body and mind with rituals and privation, the widow remained suspect because of her uncomfortable positioning in the social canvas. The Hindu Widows Remarriage Act 1856[11] had granted only legal sanction to remarriage for young widows, but failed to change the penal regime of social violence meted out to the rebellious widows who dared to challenge the hegemonic structure. While the Age of Consent Act of 1891 aimed at raising the age of sexual intercourse for Hindu child brides, Gandhi renounced the legal and prioritized celibacy. Though historical and literary examples amply point to the involvement of widows in consensual romantic and sexual relations, Gandhi attempted a sublimation of physical desire by emphasizing the transcendental capacity of the woman's spirit to rise above bodily craving, which also entailed the capacity for infinite suffering. Her body was re-inscribed by Gandhi as an embodiment of *ahimsa* or non-violence.[12] The widow is Gandhi's model *satyagrahi* (an ideal fighter for truth), and the very incarnation of suffering and fortitude. He glorifies and essentializes the Hindu widow as a 'treasure' and as 'one of the gifts of Hinduism to humanity' (Gandhi 1951–95, 31: 314). If an awareness of male injustice to women grew with the various reforms for women, there was relentless counter effort to sublimate her sexuality through a re-inscription of her body. Any analysis of Tagore's widows will have to be placed in the context of this intensely fraught discursive terrain.

Although the reforms for ameliorating the abject conditions of widows in colonial times did not usher a radical transformation of the hegemonic structure, yet these achieved something of immeasurable value for women: first, it brought to the fore women's status as victims of male injustice and violence; second, from this awareness followed the realization that women's basic rights as human beings were regularly violated. As we undertake the task of looking into the widow's problematic positioning in colonial society, which entails the issues of coercion, consent, transgression and resistance, it becomes an imperative to rethink on the question of female subjecthood and agency. Feminine agency in colonial Bengal in relation to widowhood and sati is often presented either as an act of volition or simplified as resistance to the coercive structure of patriarchal hegemony.[13] A broader concept of female agency takes us beyond transgression, subversion or resistance and enables a foray into the complex forms of woman's subjectivities; it originates in the face of other forms of agency and competes with them.[14] It embraces the possibility of changing the existing power structure and might, in reality, thwart and subvert this structure. Personal experience derived from a woman's engagement with her surrounding world remains a crucial component of female subjectivity.[15] It is needless to point out that this experience is transmitted through the body and will naturally differ with the individual. Discursive construction of female subjectivity denies the space of individual experience and woman's response to the circumstances of her life, the nature and form of her resistance or volition. The body, in this revised understanding of female agency, becomes an indispensable component of social space, and it is the most crucial site for witnessing the production and reproduction of power.[16]

III

Bengali fiction of the colonial times is replete with the disturbing figure of the widow along with its focus on love or *prem/pranay*, an idea novel to indigenous culture. As understood in Bengali society, the very nature of love was illicit, beyond social acceptance and also outside the safe domain of domesticity. What was widely recognized as acceptable or legitimate heterosexual emotion was the affection between husband and wife.[17] The world of love was thus relegated either to the widow or the whore as in novels such as Bankimchandra's *Bishabriksha* (1872), *Krishnakanter Will* (1875), Rabindranath Tagore's *Chokher Bali* (1901), Saratchandra's *Baradidi* (1907), *Pallisamaj* (1915), which were severely criticized for their portrayal of the widow's love. In fact, Tagore's fictional world has a number of widows—nubile, intelligent and attractive. In his first novel *Karuna* (1877), Tagore introduced the child widow Mohini, who can be regarded as the predecessor of *Chokher Bali*'s Binodini. The man who gets attracted to her beauty is also named Mahendra, and like Binodini, Mohini also embraces an ascetic life after uniting Mahendra with his wife Rajani. The similarities between the predicament of the widows in *Karuna* and *Chokher Bali* are indeed striking. In both, Tagore has prioritized the claim of conjugality over transgressive prem, and in avoiding any radical resolution on widowhood, he has respected popular Hindu sentiment.

The treatment of the complexities of heterosexual relationship in Tagore's *Chokher Bali* (Eyesore) published in the year 1903 makes it unique and avante garde in the context of its time. Tagore's *Chokher Bali*, set between 1902 and 1905, recounts the story of Binodini—a beautiful, educated woman, trained in western learning under the tutelage of an English governess and then subjected most unjustly to the cloistered, unenlightened life of the Bengali women of her day. Through Binodini, Tagore explores the consequences of the abject life and carnal frustrations of a young Hindu widow. However, the end of the novel shows Tagore succumbing to accepted social practice in dismissing Binodini to an ascetic life of self-imposed penance in Benaras or *Kashidham*. This was, surely, the acceptable way of bringing her within the hegemony of the Hindu patriarchy. The novel evoked various kinds of responses. When it was serialized in *Bangadarshan*, the characterization of Binodini created severe discontent among the conservative Hindus as Tagore made Binodini desire sexual fufilment. The novel acquires historical importance by offering valuable insights into the problematics of configuring gender as a national imperative to counter British imperialism.

Binodini was rejected by Mahendra when his mother Rajlakshmi proposed a match between the two. She then approached her son's closest friend Bihari, but he also disappointed her by refusing to marry Binodini. Binodini was then married off and sent to live with her in-laws in a remote village. Widowed within a year of marriage, Binodini comes to Mahendra's house as a companion to his mother. When Binodini sees Mahendra's love for his uneducated, naïve wife Ashalata, her repressed sexual desire is aroused.

> Asha badly needed a female friend and a companion. Celebration of love lacks repletion when confined to two partners only.... Binodini on her own part avidly drank in the love tales of a young bride. Her arid and thirsty heart vicariously sought to quench her unsatisfied passion like an inebriate, imbibing strong and heady wine. The drink went into her head and incited her body.... Her whole body was feverish, and all nerves tingled with desire. Her eyes emitted fiery sparks. This happy home with such a loving husband, all these could have been mine, she contemplated. (*Chokher Bali*, 48–50).

The more Binodini comes to know Asha, her rejection by Mahendra appears all the more unjust. Apparently, Binodini might appear to be a helpless widow left at the mercy of others, yet she is far from being a passive, hapless victim who could be easily wished away.

Bihari sees in her that dangerous spark that can turn into a confla-gration if she is not readily sent away to her rural home. And yet, 'he knew well that this woman could not be treated as a plaything, and that she could also not be brushed aside' (ibid.: 53). Binodini, thus exists as a force to be reckoned with by the other men and women in the novel. Her enlightened mind refuses to accept her social abject-ness; instead she feels that she has every right to be treated and honoured as a human being. Mahendra's initial disinterest infuri-ates her: 'What was behind this calculated disdain? Was she not a live human being? Why treat her like an inanimate object? She was also a woman, and had he cultivated her he would have appreci-ated the gulf of difference between herself and his adorable Chuni [Ashalata]!' (ibid.: 58) What makes Binodini so irresistible to poster-ity is that within her Tagore depicts an incessant tussle between her interpellated social position and her individuality. Her resistance to social coercion is the outcome of intimately personal experience, envy and vengeance. Binodini's personal agenda of revenge centres round Mahendra, Ashalata and Bihari, and brings out the complex and enigmatic nature of female subjectivity. In Rituparno Ghosh's adaptation of the novel, a song from Tagore's dance-drama *Mayar Khela* plays in the background whenever Binodini appears on screen: *Mora jale sthale kato chhale maya jaal ganthi* [We weave spells in water and on land with our wiles]. Like the group of enchantresses in the dance-drama, Binodini is indeed an enigma for all. Rajlakshmi describes her as *mayabini*—an enchantress, who deftly ensnares Mahendra and wreaks havoc with his life. With a deeper insight, the pathos of Binodini's predicament generates a strange ambivalence: situated at the limen of social possibilities, Binodini desperately tries to occupy a space that could never belong to her. She might entrap others in her charms, but she herself is also a pursuer of an illusion. Even while portraying her destructive moves, the pathos and despair of her social situation never escapes Tagore.

As Binodini starts capitalizing on Ashalata's naïveté to access Mahendra, the two women become close friends and start calling each other '*chokher bali*' instead of the widely used Bengali word '*soi*' (friend). Little does Asha realize that the apparently innocent words of endearment suggest competition and rivalry between the two, and embody Binodini's real attitude to Ashalata. Ashalata is too inexperienced to gauge Binodini's subtle strategies and when realization dawns, Binodini has already trapped Mahendra in her snare. She starts playing a dangerous game by pitting the two friends, Mahendra and Bihari, against each other, and continues to provoke Mahendra's envy by her frequent indulgences towards Bihari. The novel displays a complex interplay of human desire in which we witness two dangerously poised love triangles: on the one hand, Ashalata and Binodini struggle for possessing Mahendra; on the other, Mahendra and Bihari compete for Binodini. The reason behind Tagore's triumph in creating a psychologically complex character like Binodini lies in humanizing her so thoroughly. Her depraved body is like a cauldron of unrequited passions, envy and desires. On the mental level, Binodini is found to struggle with her intense feelings, confused at times and unable to decide if her passion for Mahendra is love or jealousy. Bihari's sympathy for Asha inflames her anger at the injustices she has been subjected to in life and strengthens her resolution to ruin both Mahendra and Bihari:

> Bihari could not see her face in the dark, but were he able to do so he would have seen a face embittered with intense resentment. Bihari's heart was full of compassion and concern for Asha, but what about Binodini? She was nobody, just did not count.... Just you wait, Mahendra-*babu*, and you Bihari-*babu* as well, Binodini by demolishing both of you would open your eyes to the gulf of difference that was between herself and Asha. They would then know the true worth of Binodini. An adverse turn of fate had denied Binodini the opportunity of winning any man's heart by the use of her talents, so she must assume the role of the predator, armed with deadly missiles! (ibid.: 94)

> ... If she could find no happiness, then whoever stood in her way to frustrate her, whoever was instrumental in depriving her from all that she deserved, whoever conspired to deny her what were her rightful dues, would be mercilessly crushed and humbled (ibid.: 126).

It is difficult to see Binodini as an anti-heroine; nor does Tagore want us to regard her as a typical vamp against Asha. In fact, as a contrast, Ashalata is too passive and non-individualized in the novel. She is just another unenlightened woman of her time whose social acceptance is hinged on the fact that she is the perfect product of 'hegemonization and homogenization' that constituted colonial Bengali womanhood. Contrarily, Binodini is a rebel. She possesses sharp intelligence, she is sensitive to every situation, to the weaknesses of men, and can devise her subtle strategies of usurpation. A son spoilt by his mother's thoughtless indulgence, Mahendra is also too immature and tactless to match up to her. Though triumphant in her revenge, Binodini instantly realizes that he is incapable of understanding the demands of their relationship and also lacks the maturity to withstand social pressure: 'I do admit that shamelessly Mahendra may love me, he is so foolishly blind that he does not really know me' (ibid.: 187). She snubs Bihari when he accuses her of ruining Mahendra's home: 'That is your holy scriptures talking and I am sorry I am in no mood to listen to your sermons' (ibid.: 186). Throughout the novel Binodini demands recognition as a sentient, living, bodily entity, who cannot be bound by doctrinal prescriptions. Her desire for revenge might have been ignited by her envy towards Ashalata, but the real impulse seems to be a craving for recognition. When Bihari reprimands her for behaving like the heroine of a play who cannot be accommodated in real life, Binodini's spirit collapses. She begs for Bihari's love and, when refused, does something unexpected:

> She commenced showering kisses on Bihari's feet.... She knelt before him, and locking her arms round Bihari's neck, spoke tenderly to him. 'My dearest, I know you will never belong to me, but tonight do inundate me with your love, even if it be for a brief instant. I will thereafter vanish into my wilderness, with no claims on anybody. All I want is a token to remind me of you.' Binodini shut her eyes and ecstatically raised her full and inviting lips, vibrant with desire, towards Bihari's.... Bihari recovered to wake up, as if from a trance, released himself from Binodini's embrace, and contriving to make his voice sound normal, informed Binodini, 'There is a slow train early in the morning.'

> Binodini seemed lost for a while, and then collecting herself said, 'Yes, I will take that train' (ibid.: 189–90).

Binodini's craving for love is not devoid of dignity. Once she realizes that in her desperate bid to harm Asha, she has fallen in the eyes of Bihari, Binodini decides to leave for her rural home, and relinquishes all claims over Bihari. She realizes that Bihari has sentenced her to a life of penance, and his rigorous words of punishment hurt Binodini's dignity as a lover. When Mahendra comes to live with her, she is struck with blind outrage and makes him vow celibacy. Binodini is now a lover pinning away with the pangs of unrequited love, her loyalty to Bihari is unquestionable. This is a stage in Binodini's development in the novel which marks a shift from intense physicality to a gradual awakening to platonic love. When she meets Bihari in the course of her indefinite sojourn with Mahendra, Binodini unburdens her soul: 'I could have gone astray, become dissolute, but there is something in you that even though separated from you, you watched over me and protected me. I was sanctified because I had placed you in my heart. I realized how strong you were that day you sent me away from you, and I derived my strength from you to be worthy of you' (ibid.: 275). When Mahendra sees them together, he goes blind with envy and starts abusing Binodini. Furious with Mahendra, Bihari declares: 'Let me tell you that I am proposing to marry Binodini. So, take care and mind your language' (ibid.: 276). Unlike the other widows of her day, Binodini has always displayed a forbidden love for life, and flouted social norms; she has repeatedly pleaded for love but suffered rejections. When Bihari finally comes to offer her a home, a violent tempest rages in her heart, but finally leads to mental calm. She realizes that if she burdens Bihari with domesticity, his public work will suffer. Moreover, he will also lose social esteem by marrying a widow. Binodini finally leaves for Kashi to lead the kind of ascetic life widows were expected to live in her days.

As I read *Chokher Bali* from a temporal distance of more than a century, it appears that Binodini's decision to leave Bihari invests her with greater agency: 'You will not be happy if you marry me, on the other hand, you will lose your stature, and with you I will lose the glory with which you have invested me. You have always remained detached and uninvolved, yet contented. Keep that way. I will keep away from you, but will do whatever you ask me to do' (ibid.: 278). This is a Binodini who is not at the receiving end of things, rather she becomes superior to Bihari in renouncing the narrow limits of domesticity. Binodini seems to have awakened to the immense power of love as a sublime, regenerative emotion, which has endowed her with an infinite space of the mind. The sentimental ending of the novel with Binodini's parting plea for forgiveness conceals the magnitude of her triumph. Rituparno Ghosh's adaptation of the novel makes certain bold statements that add to my reading of the text. In Ghosh's film when Bihari proposes, Binodini has already found a space which is larger than what domesticity can offer. She has discovered a new *Bharatvarsha* which is not the colonized country Bihari has been trying to free from the clutches of the British. It is the *Bharatvarsha* of her mind, a new-found domain of immense possibilities. Rituparno Ghosh's Binodini disappears, leaving behind a letter for Ashalata and her opera glasses. Now that she has discovered a new world within herself, she no longer needs her glasses to see the outside world. Binodini's last letter to Ashalata is Ghosh's invention:

> *Dear [Chokher] Bali,*
>
> *...Do you remember asking me what desh means.... Is Biharibabu's desh same as ours? After I was estranged from you, these questions haunted me.... I realized that our cloistered life in Darzipara Street prevented us from seeing the outer world. That is why we tried to fulfil all our desires with the only man we had come across. But our desires remained unfulfilled and our small world (which you can call 'desh') was also shattered. If Lord Curzon succeeds in partitioning Bengal, then you and I will be in two countries. While living in two different countries if we think only of the insults, deprivations and sorrows we had suffered, then it would only mean that we have accepted defeat. Actually our desh is in our mind.... I came to realize what desh means on the day I stood on the ghats of Kashi* (Chakravarty 2013: 107; author's translation).

From the liminality of her interpellated position in the social hierarchy, Rituparno Ghosh's Binodini awakens to a new possibility of self-representation. Emanating from a cultural politics of difference and coercion, Binodini in the cinematic adaptation of *Chokher Bali* discovers a potent subjective space. This is where the potent change of perspective from the Victorian to postmodern is visible. Tagore's Binodini is banished to retain the normative values of middle-class society. Purging society of such seductive and self-destructive widows is a process of ethical purification. This newly conceived subjectivity enables her to transcend social hierarchy and situate herself in a position that is beyond patriarchal hegemony. Ghosh's Binodini acquires the ability to recognize far bigger goals than her limited life has offered her till then. Tagore's text surely provides an alternative space where the contradictions within the discourses on gender are exposed, yet his sympathy does not liberate Binodini from the confines of her mundane life. In Tagore, the sublimation of the complexity of heterosexual relation as a spiritual communion, a platonic emotion enshrouds the radical implication of Binodini's resistance to conjugality. The silences in the text are, therefore, significant in enabling posterity to explore the potential of marginal consciousness. Gillian Rose quoting passages from Teresa de Lauretis' *Technologies of Gender: Essays on Theory, Film and Fiction* describes these silences as 'spaces in the margins of hegemonic discourses, social spaces carved in the interstices of institutions, and in the chinks and cracks of the power-knowledge apparati' (1993: 140). In *Yearning: Race, Gender, and Cultural Politics* bell hooks detaches her identity from the hegemonic order by consciously placing herself on the margin. She also dismisses the notion of 'Woman' as the binary 'Other' created by the epistemology of difference.

> I am located in the margin. I make a definite distinction between that marginality which is imposed by oppressive structures and that marginality one chooses as site of resistance – as location of radical openness and possibility. This site of resistance is continually formed in that segregated culture of opposition that is our critical response to domination. We come to this space through suffering and pain, through struggle.... We are transformed individually, collectively, as we make radical creative space which affirms and sustains our subjectivity, which gives us a new location from which to articulate our sense of the world (1990: 153).

IV

Of the widows in Tagore's novels only Damini of *Chaturanga* undergoes remarriage. Damini is rebellion incarnate. Left by her deceased husband, Shibatosh, in the custody of Leelanandaswami, Damini is found to obtain rare pleasure from deeds unbecoming of her to the utter embarrassment to the Vaishnav guru. She is also the embodiment of irresistible sexuality: 'Damini is like the lightning which originates from the monsoon clouds. From outside she is full of the vivacity of youth; within her the fire of desire burns relentless' (*Chaturanga*: 440). Sachish writes about Damini in his diary: 'I have seen in Nanibala a new worldview—a woman who has taken upon herself the taint of sin. Sacrificing her life for the wrong deeds of another person, she endowed life with a new glory. Damini represented a different philosophy of life: she loves the pleasures of life, and believes not in sacrificial death. Like the burgeoning flowery grove of spring, she blossoms every moment with life' (ibid.). Leelanandaswami has failed to harness her desire for life with his sermons. In fact, when the guru asks Damini to listen to his preachings with the other devotees, Damini deliberately makes excuses to debunk the guru's authority; often she would shamelessly declare that she has been to the theatre in search of profane entertainments. She never dresses like a widow, nor does she live a life of ascetic penance.

Damini receives an unprecedented predominance in *Chaturanga*: almost three-fourth of the novel is about her and her relations with the three main male figures, namely, Leelanandaswami, Sachish and Sreebilash. While Leelananda remains a conduit between Damini and two other men, the life of Sachish and Sreebilash is led to their individual destiny by this apparently helpless widow. Like unabashed Nature, Damini is free, reckless and uninhibited in her longing for life's fulfilment. In the irresolvable conflict between the ideological and the rational, between abstraction and reality, life escapes. Damini is real and sentient; she evades theorizing. Like flashes of lightning Damini dazzles both Sachish and Sreebilash, and remains enigmatic to both. Sachish, who sees woman as an ideal, is unable to comprehend that Damini is life-force incarnate. His world of abstract, lofty ideas is threatened by her. She scares him; for Sachish, her irresistible magnetism exposes the vulnerability of his ideal world, made either of rational abstraction or of abstract devotion. Damini debunks the value of both. When Damini sees Sachish among the devotees of Leelanandaswami, hope of a new life begins to burgeon in her. The restless, reckless Damini suddenly slows down and with her quiet devotion and care, assumes a new self. Sachish is too overwhelmed by his new-found shelter in *bhakti* to realize the inner cravings of Damini. One day he sees

Damini banging her forehead on the floor of his room and crying, 'O, you are such a stone-hearted person! Why don't you show your mercy on me by killing me!' (442). Sachish's body goes limp in fear as he realizes that Damini is an impediment to his salvation. The dark cave where Sachish, Sreebilash and Damini take shelter during their sojourn is the correlative of Sachish's own physical desire for the sensual Damini. The cold, dark recess of the cave with its moist air is like a primitive animal whose instinctive drives are beyond the grasp of civilization. In a state of trance, Sachish feels that a hairy animal has captured his feet. Terrified he starts kicking away the animal but realizes later that Damini's hair was spread over his feet. Sachish fails to see the real Damini and tries in vain to control his desire for her.

On the contrary, Sreebilash has realized with the intelligence of a man of the world that there is no escape from nature and hence Damini is invincible. She can be repeatedly renounced, but cannot be ignored; society has banished her to the margins, but she has remained at the centre of life; she can become an impediment to Sachish's spiritual growth, but there is also no salvation without her. He realized that one can transcend nature only by acknowledging its importance in life. Sachish has always abstracted himself from the real world; he has tried to think of Damini as an ideal, but the real Damini has transcended the ideal and left Sachish bewildered. Sachish consoled himself by banishing Damini from the path of his spiritual quest: 'I am looking for someone I need badly. I have no interest in anything else. Damini, have mercy on me and leave me for good' (462). Damini is sensitive and intelligent enough to understand that Sachish's attraction for her has placed him in a state of spiritual dilemma. Damini deeply loves Sachish and acknowledges him as her guru; she would not like to distract him from his spiritual quest and drag him into the narrow confines of domestic life. She leaves Sachish and reaches Calcutta with Sreebilash. Although Sreebilash marries Damini, he knows that she would never belong to him. It is significant that she insisted Sachish should give her away in marriage to Sreebilash. This, perhaps, is Damini's last and final offering to her guru: she grants him complete moral freedom to pursue his goal. Since she has given herself to Sachish, only Sachish has the right to give her to someone else. This is the only widow remarriage in Tagore's fictional world—a marriage which remains unsullied by the daily chores of domestic life. Tagore refrains from portraying the quotidian implications of the Sreebilash–Damini union and terminates their conjugal life by Damini's untimely death: 'When the full moon of the month of Magh passed onto Phalgun[18] and the sea surged up with deep sorrow, Damini touched my feet and left the world with these parting words, "My desire has remained unfulfilled; I wish you as my beloved in the next life"' (467). This is a typical Victorian ending like that of *Chokher Bali* where all problematic or unaccommodated bodies are sidelined: either they are forced outside the precincts of respectable society or they die. Tagore's colonial appropriation of western genres and moral conventions reproduces patterns of morality which were specifically Victorian. In the realm of realistic fiction in the West, the fallen woman is a generically Victorian category.[19]

V

Binodini and Damini—the two remarkable widows—defy normative widowhood. Tagore has created two fictional paradigms who are potent enough to challenge the colonial economy of gender. Both the widows are acknowledged with unabashed moral sympathy as sensual individuals, and their physicality highlighted. Yet, both have been made to transcend social life through a sublimation of love. Binodini and Damini have burnt with sexual passion for the men in their lives; both have acted as agents of consensual love and profane desire outside marriage. Again, both the women transformed their lovers into their gurus and 'elevated' their sexual desire to devotion. How are we to interpret this iterative mechanism in Tagore's treatment of female sexuality? An ambivalence is unmistakable: Tagore created powerful women characters and made them the embodiments of radical sexual energy; but refrained from being openly iconoclastic. Spiritual sublimation became a veiled mechanism of harnessing radical, disruptive sexuality of women in his fictional world. One last example from *Ghare-Baire* [The Home and the World] might further strengthen this argument. Nikhilesh is Tagore's mouthpiece, and this is also evident from his sympathy and indulgence towards Barorani and Mejorani, the widowed wives of his elder brothers. However much Nikhilesh believed that society has thrust women into a state of abjectness, Tagore's novel portrays deep ambiguity about the extent and limit of woman's freedom. There seems to be a space between the home and the world where illicit desires engender transgressive possibilities for women. In Ray's film the point is visually explicit when Bimala crosses the threshold of the andarmahal to step out into the bahirmahal. Despite their deprivations her sister-in-laws had never stepped out of ghar and hence did not have to pay for their transgression the way Bimala has to. The end of the novel does not clearly indicate whether Nikhilesh dies in the riot, but there is a subtle indication of Bimala's plausible widowhood in the beginning of the novel: Bimala thinking about the vermillion dot on her mother's forehead, as if visualizing a state of fulfilment from a distance. Ray is very strongly explicit in representing the consequence of Bimala's transgression: in the film Bimala changes from a married woman to a widow, her attire white, hair cropped. Mejorani's shrieking words of admonition—'*Rakhashi, Sarbonashi*' [Demoness, Destroyer]—ring in the background. By relegating Bimala to the liminality of widowhood, Tagore makes a covert statement about the problem of reconciling the home and the world within the colonial pathologies of gender.

NOTES

1 Quotations from *Chokher Bali* are taken from Sukhendu Ray's translation of the novel (2004). Other translations of Tagore's works including passages from *Chaturanga* are mine unless otherwise indicated.
2 Tanika Sarkar's essay. 'Something like Rights?' (2012) encapsulates the predicament of the widow in colonial times.
3 See Moore (1994) for a detailed anthropological analysis of the importance of the material body and related notions of gender.
4 See Partha Chatterjee (2009): 126–32; Ashis Nandy (2005): 32–46; Dipesh Chakraborty (1996): 50–88.
5 See Sumanta Banerjee (2000): 'The 19th century bhadralok leaders... decided to sequester the prostitutes and render the institution as unnoticeable as possible. One of the first steps they took was to try to banish them from the *bhadra pallis* (the Bengali term for the areas inhabited

by the 'respectable' and educated gentry). In Calcutta, in 1856, the Vidyotsahini Sabha, an association set up by Bengali intellectuals... appealed to the colonial administration to issue orders to the prostitutes to move out from the city to its outskirts and ply their trade there' (130). The title of Sumanta Banerjee's book—*Dangerous Outcast: The Prostitute in Nineteenth Century Bengal*—also highlights the social position of the prostitutes.

6   Widows were often called *swami-khaki*, i.e., one who has devoured her husband. The cannibalistic epithet imparted the guilt of a man's death on his hapless widow. This provided a logical ground for penalizing her with privation and death. For a detailed discussion, see Tanika Sarkar (2007): 81–115.

7   Lata Mani (1986) notes in 'Contentious Traditions' that debates over sati in colonial Bengal was 'not primarily about woman but what constitutes authentic cultural tradition' (122). For a detailed discussion on the construction of ascetic masculinity in colonial India see Chandrima Chakraborty (2011) which explores the link of masculinity, asceticism and Hinduism in India from the colonial time.

8   In the words of Tanika Sarkar, Rammohan projected 'a radical re-description of the woman, bringing in a new ethnographic gaze to bear upon her every day and her concrete, intimate, material and mental experience' (2012): 316.

9   The historical period for Manu's text is accepted as circa second century BC to circa second century AD, a period of notable political, social and economic changes that led to the dissociation of the existing order and posed a threat to it. Manu's dictates on women, which have often been unconditionally accepted as the Indian traditional views on womanhood, were formulated in the face of a threat to the older order. The imperative to preserve the challenged Brahmanical order, the *varnashram* and protect it from adulteration through the intrusion of foreign blood resulted in the formulation of several strictures on women. Manu particularly emphasized upon the control and strict management of female sexuality as promiscuous behaviour on their part would destroy the purity of the patrilineal system. See Vinita Chandra (2009) on Manu's dictates: 'Duty as a wife was considered so important that it was laid down that by violating her duty towards her husband, a wife is disgraced in this world, after death she enters the womb of a jackal.... Why widowhood was considered baneful, and remarriage condemned, needs

more to be answered' (136). Anjali Chatterji (2009) in her study of the presentations of widowhood in *Smritis* and *Puranas* notes that Manu recommended a life of strict chastity and asceticism for the widow. She further adds, 'Though the *Vasistha Smrti* did not favour the burning of a widow with her dead husband, it did not allow her to live a happy and comfortable life. There were of course restrictions on her dress, her food and her enjoyment also' (157). I quote again from Chatterji: 'Manu, the greatest jurist, is totally against widow remarriage.... But Manu declares that "a childless widow who is virtuous and chaste can go to heaven". *Visnusmrti* also supports Manu by saying that "even a sonless widow remaining *Brahmacarini* goes to heaven" (165).

10   See Sarkar (2007): 81–115.

11   This is Act No. XV, July 1856: An Act to Remove All Legal Obstacles to Marriage of Hindu Widows.

12   See M.K. Gandhi (1951–95) 71: 208.

13   For an intense critique, see Loomba (1993): 209–27.

14   Janaki Nair discusses why a reductive understanding of female agency needs to be avoided (1994): 82–100.

15   See Chris Weedon (2003): 112.

16   Hooper's views obtained from her unpublished manuscript, 'Bodies, Cities, Texts: The Case of Citizen Rodney King', as cited in Soja (1996): 111–19.

17   See Jatindramohan Singha, *'Sahitye Swasthyaraksha', Sahitya*, February–March to March–April (1921): 700.

18   The months of Kartik, Agrahayan, Paush and Magh comprise the winter months while Phalgun and Chaitra the spring time in the Bengali calendar.

19   For details see Sumanta Banerjee's *Dangerous Outcast* (2000): 126–41. Sumanta Banerjee highlights the impact of Victorian prudery on Bengali society in analysing the attitudes of the Bengali bhadralok towards prostitution. While trying to reconcile traditional aristocratic behaviour with the Victorian moral values that decried the evils of licentiousness and glorified happy conjugality, some of the bhadraloks also displayed a desire to reform the minds of the prostitutes and think of their possible rehabilitation. The shift in focus from the idea of a *beshya* (prostitute) to that of the *patita* (a woman who has fallen from grace) made room for this reforming spirit of the Bengali bhadralok and explained their 'burden' under the impact of Victorian moral values.

REFERENCES

Banerjee, Sumanta. 2000. *Dangerous Outcast: The Prostitute in Nineteenth Century Bengal.* Calcutta: Seagull Books.

Butler, Judith. 1993. *Bodies That Matter: On the Discursive Limits of 'Sex'.* New York: Routledge.

Chakraborty, Chandrima. 2011. *Masculinity, Asceticism, Hinduism: Past and Present Imaginings of India.* Ranikhet: Permanent Black.

Chakrabarty, Dipesh. 1996. 'The Difference-Deferral of a Colonial Modernity: Public Debates on Domesticity in British Bengal', *Subaltern Studies* 6, edited by David Arnold and David Hardiman. New Delhi: Oxford University Press.

Chandra, Vinita. 2009. 'Women in *Masusmriti*', *Women in Dharmsastras: A Phenomenological and Critical Analysis*, edited by Chandrakala Padia. Jaipur and New Delhi: Rawat Publications.

Chatterji, Anjali. 2009. 'Social Status of Women in Dharmasastras', *Women in Dharmsastras: A Phenomenological and Critical Analysis*, edited by Chandrakala Padia. Jaipur and New Delhi: Rawat Publications.

Chatterjee, Partha. 2009 [1999]. 'The Nation and Its Women', *The Nation and Its Fragments: Colonial and Postcolonial Histories, The Partha Chatterjee Omnibus.* New Delhi: Oxford University Press.

———. 1989. 'Colonialism, Nationalism, and Colonialized Women: The Contest in India', *American Ethnologist* 16 (4): 622–33.

Foucault, Michel. 1997. 'Technologies of the Self', *Ethics: Subjectivity and Truth*, edited by Paul Rabinow; translated by Robert Hurley et al. New York: New Press.

Fraser, Nancy. 1997. *Justice Interruptus: Critical Reflections on the 'Post Socialist' Condition.* New York: Routledge.

Gedalof, Irene. 1999. *Against Purity: Rethinking Identity with Indian and Western Feminists.* London: Routledge.

Gandhi, M.K. 1951–95. *Collected Works of Mahatma Gandhi.* 100 vols. New Delhi: Government of India.

Hooks, Bell. 1990. *Yearning: Race, Gender, and Cultural Politics.* Boston: South End Press.

Loomba, Ania. 1993. 'Dead Women Tell No Tales: Issues of Female Subjectivity, Subaltern Agency and Tradition in Colonial and Post-Colonial Writings on Widow-Immolation in India', *History Workshop Journal* 36: 209–27.

Mani, Lata. 1987. 'Contentious Traditions: The Debate on Sati in Colonial India', *Cultural Critique* 7, The Nature and Context of Minority Discourse II: 119–56; published by University of Minnesota Press; http://www.jstor.org/stable/1354153, last accessed on 13 August 2013.

———. 1986. 'Production of an Official Discourse on "Sati" in Early Nineteenth Century Bengal', *Economic and Political Weekly* 21(17): WS32–WS40; published by *Economic and Political Weekly*, http://www.jstor.org/stable/4375595, last accessed on 13 August 2013.

Moore, H. 1994. *A Passion for Difference: Essays in Anthropology and Gender.* Cambridge: Polity.

Nair, Janaki.1994. 'On the Question of Agency in Indian Feminist Historiography', *Gender and History* 6/1: 82–100.

Nandy, Ashis. 2005. 'Woman Versus Womanliness in India: An Essay in Cultural and Political Psychology', *Exiled at Home.* New Delhi: Oxford University Press.

Rose, Gillian 1993. *Feminism and Geography: The Limits of Geographical Knowledge.* Cambridge, UK: Polity Press.

Roy, Raja Rammohan. 1999. *The Essential Writings of Raj Rammohan Roy*, edited by Bruce Carlisle Robertson. Delhi: Oxford University Press.

Sarkar, Tanika. 2012. 'Something like Rights? Faith, Law and Widow Immolation Debates in Colonial Bengal', *The Indian Economic and Social History Review* 49(3): 295–320.

———. 2007. 'Wicked Widows: Law and Faith in Nineteenth-century Public Sphere Debates', *Behind the Veil: Resistance, Women, and the Everyday in Colonial South Asia,* edited by Anindita Ghosh. Ranikhet: Permanent Black.

———. 2003. *Hindu Wife, Hindu Nation.* Delhi: Permanent Black.

Singha, Jatindramohan. 1921. *Sahitye Swasthyaraksha.* Kolkata: Bhattacharjya & Sons.

Soja, Edward W. 1996. *Thirdspace: Journeys to Los Angeles and Other Real-and-Imagined Places.* USA, UK, Australia: Blackwell Publishing.

Thapan, M. 1997. 'Introduction', *Embodiment: Essays in Gender and Identity*, edited by M. Thapan. Delhi: Oxford University Press.

Tagore, Rabindranath. 1909. *Chaturanga, Rabindrarachanabali*, vol. 4. Kolkata: Visva-Bharati.

———. 1909. *Ghare Baire, Rabindrarachanabali*, vol. 4. Kolkata: Visva-Bharati.

———. 1909. 'Jibita-o-Mrita', *Rabindrarachanabali*, vol. 9. Kolkata: Visva-Bharati.

Tagore, Rabindranath. 1909. 'Sabala'. *Rabindrarachanabali*, vol. 8. Kolkata: Visva-Bharati.

———. 2004. *Chokher Bali,* translated by Sukhendu Ray. New Delhi: Rupa.

Uberoi, P .1990. 'Feminine Identity and National Ethos in Indian Calendar Art', *Economic and Political Weekly* April 28, WS: 41–8.

Vidyasagar, Ishvarchandra. 2012. *Hindu Widow Marriage*, translated by Brian A. Hatcher. Ranikhet: Permanent Black.

Weedon, Chris. 2003. 'Subjects', *A Concise Companion to Feminist Theory*, edited by Mary Eagleton. Hoboken, NJ: Wiley-Blackwell.

CHAPTER 10

'Bimala Is What She Is': Re-reading Bimala and Gender (In)justice in Rabindranath's *The Home and the World*

Dipannita Datta

This essay begins from the assumption that Rabindranath Tagore's *The Home and the World*[1] 'attracted the sort of vituperative criticism' (T. Sarkar 2003: 27) that no other work of Tagore did. This statement compels us to re-read the novel and probe the important account of Tagore's serious negotiation with highly fractured times and the *milan* and *samanjasya*—unity and harmony—that he was trying to establish between societies and cultures by making individual and collective norms and actions accountable to and measurable in terms of a speculative notion of universal humanity. It is difficult to build this worth of human relationships across national boundaries on the grounds of imperialism and its masculine civilization (Tagore 1961b). The 'common humanity of women as well as men', which Tagore was in search of and as he has described this later in 'Narir Manushatva' (Tagore 1961a), could not also be achieved through 'national egoism' or 'patriotic excitement' because either of them, according to Tagore, 'breeds sectarian arrogance, mutual misunderstanding and a spirit of persecution' (Das 1996: 273). While this is a general understanding of Tagore regarding gendered relations, which he believed was inherently destructive to the spirit of 'global unity' or even unity within a specific nation (Dutta and Robinson 1997: 85), the entire question of mutual effectiveness of shared respect and uniform gender (in)justice is vastly complex. 'All nations depend on powerful constructions of gender despite nationalisms' ideological investment in the idea of... *unity*' (McClintock 1993: 61, emphasis original). Hostility against and insensitivity to

generalizations apart, the mutual accountability of Indian nationalism and the women's question is of crucial importance. There is a
need to engage with Tagore's views about women and gender seg-
regation and analyse them in terms of cross-cultural negotiations
of common human proclivity of women as well as men as a means
to achieve human freedom and harmony. The Bimala discourse—
representative of the tensions of early twentieth-century women in
colonial Bengal—is of special significance here. This essay argues
that Tagore's insights and ideas about the women's question,
depicted in the novel, can be read as prescient metaphors for the
gender–sexuality dynamics operational in society.

In her inaugural study on patriotism versus cosmopolitanism,
Martha Nussbaum, known for her works on woman's capability and
global justice, has embraced Tagore's idea for a dialogic relationship in terms of allegiance to negotiations of common humanity of
women as well as men while arguing powerfully against the prevalent claims in the US to 'the renewal of appeals to the nation, and
national pride' (1996: 5). Emphasizing on the ideal of 'allegiance
to justice that transcends the local' in the literary text *The Home
and the World*, she has underscored the moral ideal in Nikhilesh
'whose allegiance is to the worldwide community of human beings'
(ibid.: 4) and insisted that 'what we share as both rational and mutually dependent human beings were simply not on the agenda' of
the US social philosophy of education (ibid.: 5). That Nikhilesh
in no uncertain terms insisted on commitment to his own country
and sensitively handled the 'woman question' (the issues concerning freedom and gender justice) and that both were linked with the
imposed cultural identity (on woman and nation) which Bimala
(the central narrator of *The Home and the World* and Nikhilesh's
wife) exposes, necessitates further attention along the lines of socio-
political debates on the independence of the nation and its women.

It is known that during the colonial times re-inscribing tradition
was a strategic policy of the British establishment to keep Indian
women in an inferior position, in spite of the urgent initiative of
the social reformers in the early phase of the nationalist struggle.
Simultaneously, the 'modernization' drives to abate/refashion western cultural superiority by the use of what Partha Chatterjee calls
'the ideological sieve', through which nationalists filtered European

ideas, started to have its impact on women with the official burgeoning of nationalism in the latter half of the nineteenth century (1993:
116–17). In the wake of the Swadeshi movement (the background
of *The Home and the World*), the first anti-colonial nationalist movement sparked off by Lord Curzon's arbitrary partition of Bengal in
1905, the women's position in Bengal (India) was further complicated. The tensions of power and subjectivity, which attended the
rhetoric of this movement, shaped a similar process—another form
of male patriarchal manipulation or domination of the 'nationalist
patriarchs'. Woman's position was further re-inscribed/re-invented.
Patriotic expressions were the creed of the day, but the woman was
denied access to the public sphere and remained shut-in-home. It is
impossible to analyse the discourse on women thus created without
addressing 'the notion of "the nation"…and the shifting nationalist discourses… competing for hegemony' within the contemporary
postcolonial state (and its attendant discourses on the complex interplay of a gender-culture and colonial interpellation (Yuval-Davis
2008: 4; Chatterjee 1993: 10). For, it is 'not biology but culture [that]
becomes destiny' in this discursive construction of power and subjectivity (Yuval-Davis 2008: 8; Butler 1990: 8).

A brief unfolding of the specific and fluctuating historical
structures of colonial Bengal would be useful here. The Bimala discourse demonstrates the specific complicated situation associated
with the struggle for independence and the concomitant problems
that affected women of the early twentieth-century Bengal and the
possible alternatives to the formidable days of armed conflicts and
internal repression. The 'carnivorous' and 'cannibalistic' tendencies that attended the policy of 'divide and rule' of the partition of
Bengal, created a rigid boundary in the mental outlook between the
two religious groups (the Hindus and the Muslims), and atrocities
heightened including rape and kidnapping of women. The radical
shifts in geopolitics and economy (comprising boycott and burning
of foreign clothes as depicted in the novel) resulting from the partition, which are also attributable to the growing sense of partisan
patriotism and religious nationalism, severely affected the daily life
of the masses (men, women and children of all strata of the society).
Women in particular, especially (the genteel women of the middle
rung of society), the bhadramahilas who wished to participate in

the movement were deeply affected for they had to overcome the colonial assumption of Indian women as dependent subjects (hence, stereotyped as passive victims) first and then the normative model of the nationalist pedagogy. That said, the 'woman question' was a highly complex issue and certainly it cannot be explained from any single perspective of a domination–subordination relationship.

To locate the woman's position during those volatile days of complex reciprocity, at least partially, one needs to have an idea of the culture 'of the sanctioned institutionalization of gender difference' (McClintock 1993: 61) and in particular of the material–spiritual dichotomy, which divided the home and the world into two separate domains—*ghar* and *bahir* (T. Sarkar 2001; Chatterjee 1993). The women of India were ensured freedom, but that was highly synonymous with the freedom of maintaining the traditional 'spiritual' (feminine) ethos/culture within the defined 'inner' space—the 'ghar'/the home. Predictably, the burden of carrying the ethos of the spiritual East over the material West was on women. The new model fixed, according to Partha Chatterjee, 'was now a "classicized" tradition—reformed, reconstructed' (1993: 127). With a somewhat different understanding of the normative nationalist pedagogy and the spatial practice Ashis Nandy observes 'To Tagore, the oppositions could best be handled within the format of India's "high" culture... [and that in] his world, modernity had a place' (199: 1).

The willingness to see beyond a particular matrix is the productive aspect of Tagore's vision of an alternative modernity. He tried to bring together the classical Sanskrit tradition and some aspects of the European Renaissance from which he developed his methods of Indian modernity and tried to overcome the divisive nature of the colonialism–nationalism framework. In such a situation of contestations, to develop a sense of *manusatya* (humanity) without surrendering the individual was important although not easy during those days of the colonial regime in India (and the abject and cruel condition of women across the world who survived war and conflicts). In his essay, 'Woman' (1961b), Tagore presents his views about the way nations depend on powerful constructions of gender, which seem to have come a few years after his break with Swadeshi nationalism. He asserts further in 'Woman and Home' (1922) that it is the 'unequal freedom' in the relations between man and woman, which has made the weight of life's tragedies so painfully heavy for woman to bear. Much later in 'Women's Place in the World' (1996a), he insists that though women were victims of the 'masculine civilization' they were the subjects of their own discourse. The last point is central to any articulation about woman, for it not only allows us to ponder how much space the woman had in being an actor in her own life but also directs towards a significant register of Tagore's visions of women's capability. The present attempt engages with and simultaneously interrogates Tagore's confident aspiration through Bimala's *atmakatha* (autobiographical story), which offers an intricate study of layered historical narratives of the meaning of nationhood and its implications on women. Bimala challenges the gendered assumptions, as well as examines the male ordering and proclaims:

> I am educated, and therefore, I am familiar with the contemporary times in the modern language of this age... But, having traversed from those days of my childhood to this day of my barely mid-youth, it seems I have virtually arrived at a different age (Tagore 2006 [1916]: 7).

Challenging the homogeneous 'impact of outside imagery' on Indian women, to use Amartya Sen's words and on their position as passive victims, Bimala foregrounds the problematics of the speed of the modern age, its incursion into the language of 'self-images' and culture and the complex links between tradition/s and modernity/ies.[2] Bimala insists further: 'We women are not only the deities of the household fire, but the flame of the soul itself' (Tagore 1919: 25).

This self-assertion of Bimala, while she encounters her husband's nationalist friend Sandip and his extremist move to reposition India's struggle for freedom, demonstrates the varied dimensions of her conviction with which she addressed the dilemmas that accompanied transitions and transformations in early twentieth-century colonial Bengal. Bimala not only reflects on the stereotyped social roles of wifely duties but also insists she is able to acquire knowledge of the self by introspection and relate it to the needs of the time in terms of rights to participate in the movement for the cause of the larger struggle: India's independence from British rule.

I felt the real point was, that one ought to stand up for one's rights....One day there came the new era of Swadeshi in Bengal. We had no time even to think about, or understand, what had happened, or what was about to happen. My sight and my mind, my hopes and my desires, became red with the passion of this new age. Though, up to this time, the walls of the home—which was the ultimate world to my mind—remained unbroken, yet I stood looking over into the distance... (Tagore 1919: 16–17).

'The new era of Swadeshi in Bengal' that Bimala narrates is a historical phase in the annals of India's struggle for independence. It is not that complexities between the colonizers and the colonized were not known before this era, but the partition of Bengal was a new situation of crisis in the records of modern Indian history. As an expression of national integrity, the anti-partition movement— the Swadeshi movement—started. Conceived to fight both economic imperialism and communalist forces released by the British, the movement took contradictory dimensions dividing the Indian populace amongst themselves along the lines of religion. The effect was communal riots between Hindu and Muslim communities that formed the indigenous population rather than mutually and collectively against the imperial rule. *The Home and the World* puts into context the coercive colonial politics that severely impinged on the daily lives of both the communities, and the crisis is represented through the autobiographical narration of Nikhilesh-Bimal-Sandip while unfolding Bimala's capacity to respond to the discriminatory/ gendered politics operative in contemporary Bengal (India) under British rule.

It is commonplace that the Bimala discourse hinges on the nation–sexuality connotations. A woman, like Bimala, becomes the signifier of the nation as opposed to her identity as a woman. That she demonstrates a positive capability to expose multiple experiences of a woman with the birth of the nation is completely erased not only from the debates on the distinctive nature of the 'woman question' in the historical narratives of India and nationhood but also in discursive/philosophic cognizance of women's various deprivations and gender asymmetry. Bimala could look beyond the walls of the home while keeping the home in its place; and, while being at home, she provides a discursive space to the important interrelationship between contests and complicities in the movement towards public resistance to patriarchal norms both indigenous and those held as modernity under British administration.

However, it is unreasonable to probe into the prescriptive assertions about sexual equity without having an understanding of the historicity of the Swadeshi movement. Swadeshi patriots (mostly not of the extremist variety), like Tagore himself, primarily encouraged indigenous growth of economy (*atmasakti*)[3] against the 'motive forces' of colonialism. The colonial regime, as Bipan Chandra (2010) comments, deliberately followed 'discriminatory policies' 'making India its agrarian hinterland for the sale of its manufactures and purchase of India's raw materials... and the suppression of Indian capital'.[4] Bimala's *atmakatha* unfolds the sensitive moment in the space of the nation and in a woman's life, which is deeply entwined with the history of India, from the partition of Bengal to solving India's problem. Bimala does not negate the material agency of 'political economy' that would in turn facilitate support for the villagers in Nikhilesh's estate (Tagore 1919: 25), but to resist the colonial status was important to her, and she narrates:

> From the time my husband [Nikhilesh] had been a college student he had been trying to get the things required by our people produced in our own country. There are plenty of date trees in our district. He tried to invent an apparatus for extracting the juice.... [He also attempted] reviving our industries... and also took it into his head to teach his countrymen ideas of thrift, so as to pave the way for a bank; and then he actually started a small bank.... My husband's list of charities was a long one. He would assist to the bitter end of utter failure anyone who wanted to invent a new loom or rice-husking machine. But what annoyed me most was the way that Sandip Babu used to fleece him on the pretext of *Swadeshi* work (ibid.: 18).

It is clear that Bimala was in search of a personal self as well as the national self. Yet, what could be Tagore's intention to display the historical phase of India's struggle for independence in the voice of Bimala? Certainly, if one was to present the tensions of confrontation between tradition/s and modernity/ies and also the modernity-project itself within which Bimala attempts to find a location for the self, the other was to suggest/emphasize that men (here the nationalists and patriots alike) were re-defined/produced by their women. Bimala does not fail to notice Nikhilesh's generous vision of Swadeshi patriotism and his practical initiatives to recover from the colonial injury. She equally records Sandip's Swadeshi politics as a self-serving impostor even if she herself gets entangled in his web of desires.

Besides, inhabiting the imaginary boundary between inside/ghar/home and outside/bahir/world, Bimala asserts her right to be heard while 'constituting herself as a project of modernity itself' (Chaudhuri 2011: 92). Nevertheless, while negotiating the boundary between the home and the world, the complex disjunctions between tradition and modernity do not allow us to settle on any side of the contradictions. On the cultural side, as mentioned earlier, rigidity was instituted by the colonial state in the name of 'traditionalization' of Indian society. This stringency continued to influence gender asymmetry at home from the late nineteenth-century to the early twentieth-century colonial India and resulted in a rigid codification of 'custom' and 'tradition' and its privileging of 'scriptural' interpretations of social law at the expense of the fluidity of local community practices (Chatterjee 1993: 31). The way the state arbitrated over women's legal rights contributed to an excessive scripturization of Hinduism (Bagchi 1995: 3–4). Bimala's capacity to engage with the sources of colonial anxiety—to look beyond the walls of the home or the domestic and challenge both colonial imperialism as well as patriarchal fetishes—invites exposition along the lines of Indian patriotism as Tagore saw it (specific to the era of Swadeshi movement and beyond) and linked that with an idealized notion of a Hindu wife's chastity (*patibrata*) and a widow's celibacy (*brahmacharje*).[5] Although the characters of the widow in the novel will not be analysed in this essay, it needs to be noted that all widows in Bengal (even in the elite families) did not share the common fate as Bororani, Mejorani did, because of their generous brother-in-law Nikhilesh.[6]

Bimala is aware that all men or 'all women could not have thought the same way' (Tagore 2006 [1916]: 8), still, she insisted on questioning the injustices on women that proliferated every layer of colonial Bengal. She draws intricate connections between rights and responsibilities of Indian women, particularly the genteel women, are the bhadramahilas, and the social impositions that restricted them from participating outside: how did these genteel women respond to the tensions of discriminatory policies operative in the early twentieth-century society and its culture, and how these collectively shaped not only the public/outside but also the private/inside.

Within the possession of normative function, during the days of the anti-colonial struggle, especially the second phase—during the last quarter of the nineteenth century and the early twentieth century, as Vina Mazumdar observes, 'the independence of the country and of women [had] become so intertwined as to be identical' (Mazumdar 2001: 135). Women also claimed their rightful place in the field of anti-colonial politics. Bimala declared: 'As soon as the Swadeshi storm reached my blood, I said to my husband (Nikhilesh): "I must burn all my foreign clothes"' (Tagore 1919: 19).

Tagore's foraying into the women's movement—'the passion of this [Swadeshi] new age'—and along the lines of the woman question, which are central issues in the novel and that both of which were an integral part of the struggle for country's independence have often been misinterpreted or have received censorious attention. Sumit Sarkar has elaborately described the 'sharp criticism' in terms of *Ghare-Baire in Its Times* (2003: 143–68). Amartya Sen observed, 'The story had many detractors not just among dedicated nationalists in India' (2005: 109). Tanika Sarkar's balanced response to Lukács' condemnation is useful here. She remarked, 'he got the anti-colonial politics within India woefully mixed up' (T. Sarkar 2003: 27). However, back at home nationalists of the extremist variety saw in it 'a compromise with imperialism' (ibid.). These critical receptions of *The Home and the World* show that the reactions were entirely symptomatic of the conflicting experiences of the time and confirm how colonial and anti-colonial imperatives indeed competed to weave a complicated pattern on Rabindranath Tagore and his work. Nevertheless, Bimala exemplifies the poignant and adventurous perception of ways in which women challenged themselves and questioned society and merits to be located in reading a subversive space: Bimala 'discarding the posture of obedience and subjection' (ibid.: 35). Was that Tagore's sole objective—to portray an independent-minded and autonomously acting woman?

Even if not the only one, the readers are certainly reminded of the fact that women are not puppets in the hands of their gods, neither are they an agent of socialization: the 'home-made Bimala, the product of the confined space and the daily routine of small duties' (Tagore 1919: 43) is free to see herself outside the idealized/ essentialized notion of purity of becoming a *patibrata*. She exercises her choice beyond the realms of the conventional aesthetic and obligation of Hindu households into a creation of a space for herself. As several commentators have observed the choice of exercising her freedom was granted to Bimala by Nikhilesh. Still, it is necessary to consider that the Bimala discourse needs to be located at a particular time of the political movement in Bengal when social innovations regarding the woman question within Indian modernity, too, had to contend with certain deep-seated notions that constituted its own cultural context. A woman's identity itself was a vexed term. Tagore himself has observed this referring to the 'literary debates of the times'.[7] 'Any different form of imagining' had to be 'thwarted as anti-national' (ibid.: 43). Thereby, the gender question, to use Lucy Irigaray's term, never seemed to manage an escape from its 'inter-dict' position (1985: 22).

Under such a complex situation, rather, Bimala's projection of her thoughts for the country's independence is emblematic of a strong and courageous woman though she was not free of her subjectivity, which was already constructed as a typically feminine figure split between two conflicting ideologies of patriotic national-isms (cultural nationalism and religious/ethnic nationalism) repre-sented by the two male protagonists Nikhilesh and Sandip. Even if Nikhilesh's concern to uplift Bimala from the clutches of social prej-udices was potent and Sandip's jingoistic articulations made her feel that she was the 'Queen Bee', Bimala's stance was to take the dif-ficult middle path between *samarpan* (devotion) and *sangram* (revolt).

> The thing that was agitating me within was merely a variation of the stormy passion outside, which swept the country from one end to the other. . . . Through all my past I had been consistent in my devotion-but when at length it came to receiving the boon, a different god appeared! And just as the awakened country, with its *Bande Mataram*, thrills in salu-tation to the unrealized future before it, so do all my veins and nerves

send forth shocks of welcome to the unthought of, the unknown, the importunate Stranger. . . . One night I left my bed and slipped out of my room on to the open terrace. . . . Through the gaps in the village groves to the North, glimpses of the river are seen. The whole scene slept in the darkness like the vague embryo of some future creation. . . . In that future I saw my country, a woman like myself, standing expectant. She has been drawn forth from her home corner by the sudden call of some Unknown (Tagore 1919: 135–36).

Bimala had made her point clear that it was a 'a situation of crisis' for her: she was torn between devotion to her domestic duties (which she wished to maintain while remaining open to the negotiations with modernity) and the stormy passion of the new era that left her with little or no trace of a way to return to conventional ways of life. What she urged was to uphold the cultural continuity of the conventional innate piety at home—a quality she inherited from her mother—which Tagore idealized and wished to portray as a shift in the 'ideal world' (Das 1996: 741). She also felt that it was her right to respond to the call of the nation—*Bande Mataram*! But to sustain through both was difficult. As Jasodhara Bagchi puts it, 'the affective empire of the woman's home [was] suddenly faced by the challenge of the world' (Bagchi 2003: 181). It is this gendered nature of reality (displayed through two different perspectives—Sandip's power politics casting a hypnotic spell on her, which would confine Bimala as woman as goddess of the nation and Nikhilesh's idealist-turn—practical understanding of inclusive Swadeshi patriotism, which has a scope to link with the overlapping of social spaces—(the home/private sphere and the world/public sphere), which is so significantly portrayed in the novel, yet remains unexplored. This is perhaps because the imperceptible authorial voice flows in smoothly into the irreversible passage of time, and its consequence—a sense of loss and void of the partition of Bengal—that Bimala experiences is brilliantly revealed to us by the use of stream of consciousness technique. The way Bimala survives the struggle for herself and for the country/ nation/world without harbouring any rancour about it comes to us filtered through her own consciousness with timeless reality represented by the 'glimpses of the river' (ibid.: 136).

In engaging with the river, Bimala remains ambivalent in her assertion. The river marks an important boundary, crossing which was made difficult by the suggested partition of Bengal. The negotiation (of absence and presence) of Bengal is epitomized in the river symbol, which puts into relief the question: what it meant for a woman like Bimala to negotiate with the injustices of the brute forces of a masculine civilization and to produce (bring into being) a representative self in a densely wild and antagonistic environment. Besides symbolizing boundaries, the river also symbolizes pathways into the heart of civilization or away from it. Bimala responds to the call of the nation, which is 'unknown' to her, and, simultaneously takes recourse to the Vaishnava Poets. Bimala understood that the freedom of village life that Bengal's rivers connote was replaced by greater oppression and injustice. She wished to associate herself with the life of the poor and the ordinary people (like Pachu and Mirjan) living in the rural backwaters of the Bengal province but the colonial situation and the political aggression associated with it (as depicted in the last scene) made her a captive of the masculine powers operative in society.

But Bimala was hopeful. She knew rivers symbolize pathways into the heart of civilization or away from the heart of civilization besides symbolizing boundaries. She, thus, like the river, tried to give life to the disjointed past. In trying to survive the effects of political and social oppression, Bimala responds to the call of the Nation, which is 'unknown' to her, and, simultaneously takes recourse to the Vaishnava Poets (ibid.). Even if looking backward may seem problematic within western paradigms of modernity, Bimala's reconstruction of the past gave her the forte to relate herself to the present, decolonize the mind and seek freedom in action to initiate future changes. That Bimala returns to the past is 'power re-membering, a putting together of the dismembered past to make sense of the trauma of the present' (Bhabha 63), The past does inform Bimala's thoughts in several ways and the course of action she takes, but while looking back she reaffirms her political self and the choice she exercises was entirely her own. This enables her to defy the paternalistic feminism of her husband Nikhilesh on one hand and challenges the idea of nationhood that Sandip upheld on the other. Bimala demonstrates that the women of India had a choice to clear certain 'unfreedoms'[8] and exercise the choice of 'willingness' to draw the world within the ambit of home. She could choose to serve her own personal needs without sacrificing 'self love' or 'enslaving or killing' her individualities (Tagore 2004a [1909–10]: 45). As far as the woman question in fashioning a 'modern' national culture was concerned, Tagore forcefully observes, 'War has been declared between man and woman' (Tagore [1917] in Guha 2009: 38). This points to the notion that 'No nation in the world gives women and men the same access to the rights and resources of the nation-state' (McClintock 1993: 61). Tagore was never comfortable with the new reality that was endangered by 'exclusive political interest' (Tagore [1917] in Guha 2009: 64). This path, although colourful, legitimized disregard for human (especially women's) rights as well as what Martha Nussbaum puts it as 'fundamental allegiance to the world community of justice' or 'aspirations to justice' (1996: 8). Therefore, Nussbaum reads *The Home and the World:*

> These qualities [like aspirations to justice, and goodness and their capacities for reasoning in this connection] may be less colourful than local or national traditions and identities— it is on this basis that the young wife in Tagore's novel spurns them in favour of qualities in the nationalist orator Sandip (ibid.: 8).

In her reading of nationalism and its corollary patriotism, as Nussbaum sees it, Bimala is dismissed from the discussion on the ground that she finds her husband, Nikhilesh, 'boringly flat' (ibid.: 5). Tagore might seem indecisive in his treatment of female sexuality but such a neat closure of Bimala's agonizing and tedious *experience* from the gendered narrative of history demands further study Was not Tagore questioning the society and the place of a woman in the modern society through Nikhilesh? Moreover, Bimala loved her country as much as Nikhilesh did and any pretext to suppress her anxiety for the cause of India's independence could not be 'constrained to a narrowness of sphere' (Tagore 1996a: 676). So, Bimala should come outside of the narrow nationalism, or, to use the words of Tapabrata Ghosh, the 'communal toxin' (2003: 74) that divided the man–woman relationship, but she was free to take her decisions. Bimala does get enticed by Sandip's wonderful skill of patriotic oratory and imagines herself to be the face of a newly awakened country and the gaze of that new world rests upon her, but she realizes soon that Sandip's 'world of reality' was only to provoke the power of the mighty man to win over the hearts of women and that his love for the country was false (Tagore 1919: 47). Moreover, Bimala was sensitive, intelligent and knowledgeable enough to grasp the power of the rationality of the anti-colonial struggle even before Sandip presented a political image of nationalism for her. She even realized from within that Nikhilesh, in spite of having wealth, both the monetary wealth and the wealth of education 'did not use [or misuse] his power, just because he had it' (ibid.: 17). It reminds one of Foucault's *History of Sexuality* where he famously points out the intellectual obligation to locate within specific material conditions of the need 'to discover who does the speaking [and] the positions and viewpoints from which they speak' (1980a: 11).

Bimala is a new aspirant in her struggle for 'freedom' in the overarching atmosphere of colonial imperialism asserting definition of rights of a woman's individual self as well as of the nation. She represents a section of early twentieth-century women in British India who could not right away accept the westernization of Indian culture or reject the necessity for openness in the pursuit of knowledge. Bimala, rather, perceives the necessity of woman's 'rights' (Tagore 1919: 16) and negotiates it in the light of the colonial tensions of the time and what future of the country may hold. While she insists on retaining of justice in a woman's life, she chooses to appropriate the Swadeshi patriotism into the Sukhasayar household after her marriage with Nikhilesh, particularly after meeting his friend Sandip. She also identifies herself with Sandip's patriotism (if that was so) 'I shall simply make Bimala one with my country' (discussed later). The innocence of young Bimala did not allow her to understand immediately the deceitfulness and unscrupulous stance of Sandip, but that gave way to more real-life instances, surfacing new complexities in the face of the new social and political hierarchy. Although no simple evaluation of the characters is possible, it can be safely said that Tagore seemed no longer obliged to make Bimala conform to the conventional notion of morality.

In his book on Tagore, Mohammad Quayum commented that Tagore was a realist, and was also a reformist who looked into the future to bring change:

> He showed a remarkable understanding of women's psyche perceived the injustice of an unequal social structure, and advocated for greater freedom and decision-making power for women in family and the larger society. He was of the view that women could not be held captives for ever, nor could they be crushed by male aggression and arrogance because they were endowed with *Shakti*, a vital charm, 'the living symbol of divine energy' (Tagore 'Women's Place in the World' 1933: 676), without which the masculine powers would remain inactive and dormant. Therefore, giving women their freedom and rights, instead of forcing them to submission, was the only way to create a balanced and meaningful civilization in which man and woman could complement each other's attributes... (2011: 18–19).

Bimala's choice exemplifies that freedom of mind is not the only preserve for men. Bimala is aware of the political movement of challenge and resistance to colonial imperialism as much as she was keen on adapting to the social movement directed towards reforming the existing traditional structure with a concern for women's liberation. Bimala responded to the call for modernity with personal sensitivity. She learned the English language privately from Miss Gilby and was not bothered whether Miss Gilby was European or Indian, until the point when the impulse of Swadeshi patriotism brought a radical change in her. She even read out western novels to Nikhilesh's grandmother with care as much as she learned certain new cosmopolitan etiquette from Miss Gilby. Her response to the practical demands of the time—the need to support the political cause of national movement against the irreparable forces of colonial imperialism—is also significant.

But her attraction towards Sandip could not have been taken in the right light during the days of anti-colonial nationalist movement for her excursion into the outside world threatened the 'naturalized' (Yuval-Davis 2008: 67) conjugal space. Bimala's challenging journey defies this gendered notion of women's position in relation to men and suggests that women are not usually (though not

exclusively) 'non-participants in the determination of gender relations' (ibid.: 8). Moreover, the journey she undertakes on a personal (spiritual, cultural and even psychological) level to support
the cause of the Swadeshi home rule movement needs an understanding that Bimala's voice of patriotism is simultaneous with a
voice for the cause of India and for the sake of the human race,
just as Nikhilesh's is. In the days of the colonial regime, as Nirad
C. Chowdhury observes, 'the search for the "woman" turned out
to be man's quest for ambitious, but personal goals' (1988: 130). To
a certain extent, Chowdhury's observation is analogous with what
Chatterjee described as the 'preferred goals' of the nationalist patriarchs (Chatterjee 1993: 117). However, overcoming the thresholds
of the male–female dichotomy and the gendered division of the
social space into inside and outside was important to Tagore and
continues as a dominant aspect in *The Home and the World*, questioned strategically in the web of desire and jealousy between the
protagonists Nikhilesh, Bimala and Sandip. Bimala confirms that
women of India are not uniformly marginalized and can attend to
the dilemma when an individual faces with new values, ideas or
norms. Of course uncertainty continues to rule over Bengal and in
the life of women but Bimala informs her readers that the human
mind can train itself to see beyond discipline into free enquiry.

Bimala does not escape her family responsibility but exerts her
demand on exercising freedom to engage with the independence
struggle. Her conviction is also the beginning of a new discursive
process that establishes a meaningful relationship between the home
and the world, where family narrative is recognized as an inclusive
domain of patriotism as well as one way of exploring the margins
of the nation. The persuasion of Bimala to reclaim an agency for
the self as well as in terms of both the country's needs and women's
rights becomes problematic because the division of social space into
ghar and bahir intensified the already existing social division.

As discussed, Bimala adequately exposes the dilemmas of
a Bengali modernity in terms of spatial strategy and also the new
consciousness that was tormented by conflicts and tensions of love
and gender bias on the one hand and nationalist patriarchy on the
other. Bimala is a thinking individual, had the capacity to look 'over
into the distance' (Tagore 1919: 17) and move beyond the realms of

colonialism-nationalism binaries exposing a new sense of 'the elements of its articulation' (Foucault 1980b: 98). Embracing a politics
of violence, for example, the violence that attended the rhetoric of
Swadeshi extremism, or the viciousness of 'this destructive excitement' (Tagore 1919: 20) according to Tagore, could not be endorsed
even if it involved a concern for justice beyond the sanctioned social
roles. A violent anti-colonial struggle defies justice, which is needed
for the continuity of human relationship, and aggravates violence.[9]
What needs to be noted is that Tagore's dissenting voice was placing the moral fulcrum of society on what has been categorized as
feminine values. Violence, destructive agitation and actions of that
ilk were abhorrent to Tagore as means for achieving a gender justice
and hence a transformation of society. Instead, by focusing on values
that have been associated with the feminine, Tagore challenged the
gendered bases of the nation and its modes of incorporating members. He insisted that a woman cannot be held hostage of the 'golden
wands of wealth' nor can she be pushed into the controls of 'iron
rods of power' (in Das 1933: 677). Thereby, he not only rejected the
excess of traditionalization, the depiction of stereotypes of a feminized nation (the female to embody the nation) but also the revival
of the Indian national pride of spiritual superiority, which got intricately linked with the nationalist movement. For Tagore, if women
were labelled as the repositories of the 'spirituality' of the home/
nation, the responsibility on them to retain the traditional culture
of the nation would further galvanize the process of marginalizing
women and subverting their voices. His method of overcoming the
colonial situation was to draw together diverse traditions and ideas
into a new reality, which he saw could not be achieved until gender
justice was realized as an essential component of social change.

Therefore, without ignoring it, he deliberately raised gender
issues at home, which were shaped by economics, politics, and
culture outside; and while foregrounding the crucial links of
inside–outside, attempted to challenge the conflicting paradigms of
tradition and modernity but also the frontiers of social (in)justice.
Any challenge to the fundamentals of normative discourses, nevertheless, was resisted: 'the weak dared not be just' (Tagore 1919: 44).
As a defence against the mounting cultural challenge of the modern
West that came on the colonial back and dominant patterns of the

traditional Hindu order, Tagore moved ahead of the narrowness of colonialism and its binary nationalism and primarily the religiosity that got attached with the local/ethnic nationalism and problematized (or externalized) the issues concerning gender (in)equality in social relations in Bengal. Against the system of injustice that ruled over indigenous gender identities and problems of gender relations, Tagore thus puts it through Nikhilesh that Bimala should discover her capability in the public — 'more fully in the outside world' (ibid.: 12). Similarly, Nikhilesh as a self-conscious individual should 'often try to take an outside view'. To put in his own words—'to see myself as Bimal sees me' ((ibid.: 83). This performative act of interaction between the male and the female in public space, between the inside and the outside boundaries of the home and the world leads not only to overcoming of the (en)gendered self but also realizing of the self with the other in a web of social relations (in the public space). The creation of this public space shapes into existence its 'other', the private sphere, where emotions and sentiments remained firmly rooted in home.

> What I really feel is this, that those who cannot find food for their enthusiasm in a knowledge of their country as it actually is, or those who cannot love men just because they are men… shout and deify their country in order to keep up their excitement—[they] love excitement more than their country.

> To try to give our infatuation a higher place than Truth is a sign of inherent slavishness (Tagore 1919: 45).

Supplanting Tagore's ideas of country, justice, truth, love into the Bimala discourse, one can easily see that the redefinition of the 'other' is done not by a remote and long perspective but by delving into the life of the andarmahal, by changing the lens with which this world of women was viewed during colonial times. And it is the power of this lens, which brings forth the vision of a Bimala, the revolutionary, and who has decided to live optimistically in a cruel world. Although seemingly idealistic, this is indeed a very strong proclamation of Tagore's patriotism and the steps he took for women's empowerment.[10] His insightful assertion does underline his love for his country (and its women) and a vision of modernity where emotion and reason intersected. It also underscores his deep engagement with building the capacity for self-government to overcome the colonial situation—a vision of Indian modernity that remained firmly rooted in her own cultural resources without negating what was good of the West. Under the tensions of colonial imperialism and local religious nationalism (which he believed was also influenced by the western concept of aggressive masculine nationalism), what Tagore envisaged was indeed a hybrid modernity where a considerable autonomous space for the survival of cultural *difference* was left. In the words of Partha Chatterjee, the cultural project of newly derived Indian nationalism was 'to fashion a "modern" national culture' that was still not western (1993: 6). This construction of national difference might put Tagore in an ambivalent position for hegemonic cultural projects often go against the interests of women. Tagore had no intention to resist the modern culture and literature of the West but quite contrarily he was never at ease with the West's readiness to 'assert that [women's] difference from men is unimportant' (1922: 40). He emphatically stood against the ideology of colonial modernity that sought to establish superiority over India by casting a hypnotic spell of aggressive nationalism that not only divided countries but also divided human relationships between men and women just for the sake of greed and profit that nation-states promote.

He did not submit to the slavery of taste of the new age of colonial modernity and yet sought to remove dark areas of traditions. As well, we will have to remind ourselves that traditions in India as in other counties once colonized were inflected by colonialism. Tagore understood that the identity of modernity and the belief in the linear progression of time that had been initiated with the birth of the Nation, in the form of imperial nationalism/colonial nationalism, was irreversible—'new elements have been introduced, and wider adjustments were waiting to be made' (Tagore 1917: 35). Therefore, he insisted on (ex)change of ideas, which, as he comments at several places, will only happen when we decide to improve our circumstances—not by sacrificing women's right to freedom by upholding them as goddesses (which was an exclusionary process), but by negotiating the values of justice that encourage the basic tenets of human rights and by persistently working towards that to remain free from enslavement to circumstances.

What needs to be noted here is that the nationalist discourse gave birth to the idea of Nation-as-motherland/Nation-as-mother-goddess. This concept of idolatry of the Nation got further coalesced with the glorification of woman as goddess, which produced the specific ideological form of the Indian women.[11] The construct of 'goddess in the womanhood' in modern literature in the context of a culture coeval with the era of nationalism is deeply interwoven in Bimala–Sandip relationship. Tagore's idea of love (as represented by Nikhilesh) of country and women's liberation in general and particularly Bimala's freedom went against Sandip's 'worship' of his country and adulating Bimala in the image of the Nation, which also took the form of violent assertions and patriotic militancy. Sandip quips:

> I shall simply make Bimala one with my country. The turbulent west wind which has swept away the country's veil of conscience, will sweep away the veil of the wife from Bimala's face... flying the pennant of *Bande Mataram*, and it will serve as the cradle to my power, as well as to my love (Tagore 1919: 119).

Sandip's clever pronouncement of liberating Bimala from 'the veil of the wife' and his quickly juxtaposed resolve to dedicate the primordial power of Bimala to the cause of Swadeshi (love of one's own country) against 'the turbulent west wind which has swept away the country's veil of conscience' is an avant-garde move that Tagore resorted to during his days with *Sabuj Patra*.[12] Tagore perhaps could have done without this intensely phallocentric description, which invited unwanted criticism. As Ashapurna Devi, who has consciously analysed the tensions of the long colonial rule and the emerging nationalism and their combined effect on the double subjugation of women, perceptively observes,

> By writing the extensively debated . . . novel *Ghare-Baire*, Rabindranath had to stand a wide criticism and scathing judgements on ethico-moral grounds from the conformists of his time. It is because revolutionary Rabindranath, in this book, has struck a severe blow on the established sense of values of the society . . . [primarily] on the notion of chastity of women. Love for a man other than husband is nothing new as the subject of a novel; but the author would rarely pardon that infatuated woman;

rather, it was usual to transform her into a demon in the end. Bimala in
Ghare-Baire is an exception to that (1980: 35).

Ashapurna's comment is particularly pertinent in the context of contemporary gendered narrative of the nation and its attendant discrimination (in India as well as in parts of the postcolonial world),
which continues to influence society to date. More importantly, she
has powerfully written about the clamorous private sphere from
where women themselves made their way to public presence. The
negotiation and opposition of the private and public was difficult
and complex during the colonial times. And, the concerns of both
the authors regarding the invisibility of women brings out clearly
that both the male author and female author were equally concerned
about strengthening the status of women outside the essentialized notions of chastity, which were used by the colonial masters
to keep women in a subordinate position so that by maintaining it
they could show that India was not yet fit for independence. On the
other hand, both the authors loved their India and thus stood against
religious nationalism that divided the man–woman relationship in
the name of authentic culture. Tagore was conscious that the novel
would invite unfair criticisms because of the internal authoritarian-
ism and more so because of the conflicts of the time in which it was
written. He wrote: 'literary debate turns around whether or not a
character fits in with the ideals of the true Hindu woman' and further observed that moulding the characters according to the requirements of national pride would reduce a 'kingdom of human beings
to a kingdom of puppets' (Tagore 2006 [1916]: 215–16). One may
argue against Tagore's statement both as overly precocious and
precautious, but the novel boldly portrays Bimala, as a woman of
early twentieth-century Bengal, who was determined to exercise her
choice of freedom to place claims for gender justice. That was not
unknown in culturally and historically conditioned India across ages
(as depicted by the learned Vaishnava poets and some of whom in
the nineteenth-twentieth centuries were the source of inspiration
and learning for women in Bengal, especially in the Tagore household) and scriptural tradition (as inscribed in 'Gandharir Abedan',
by Tagore).[13] The Bimala discourse underscores a very important
aspect of colonialism that was promoted as a 'white man's burden'

and how women asserted themselves to reverse the idea of the 'dependent subject'.

Without generalizing the contents of the gender discourse, it needs to be noticed that Bimal—(meaning 'pristine', as Nikhilesh calls her)—in particular, underscored the need for change in terms of modernization congenial to Indian society and not on reinstituting the alien inflexibility of the British establishment. This new complex historical treatment need not be pitted against the historic traditions of 'the Badshahs... of the Mughals and Pathans,... of Manu and Parashar' that shaped Indian cosmopolitan cultural conditions laterally for ages (Tagore 1919: 4). This postulation of differing/different notions of cultural tradition, received through the ages in India, though, is not to foster the idea that injustices towards women were not in practice in different phases of history even in the modern age (in the nineteenth century or in the early phase of twentieth century). In the novel, Bimala exposes the subtext of the gendered society—how the depletion of the agrarian economy negatively affected the life of bhadraloks (like Nikhilesh's brothers who idled away their time in every possible wrong way, although there cannot be any generalization as such). They not only gave in to 'dissipation' (ibid.: 4), which did upset their family life (the daily tears [of their wives] being drowned in the foam of wine, and by the tinkle of 'dancing girls' anklets (ibid.: 9), but also were scrutinized as identities enacting gendered violence against their women. Bimala shows how by the effect of political process these men become both victims and agents of the gendered system and that the 'narrative of Hindu marriage could no longer use the language of love; it had to be rewritten in terms of force and pain' (T. Sarkar 2001: 43).

Way back in 1904, Margaret E. Nobel, known for her Swadeshi patriotism and her friendship with Tagore and other patriots of the time, described in what tortuous ways the web of Indian life was disrupted by colonial imperialism. The result, however, was encouragement of re-invention of cultural norms on the part of the colonial government that influenced unevenness in gender relations. In turn, the nationalist patriarchs (mostly the moderates) took up to restructure the place home, though the logic was exercised, as discussed, according to their *preferred goals*. Given that, one cannot help being cautious of or help noticing the fact that women became the site for cultural contestation of traditions and/or modernities of patriarchal discourses on which the narratives of community and nation were written.

In her *atmakatha*, Bimala articulates the tensions of being a colonized woman and the question of becoming independent in an overarching colonial atmosphere. Not only that, by responding to the clarion call for protest, against the partition movement, strengthened by the song *Bande Mataram*, she offered to show how literature can give life to political movements and how material conditions inscribed in such movements get transported through literature. More importantly, in her continuous search for the self, in her understanding of the quest for an independent nation or *desh* and its people (irrespective of their class/caste, race and gender), she offers a new space within the different strands of an anti-colonial nationalist programme (as exemplified by Nikhilesh's constructive Swadeshi and Sandip's violence and boycott-centred extremism) and within the interplay of consent and coercion that constituted the hegemonic process of marginalizing women. She introduces the values that emerge from participation in a shared space of empathy, understanding and equality. As discussed, this is an arduous and continuous process, and I would like to call it a *samajik* method after Tagore, which allows a continuously evolving analysis of the ways gender relations affect and are affected by a nationalist project and process.

This method of inclusive political principles is explained by Yuval-Davis's terms, the ways 'shifting' and 'rooting' take place in a social space creating areas of contestations beyond the immediate private sphere without tearing off the roots (2008: 88–92). Although Bimala takes quite a long time to make a conscious articulation of this transformative process, she exemplifies a *samajik* method of creating possibilities of not capturing the hegemonic power while opening up ways to mitigate social deprivation. Bimala sustains and reinforces this inner creative strength and affirms that the woman's 'right' to self-determination was as important as national determination, and she reaches out to 'humanity as a whole' by going through a complex experience of love (Nussbaum 1996: 9). Thereby, Bimala provides new insights into the structure and ideology of colonialism and gives new direction to anti-colonial nationalist resistance: how women refashioned social relations with a strong sense of participation in a historically challenging age.

The 'Bimala' discourse, therefore, requires a reading which is not a simple display of forbidden relationship or that of mere sexual attractions. If the amorous connection between Sandip and Bimala is the subject of discourse that provokes criticism till date, the object—the power of modernity of the new Swadeshi—is muscular nationalism that Sandip used for extreme political means and in wrong ways. What he describes as 'the turbulent west wind'(discussed above) while taking recourse to debauchery, is what Tagore critiques. In all, what needs to be noticed is that a symbol of society's sexual condition is often influenced by gender complexities, and what it takes for a woman to transcend dominant notions of Indian women (here) as passive recipients of welfare and 'non-participants in the determination of gender relation' (Yuval-Davis 2008: 8).

In the new Swadeshi era, the act of anti-colonial resistance arose from a frantic teleological rush to realize the form of nation-states. Bimala reveals the much deeper meaning of being a woman in the changing circumstances challenging her position at an ontological level as much as against the historical conflicts of the time:

Jealousy! Where the strong man shows *weakness*, there the weaker sex cannot help beating her drums of victory. So I repeated firmly: 'I really have no time' (Tagore 1919: 244).

Or

'Do you know that your *weakness* is weakening your neighbouring *zamindars* also?'

'I did not offer you my advice, Sandip. I wish you, too, would refrain from giving me yours. Besides, it is useless. And there is another thing I want to tell you. You and your followers have been secretly worrying and oppressing my tenantry. I cannot allow that any longer. So I must ask you to leave my territory.'

'For fear of the Mussulmans, or is there any other fear you have to threaten me with?'

'There are fears the want of which is cowardice. In the name of those fears, I tell you, Sandip, you must go...' (Tagore 1919: 250–51).

Or

Sandip must have felt the shadow of approaching defeat, and this made him try to gain time by chattering away without waiting for a reply. I believe he knew that I had sent the messenger for Amulya, whose name the man must have mentioned. In spite of that he had deliberately played this trick. He was now trying to avoid giving me any opening to tell him that it was Amulya I wanted, *not him*. But his stratagem was futile, for I could see his *weakness* through it. I must not yield up a pin's point of the ground I had gained.

'Sandip Babu,' I said, 'I wonder how you can go on making these endless speeches, without a stop. Do you get them up by heart, beforehand?'

Sandip's face flushed instantly.

'I have heard,' I continued, 'that our professional reciters keep a book full of all kinds of ready-made discourses, which can be fitted into any subject. Have you also a book?'

… 'You had better go back and look up your book, Sandip Babu. You are getting your words all wrong. That's just the trouble with trying to repeat things by *rote*' (my emphasis; Tagore 1919: 281–82).

Bimala's confident self-discovery made her see that the modernity of Sandip was questionable. While romantic love (where radical imagination could swim expansively) between Bimala and Sandip is crystalized as one of the bases of the man–woman relationship, Bimala's particular sensibility to perceive the world within which she sees India echoes a woman's capacity to resist dominant convention and make decisions about her own life. Bimala loved her country as much Nikhilesh did and though she is left in total uncertainty, at the end she specifically addresses the question: why did the gender system survive within this paradigm of colonialism and its modernity, not just as an issue of social justice, but as a way of life. Thereby, Bimala comes out of her interdicted position; she repositions her location in-between the signs of competing discourses, like the reified binaries between traditions and modernities, primitive and civilized and creates a discursive third space, which has the potential to limit and to exceed the limits of gender difference—a social space of shifting and rooting beyond the prescriptive sexual roles, which is of strategic importance in binding the immediate everyday life to distant and future macro-structures of life. What she experiences is 'deathless', as she claims (Tagore 1919: 421). In this process of negotiated self-making, Bimala reclaims her agency in non-normative ways. At the same time, she manifests certain emancipatory potential within normative patterns by claiming a voice of resistance and freedom and realigning them for her struggle. Bimala sustains the requirements of a modern material world and betrays the misrecognition of respectability of a veiled or hidden sexuality within the historical structures of domination.

NOTES

All translations are mine unless mentioned.

1   *Ghare-Baire* is the original Bengali version of *The Home and the World* (first published, London: Macmillan, 1919; translated by Surendranath Tagore). The Bengali novel was serially published in the avant-garde journal *Sabuj Patra* between May 1915 and February 1916. Henceforth mentioned as *H W*, it was first published serially as 'At Home and Outside' in Kolkata in the *Modern Review* in 1918 and then in book form in London: Macmillan, 1919.

2   For more on how 'the self-images' of Indians have been much affected by colonialism, see Sen (1987); Chatterjee (1989b).

3   Tagore's *atmasakti*—a non-violent anti-colonial movement is a mark of patriotism. He did not reject the British/western merchandise but insisted on rights to private enterprises and education both of which were sought on private initiatives. This alternative method would direct towards developing atmasakti or self-empowerment and enable the country/nation to regain its lost potentials. At the height of the Swadeshi movement, thus, Tagore strongly warned against cultivating the weakness through violence, for the forces of imperialism work on this weakness on the world stage, which is explicit in several of his works like in the essay: 'East and West in Greater India' (Tagore 2004a). For discussion, see Datta 2013: 439–68.

4   For more on colonial extraction of Indian economy, the colonial governments anti-growth policy and the consequent anti-colonial stance, see, Bipan Chandra (2010[1981]): 23, 213, especially.

5   See Rabindranath Tagore, 2006 [1916]: 7.

6   For more on widow, as a symbol of the purity of a national culture and should remain uncontaminated by colonial subordination, see Tanika Sarkar (2001): 41–2.

7   For more on the literary debates, see Sumit Sarkar (2003): 143–73.

8   See Dipannita Datta 2013: 439–68. The term is taken from Amartya Sen's philosophy of the pursuit of justice 2009, which Sen has developed from his 1999 study on freedom. His 2009 book is a major rethinking on the changing perspectives of female subjectivity and agency and related notions of gender justice. Also see Yuval-Davis: 'not all women are oppressed and or/subjugated in the same way or to the same extent, even within the same society at any specific moment' (2008: 8).

9   See Datta, (2013): 439–68.

10 Around the time *Ghare-Baire* was written, Tagore started addressing the issue of women's education in a renewed way. In his essay '*Strisiksha*' (First published in Bengali in the journal *Sabuj Patra* (Bhadra-Ashwin 1322) and translated as 'The Education of Women' in August 1915) he underlined that there should be an impartial education policy in the 'sphere of practical utility'. 'Women should acquire pure knowledge for becoming a mature being and utilitarian knowledge for becoming true women' (Tagore [2010]: 139). That would strengthen the much-challenged gendered space, and simultaneously preserve rights for a greater cause, which cannot be impeded by coercive means. Challenging the gendered nature of reality Tagore, thus, perceptively moved towards promoting the modern education policies for women.

11 For further study on the gendered construct see Partha Chatterjee 1993: especially, 131.

12 For more on *Sabuj Patra*, see Datta (2003): 7.

13 I have discussed this in '*In Search of Fairness of Justice*', 2013: 439–68.

REFERENCES

Bagchi, Jasodhara. 2003. '*Anandamath* and *The Home and the World*: Positivism Reconfigured', in The Home and the World: *A Critical Companion*, edited by P.K. Datta. New Delhi: Permanent Black, 174–86.

———. (ed.). 1995. 'Introduction', in *Indian Women: Myth and Reality*. Hyderabad: Sangam Books.

Bhabha, Homi, 1994. *Locations of Culture*. New York: Routledge.

Butler, Judith, 1996. 'Universality in Culture', in *For Love of Country? In a New Democracy Forum: On The Limits of Patriotism*, edited by Martha C. Nussbaum. Boston: Beacon Press: 45–51.

———. 1990. *Gender Trouble: Feminism and the Subversion of Identity*. New York: Routledge.

Chandra, Bipan. 2010 [1981]. *Colonialism and Nationalism in Modern India*. New Delhi: Orient BlackSwan.

Chatterjee, Partha. 1993. *The Nation and Its Fragments: Colonial and Postcolonial Histories*, Princeton: Princeton University Press.

———. 1989a. 'The Nationalist Resolution of the Women's Question', in *Recasting Women: Essays in Colonial History,* edited by Kumkum Sangari and Sudesh Vaid. New Delhi: Kali for Women.

———. 1989b. 'Colonialism, Nationalism, and Colonized Women', *American Ethnologist*, 16(4): 622–33.

———. 1986. *Nationalist Thought and the Colonial World: A Derivative Discourse*. London: Zed Books.

Chaudhuri, Supriya. 2011. 'Dangerous Liaisons: Desire and Limit In *The Home and the World*', in *Thinking on Thresholds: The Poetics of Transitive Spaces*, edited by Subha Mukherji. London: Anthem Press, 88–99.

Chowdhury, Nirad, C. 1988. *Atmaghati Bangali (Self-destructive Bengali)*, vol. 1. Kolkata: Mitra & Ghosh.

Das, Sisir Kumar (ed.). 1996. *The English Writings of Tagore*, vol. 2. New Delhi: Sahitya Akademi.

Dasgupta, Sanjukta, 2013. *Rabindranath Tagore*, translated by SWADES. Kolkata: Visva-Bharati.

Datta, Dipannita. 2013. 'In Search of Fairness of Justice: Contemporarising Tagore and *The Home and the World*', in *Contemporarising Tagore and the World,* edited by Imtiaz Ahmed, Muchkund Dubey and Veena Sikri. Dhaka: The University Press Ltd, 439–68.

Datta, P.K. 2003. The Home and The World: *A Critical Companion*. New Delhi: Permanent Black.

Devi, Ashapurna. 1980. 'Novels of Tagore', in *Nirmok*, vol. 2, Kolkata, 34–6.

Dutta, Krishna and Andrew Robinson.1997. *Selected Letters of Rabindranath Tagore*. Cambridge: Cambridge University Press.

———. (eds). 1995. *Rabindranath Tagore: The Myriad-Minded Man*. London: Bloomsbury.

Forster, E.M. 1983. *Abinger Harvest*. London: Edward Arnold & Company, 365–67.

Foucault, Michel. 1980a. *History of Sexuality*, vol. I: *An Introduction*, translated by R. Hurley. New York: Vintage.

———. 1980b. *Power/Knowledge: Selected Interviews and Other Writings 1972–77*, edited by Colin Gordon. Hertfordshire: Harvester Press.

Ghosh Tapabrata. 2003. 'The Form of *The Home and The World*', in The Home and The World: *A Critical Companion*, edited by P.K. Datta. New Delhi: Permanent Black, 66–81.

Guha, Ramchandra, 2009. 'Introduction', in *Rabindranath Tagore: Nationalism*. New Delhi: Penguin Books.

Hay, Stephen N. 1962. 'Rabindranath Tagore in America', *American Quarterly*, 14 (3): 439–63.

Irigaray, Lucy. 1985. *Spectrum of the Other Woman*, translated by Gillian C. Gill. Ithaca. Cornell University Press.

Lukács, Georg. 1983. *Review and Article for* Die Rote Fahne, translated by Peter Palmer. London: Merlin Press, 8–11.

Mazumdar, Vina. 2001. 'Whose Past, Whose History, Whose Tradition?: Indigenising Women's Study in India', *Asian Journal of Women's Studies (AJWS)* 7(1): 133–53.

McClintock, Anne. 1993. 'Family Feuds: Gender, Nationalism and the Family', *Feminist Review* 44, Summer, 61–78.

Miller, Hillis J. 1975. 'Deconstructing the Deconstructors', *Diacritics* 5: 24–33.

Nandy, Ashis. 1994. *The Illegitimacy of Nationalism: Rabindranath Tagore and the Politics of Self*. Delhi: Oxford University Press.

Noble, Margaret E. (Sister Nivedita). 1906 [1904]. *The Web of Indian Life*. London: William Heinemann.

Nussbaum, Martha C. 1996. *For Love of Country? In a New Democracy Forum: On The Limits of Patriotism*. Boston: Beacon Press: 2–20.

Pal, Prashanta Kumar. 1977. *Rabijibani*, vols 7 and 8. Calcutta: Ananda Publishers.

Quayum, Mohammad A. 2011. *The Poet and His World: Critical Essays on Rabindranath Tagore*. New Delhi: Orient BlackSwan.

Radhakrishnan, Sarvepalli. 1918. *The Philosophy of Rabindranath Tagore*. London: Macmillan.

Roy, Mohit K. (ed.). 2004. 'Tagore in *Ghare Baire*: Aesthetics in Command', in *Studies on Rabindranath Tagore,* vol. 1. New Delhi: Atlantic Publishers.

Sarkar, Sumit. 2003. *'Ghare-Baire* in its Times', in The Home and The World: *A Critical Companion*, edited by P.K. Datta. New Delhi: Permanent Black.

———. 1997. *Writing Social History*. New Delhi: Oxford University Press.

Sarkar, Tanika. 2003. 'Many Faces of Love: Country, Woman and God', in The Home and The World: *A Critical Companion*, edited by P.K. Datta. New Delhi: Permanent Black.

———. 2001. Hindu Wife, Hindu Nation, Community, Religion, and Cultural Nationalism. New Delhi: Permanent Black.

———. 1995. 'Hindu Conjugality and Nationalism in Late Nineteenth Century Bengal', in *Indian Women: Myth and Reality*, edited by Jasodhara Bagchi. Hyderabad: Sangam Books.

———. 1987. 'Nationalist Iconography: The Image of Women in 19th Century Bengali Literature', *Economic and Political Weekly* 21 November, 2(47): 2011–15.

———. 1985. 'Communal Riots in Bengal', in *Communal and Pan-Islamic Trends in Colonial India*, edited by Mushirul Hasan. New Delhi: Oxford University Press.

Sen, Amartya. 2009. *The Idea of Justice*. London: Allen Lane.

———. 2005. 'Tagore and His India', in *The Argumentative Indian*. London: Penguin Books.

———. 1987. 'Indian Traditions and the Western Imagination', *Daedalus*, Human Diversity (Spring), 126 (2): 1–26, MIT Press on behalf of American Academy of Arts & Sciences.

Tagore, Rabindranath. *'Strisiksha'*. 2010 [1915]. *Shiksha*. Kolkata: Visva-Bharati.

———. *Ghare-Baire*. 2006 [1916]. Kolkata: Visva-Bharati.

———. 2004a [1909–10]. 'East and West in Greater India' [EWGI], *Greater India*. New Delhi: Rupa: 447–60.

———. 2004b [1922]. 'East and West', *Rabindranath Tagore: Selected Essays*. New Delhi: Rupa.

———. 1996a [1933]. 'Women's Place in the World', *The English Writings of Rabindranath Tagore*, vol. 2, edited by Sisir Kumar Das. New Delhi: Sahitya Akademi: 676–79.

———. 1996b [1921]. 'The Union of Cultures', in *The English Writings of Rabindranath Tagore*, vol. 2, edited by Sisir Kumar Das. New Delhi: Sahitya Akademi: 426–38.

Tagore, Rabindranath. 1996c [December 1918]. 'The Object and Subject of a Story', *The English Writings of Rabindranath Tagore*, vol. 2, edited by Sisir Kumar Das. New Delhi: Sahitya Akademi: 437–42.

————. 1961a. [April 1928]. 'Narir Manushatva' (Woman and her Humanness), *Rabindra Rachanabali*, vol. 13. Kolkata: Government of West Bengal, 28.

————. 1961b [Nov–Dec 1936]. '*Nari*' (Woman), *Rabindra Rachanabali*, vol. 13. Kolkata: Government of West Bengal, 377–80.

————. 1919. *The Home and The World*, translated by Surendranath Tagore. London: Macmillan.

————. 1917. 'Nationalism in the West', in *Nationalism*. U.S.A: Berwick & Smith Co.

Yuval-Davis, Nira. 2008. *Gender and Nation*. New Delhi: SAGE Publications.

PART V

WOMEN IN TRAVEL WRITINGS

CHAPTER 11

The 'Other' Women in Tagore's Travels to Europe

Jayati Gupta

Rabindranath Tagore's first journey to Europe was in 1878 as a seventeen-year-old teenager. In the letters that he wrote home, he comments on his encounters with people and places and observes life as it was lived abroad. Inevitably, his attention was focused on women and the role of women both in the home and in the world. The women in the Tagore household at Jorasanko were unusually gifted and talented, educated and liberal. Consciously or otherwise, Rabindranath drew on his knowledge of these women to construct a critique of the European women he first met on his voyage. At a juncture when women's education and emancipation were key issues in Indian society, Rabindranath's comparative analysis of the roles of the traditional Indian woman and the Englishwoman in a different social ethos provides interesting insights. In later times, the poet was feted by the world as the Nobel Laureate, a sage and a guru, and when he travelled to foreign destinations to deliver lectures, he made the acquaintance of several women, which was in stark contrast with his initial reaction to women as a shy first-time traveller. This essay will try to understand and comment on Rabindranath's encounters with women on foreign shores.

The familiar shores of Bombay that represented the much cherished homeland, receded as the steamer *Poona*, which Rabindranath Tagore and his elder sibling Satyendranath had boarded, set sail from the harbour for foreign shores on 20 September 1878. As Rabindranath looked across the horizon, his adolescent anxiety regarding travel and encountering new lands and peoples surfaced as a pathological condition: 'I confess that I was feeling somewhat listless, melancholic, drained of life and vigour...' (2008: 23).[1]

This shy teenager's first journey to Europe or *bilet* was under family compulsion—the agenda was to train this school dropout in the English language and etiquette, English social observances and practices. Also he needed to learn a profession, to read for a degree in law so that he could return to pursue a prestigious occupation suited to the educated Bengali bhadralok. 'Bilet' in nineteenth-century Bengali parlance referred not to Europe but to England and metropolitan life in London and its peripheral towns, that encapsulated what was considered the progressive civilization of India's colonizers. The trope that Rabindranath used in *Amar Chelebela* (*My Boyhood Days*) about his temporary relocation and displacement is of being 'torn up by the roots and transplanted from one soil to another...' (ibid.: 183).[2] The violence embedded in the imagery of uprooting is balanced by the idea of transplanting and finding a new soil to grow in. This is an image that is in tune with the nineteenth-century idea of embracing western thought and knowledge to refashion the self into a modern entity that counters the idea of being in perpetual exile.

In the discourses of nineteenth-century colonial Bengal, the upper-class Bengali bhadralok as well as the wealthy zamindar faced a dilemma that centred on the idea of rejecting age-worn superstition and rigorous cultural traditions that stymied the avenues of modernity, social change and reform. Though Rabindranath speaks of foreign lands and societies as 'strange surroundings', his grandfather, Dwarakanath, was, like Rammohan Roy, an early sojourner to England (1843). The Jorasanko home allowed the winds of change and transformation to sweep through it. A quasi-liberal environment prevailed, though in the andarmahal, the preoccupation and participation of women in indoor and outdoor activities were conservatively monitored. Noted historian Sabyasachi Bhattacharya finds the value systems of Maharshi Debendranath, the paterfamilias, dedicated to the reformist Brahmo Samaj movement, somewhat ambivalent.

His attitude to the womenfolk of the family was conservative and backward-looking. Significantly, his wife, Sarada Devi, was a shadowy figure in the remote recesses of the 'inner quarters'. Born in a conservative Hindu family, she was far from being a Brahma Samaj enthusiast like her husband. She gave birth to no less than fourteen children. Understandably, the children were left to the care of servants, and she scarcely appears in the reminiscences of Rabindranath (Bhattacharya 2011: 59).

Set off against this family background was Rabindranath's sister-in-law, Jnanadanandini Devi, married to his second eldest brother, Satyendranath, the first Indian to be selected for the prestigious Indian Civil Service, who had travelled to England with her two children, Surendranath and Indira, months prior to Rabindranath's journey, in order to set up home in Brighton. Despite having a home away from home, the poet's sense of displacement, his perception of being exiled and the sentiment of loss were acutely felt. His poetic psyche was challenged by a restlessness that focused on the romantic quest for the remote and the far and simultaneously suffered from estrangement from the self. Rabindranath's early cross-cultural encounters cannot be reduced to simple relations of power—of domination and subordination. The poet-traveller begins by participating in the typical expectations associated with colonial travel, of encountering colonists in their own country and imbibing the progressive influences one was likely to be exposed to. At the core of several of these letters addressed probably to Kadambari Devi, wife of his elder sibling Jyotirindranath, are candid observations, provocative experiences, curious adventures that document and transmit a reality that respects the plurality of human interactions. The spirit of this early travelogue *Letters from an Early Sojourner in Europe; Europe Pravasir Patra* is underlined with wit and humour, often critiquing social practices that represented what was proverbially a more 'civilized' area of the world.

Several of these early letters record a teenager's reactions to the gendered 'other'. There were several English and European women among the ship's passengers and the youthful Rabindranath was self-conscious and wary of them. With characteristic tongue-in-cheek humour he observes:

> I am by nature fearful of 'ladies'. To venture close to them means the possibility of so many dangers that if the scholar Chanakya had been alive, he would have advised me to keep distance from them. On the one hand, there is the possibility of various grave mishaps occurring in the realm of the mind—and besides, I am always wary, lest in meaning today one

> thing I say another, and our fragile, tender-natured ladies, unable to bear
> the slightest infraction of etiquette, should swoon from sheer disgust and
> shame, and ten gentlemen should descend, in an uproar, from ten direc-
> tions (Tagore 2008: 25–6).

Awkwardness in encountering women is only natural in a youth
attempting to negotiate cultural difference. Yet the underlying fear
of western women centred on the social sophistication expected of
a gentleman and the sense of lack experienced by a male psyche
not used to European social practices. Rabindranath expresses his
nervousness about tripping on ladies skirts or carving his own finger
instead of the chicken served at mealtimes.[3] Rabindranath's initial
observations about women, beauty, youth and gender relationships
in the context of Europe are invariably laced with wit which critiques
the European involvement in external aspects of life and living.
Rabindranath's humorous, caricature-like verbal portrayals of the
ladies on the steamer who were neither 'youthful' nor 'comely' lead
on to observations that contrast the essence of womanhood in the
East and in the West. His penetrative perceptual powers were akin
to what art historian E.H. Gombrich calls:

> The gift of vision which enabled him [the artist] to see the everlasting
> truth of ideas beyond the veil of nature…the portrait painter's task was to
> reveal the character, the essence of the man in an heroic sense. The cari-
> caturist has a corresponding aim. He does not seek the perfect form but
> the perfect deformity, thus penetrating through the mere outward appear-
> ance to the inner being in all its littleness or ugliness.[4]

Rabindranath's reactions to his alien human environment on
the ship, in Europe and in England, display what has been termed
'the peak shift effect' (Ramachandran and Hirstein 1999: 134) in
art which, as a principle, effectively takes into consideration human
pattern, recognition and aesthetic preference that is socio-culturally
determined. The expectations of what it was to be feminine was pre-
determined by images that were linked to memories of women he
had known and seen in the familiar environs of his Jorasanko home
or in surrogate homes in Ahmedabad and Bombay.[5] Confronted by
disparate forms of 'otherness', the poet's imaginative temperament
guided his reactions to external stimuli enabling him to formulate

cognitive impressions that played with, reshaped, modified immediate sensory experiences that were then translated into verbal or
visual forms—his writing and later his paintings.

The complex dynamics of reality and imagination in perceiv-
ing Europe became apparent to the young Rabindranath as he
documented his excitement on having 'stepped on European soil'
at Brindisi (2008: 31). 'I had thought a marvellous sight would
open up in front of my eyes as soon as I reached Europe!' he writes
(ibid.). The gaping disparity between fantasy and experience that
lies at the heart of the romantic sensibility was itself a recognition of his ambivalent poetic search for beauty. He goes on to
describe his aesthetic delight in the Mediterranean landscape that
he sees from the train, travelling from Italy to France—vineyards
and fields, mountains, rivers and lakes, church spires and tiny villages. The picturesque beauty of the landscape was intangible, 'like
a poet's dream', linguistically inexpressible and 'far too exquisite
for words', and a source of pleasure 'as if we were reading poetry
all the way' (ibid.: 33).

Discerning pleasure and poetry in everyday reality was habitual
for Rabindranath. His description of beauty in Italian girls hinges
on culturally embedded structures of perception and familiarity.
'They greatly resemble the girls of our country. Lovely complexion,
black tresses, black eyebrows, black eyes, and their facial structure
are indeed marvellous. We merely saw girls of the working classes
on the streets, but it is difficult to express how comely even they are!'
(ibid.: 33). In stark contrast, Rabindranath's observation of upper-
class Anglo Saxon women on board the steamer were projected as
largely negative encounters with difference and alterity.

During the season of 1879, spent in London, the bewildering
encounters with foreign women at evening invitations, fancy dress
parties, dances and ballrooms were terrifying for Rabindranath who
was still trying to master dress codes, etiquette and manners acceptable by the British whom the 'native' was expected to ape perfectly.
Elsewhere, the poet is scathing in his criticism of the Ingo-bongo
community, anglicized Bengalis, who had taken aping to such a
level that they were contemptuous of every indigenous practice
and unduly deferential to the *gora* sahib. Compelled, during his
stay in England to attend certain social events, the poet recounts
his startling entry into a ballroom and how 'amongst a hundred

fair-skinned ladies, there was present one of our dusky Indian ladies. My heart leapt when I saw her. It is difficult to say how much I fancied her' (ibid.: 34). His sense of loss and alienation, his inward hankering for comfort in a situation where he was acutely conscious of separateness, become evident in these reactions. His realization that 'English girls are a completely different race', fair-skinned 'otherworldly creatures' is countered by a feeling of kinship that he experiences when he notices a dark face 'radiant with the innocent humility our Bengali girls have' (ibid.: 46). Very obviously the self was connected to modes of feeling, saying and doing that evoked a positive sense of community, communion and unity that remained important parameters of judging the 'other'. In the Second Letter, Rabindranath records his deep disappointment with the preoccupations of young Englishwomen who were 'goddesses in the realm of fashion and akin to playthings for young men' (ibid.: 37). The concern with physical beauty and clothes engages the women in several forms of affectation that characterized their single-minded aim to 'captivate men'. What is called in question here is the assertion of the 'independent entity' (ibid.: 38) of women, their emancipation from the norms of a predominantly patriarchal society.

Rabindranath's own response to Englishwomen is in sharp contrast to that of the Ingo-bongo youth who were dazzled by 'the external glamour' (ibid.: 66) of life in England. It is the opportunity of 'mingling with the women' (ibid.: 67) that they especially enjoyed. It is the forwardness in conversing with the opposite sex, 'their gestures and behaviour free of a certain veil of painful reticence' (2008: 67) that marked the difference of Englishwomen with women back home which was attractive to the young men. The poet scathingly satirizes the petty trivialities that underlie the English-returned bhadralok's critique of Indian womanhood, which is significantly removed from the social-reformist movements, focusing on women's education and emancipation in colonial Bengal. It is pertinent to observe here that 'with some exceptions, the women of the Tagore family remained in an enclave of home-education with no contact with the external world and the institutions of formal education' (Bhattacharya 2011: 62). When Tagore set up his own educational establishment in Shantiniketan, the tradition of 'antahpurshiksha' or zenana education was replaced by a more liberating scheme of educational instruction.

While Rabindranath relentlessly critiqued the affectation, arti-ficiality and blatant consumerism of Englishwomen, he expressed his disappointment with their lack of intellectual pursuits. Life in western society was marked by bustling activity and elaborate social observances that Rabindranath detested. Yet in one of the later let-ters of his travelogue he supported the idea of free mixing and wrote about the liberation of Indian women who were 'chained docilely to the walls of the innermost chambers of the houses' (2008: 88), an idea that was challenged by the editor of *Bharati*, the journal (where the letter was first published) edited by Rabindranath's eldest brother, Dwijendranath. There were several ideational conflicts that surfaced in Rabindranath's creative writing regarding tradition and modernity, the forces of change and stagnation in society, selfish individualism and humanist universalism. In his early interactions with western women he had tried to understand their role within the home and in the world outside and concluded that:

> By banishing women from society, we deprive ourselves of so much hap-
> piness and progress that can only be comprehended when we come into
> contact with British society. We cannot imagine many things from afar
> which we have not witnessed with our own eyes—it is difficult to even
> believe them. What first caught the attention of all the Indians who ever
> came to England?—the indispensable contribution of the ladies towards
> the pursuit of well-being and success in the society. Those who were once
> against the liberation of women must surely have undergone a complete
> change in their attitude upon coming to this country (ibid.: 89).

Rabindranath's later travels opened up his mind to the benefits of exposure to various forms of knowledge and to a cosmopolitanism that was liberating. 'When one mingles in society, a clash between different opinions presents itself; therefore, one is able to see a single matter from many different angles.' The participation of western women in several of these debates and conversations enabled Rabindranath to conceptualize the ideal role that he would like to assign to women in his own society where 'many centuries of piti-less customs, and their disciplinary torture, oppression and restric-tion . . .would make one recoil in horror' (2008: 88) The editor of *Bharati* cautions readers about Rabindranath's idea of women's lib-eration. He believes that it is the nature of the country, its history, customs and culture that should be respected and considered in this context. At a time when Indian society lacked political freedom, educational opportunities or independence of taste, 'women's liberation would amount to waywardness, to tomboyishness and loquaciousness' opined Dwijendranath.[6] Rabindranath's altercation with the editor and the rejoinder hinges on the misinterpretation of his words and ideas concerning the emancipation of women which was related to experiences of realistic social situations in a foreign country. Rabindranath's fictional women characters in his novels and short stories however reflect various facets of the 'new' woman— independent, discursive, reasoning, inspiring, yet humble, simple and respectful in deference to traditional ideals of Indian womanhood.

For Rabindranath, the idea of the woman was separate from the real women whom he encountered within the home, in his own society and across the oceans. Suniti Kumar Chatterjee writes that 'Rabindranath's *Jivana-Devata* has inspired as well as played with the poet all through his life. She is a woman dwelling afar, beyond this world of ours, who in her various moods met the poet and participated so to say in the drama of his life' (Chatterjee 171: 78). From the literal to the metaphorical to the mystical, women occupied in his life, writings and consciousness an ambivalent space that is difficult to map and territorialize in corporeal terms. In his travelogues and correspondence Rabindranath's encounters and acquaintance with several women are often only cursorily documented in his own words. These are women of flesh and blood, historicized and contextualized, records of interactions celebrating friendships or expressing the worship of devotees to a mentor and a sage. Often he had not met the ardent admirers who corresponded with him, occasionally he had been introduced to them only briefly on one of his innumerable foreign sojourns, but his personality attracted homage and devotion. Such foreign women named by Ketaki Kushari Dyson (1992) include the Spanish transcreator of his poetry, Zenobia Camprubi, the French artist Madame Andrea Karpeles, his devoted German translator and correspondent Helene Meyer-Franck and the Hungarian painter Elizabeth Brunner, a truly transnational group from Spain, France, Germany and Hungary.

On his first visit to Europe, Rabindranath's initial observations on the trivial preoccupations of European women, leads to a deeper sympathy with them once he is able to observe them within the domestic context of their home and hearth. He spent some time as a paying guest in the Bloomsbury home of Dr. Scott whose wife took special care of him. The four Scott sisters became close friends and what he picked up from the enjoyable evenings spent with them in terms especially of the music and songs that he heard, remained with him as strains of memories that could be evoked many years later in his creative endeavours. The transference of the sensuous into the spiritual, or the translation of beauty into images and symbols followed no discursive formula but its own poetic logic. About this friendship Ketaki Kushari writes:

> The third Miss Scott sang and played on the piano, and taught him English and Irish songs. Possibly it was she who expressed a wish to learn Bengali and had lessons from him. It is likely to have been his good-bye to these sisters which was recalled in a tenderly romantic poem in *Sandhyasangit* entitled 'Dui Din' (Two Days) (1992: 56).

One of the lasting friendships of Rabindranath's twilight years was forged with the Latin American writer, poet and intellectual, Victoria Ocampo (1891–1979) whom he lovingly rechristened Vijaya, literally a Bengali translation of her first name. Ketaki Kushari Dyson has written extensively on this friendship of intellectual peers, whose ages were vastly disparate; Rabindranath was old enough to be a father-figure to the young and charming Argentinian socialite (1997 [1985]; 1988). Dyson writes:

> I realized that of all the gifted and attractive women with whom Tagore had come into direct contact in his long life—and there must have been quite a few of them—Ocampo had possibly been the most distinguished. When her own long life and its work are considered in their entirety, she is the closest to him in stature. It is only when the two vitae are placed side by side that we realize how unique a meeting theirs was (Dyson 2001).

It was almost an accident that brought the poet and Victoria into proximity in 1924–25. Rabindranath was in Buenos Aires en route Peru to deliver a lecture celebrating the hundredth anniversary of Peru's liberation from the Spanish. He was staying at a hotel with Leonard Elmhirst who was travelling with him when he fell ill. He was visited by Victoria Ocampo and was invited to stay on in a villa that belonged to a relative to recuperate his health. The beautiful villa in the suburban district of San Isidro overlooked the Rio de la Plata and very clearly was a fascinating site where the river could be viewed from the balcony. What began as a week-long stay turned into a two-month interlude. Victoria proved to be extremely resourceful and looked after every need of the poet, visiting him everyday from her home a few blocks away. What began as admiration and devotion for the poet whose *Gitanjali* Victoria had first read in the French translation of André Gide, turned into an intense friendship. It was the spiritual core of his writing that had a lasting impact in her personal search for peace and evoked her veneration for the master. When Tagore parted from Ocampo in January 1925, he had planned to meet up again in Europe but that never happened until 1930 when they briefly met in Paris where Rabindranath's first exhibition of visual art was quickly arranged. Ocampo, like Helen Meyer Frank, his German translator and admirer, never visited India or Tagore's cherished ashram in Shantiniketan. To explore these platonic friendships with foreign women is to delve into the loneliness, the sense of loss and exile, the desire for something afar that formed the nucleus of the poet's romantic sensibility.

Rabindranath's *Purabi* (1925) poems, several of which were recollections of his sojourn in Argentina may be reworkings of emotions generated by encounters that left a lasting impression on his creativity. There are critics, however, 'who refused to consider the direct influence of the human experiences, especially his relationships with various women, on some of Rabindranath's greatest lyrical pieces, or considered any attempt to probe into them irrelevant, irreverent, or irresponsible'.[7]

Though it is futile to try and locate a specific muse for every composition, Rabindranath's *Purabi* poems, going by the timespan during which he was writing these lyrics, mark his first encounter with Victoria Ocampo. The growing intimacy and painful parting that characterizes this friendship can certainly be traced in the volume dedicated to Vijaya. On 14 March 1939, Rabindranath wrote to Vijaya of 'some experiences which are like treasure islands detached from the continent of the immediate life, their charts ever remaining vaguely deciphered', going on to record that 'my Argentine episode is one of them' (Alam and Chakravarty 2011). For Rabindranath, it was not the transient relationship with his Argentinian hostess that left its indelible impression on his creativity. It was the memory of that encounter that remained with him. On 17 November 1924, during his stay at Villa Miralrio, San Isidro, 'that building near the great river' where he was 'housed . . . in strange surroundings with its cactus beds that lent their grotesque gestures to the atmosphere of an exotic remoteness'(cited from ibid.) Rabindranath wrote:

> On a lonesome trail I was, when you came along,
> your eyes set on my face.
> I thought I'd say, 'Why not come with me?
> Say something to me, please!'
> *Bijonpathe chole chilam, tumi ele*
> *Mukhe amar nayan mele.*
> *Bhebechilem boli tomay, 'Songe chalo,*
> *Amay kichu katha bolo.'*[8]

These women in Rabindranath's life, the enchantresses from foreign shores are at once real women, ideal figures and elusive fantasies—all fused into one—who may be versions of his *Jivana-Devata* as is often conjectured from his long narrative poem *Sindhu-Pare* or 'By the Ocean' composed in 1895. While Rabindranath was in Argentina, he also started doodling, cutting out lines of poetry and creating images, intuitively constituted out of crossed-out words in the manuscripts. These doodles led his literary imagination to find a visual dimension of expression in his paintings that represent an inner consciousness rather than being imitations of real faces that he knew. Several of the faces of the women that he painted are veiled, mysterious, unidentifiable, metaphorically encapsulating an enigmatic concept or a mystic vision. '*Ami chini go chini tomare og obideshini/tumi thako sindhu pare ogo bideshini*' (I know you dear maiden, you live in a land afar/You live across the seas, dear lady...). The distant, alien, exotic, 'other' woman Rabindranath invokes in this song is perhaps no single, real person that he had met on his sojourns. Yet the poet has seen her and known her. She is a syncretic personality—both real and magical, sensuous and spiritual, oriental and occidental. In some ways she can be identified with the female principle of the universe and the eternal 'She' in the poet's creative fantasy.

NOTES

1 All references in the article of Rabindranath Tagore's *Europe Pravasir Patra* are from the English translation *Letters from a Sojourner in Europe* (2008). The translation of the original is by Manjari Chakravarty.

2 The page number refers to 2008 edition where there is an extract in the appendix. The translation of *My Boyhood Days* is by Marjorie Sykes, Kolkata: Visva-Bharati 1997.

3 Carving meat at the luncheon or dinner table was the male prerogative and Rabindranath is humouring his own inadequacy and the seriousness with which such typically English customs were being followed.

4 Gombrich and Kris (1938), cited from: https://gombricharchive. files.wordpress.com/2011/05/showdoc85.pdf, p. 2; accessed on 26 December 2012.

5 Here surrogate homes refer to Satyendranath's home in Ahmedabad where he spent six months prior to his westward voyage. In Bombay, he spent a month in the home of Dr. Atmaram Padurang Turkhud, renowned physician and social reformer. His daughter Annapurna or Ana was given the responsibility to improve Rabindranath's conversational skills in English.

6 These letters were printed serially in the Bengali journal *Bharati* between Baisakh 1286 B.S. (1879 and Sravan 1287 B.S. (1880). In the Sixth and Seventh Letter especially this debate comes to the fore. Dwijendranath made caustic comments in the sixth letter and Rabindranath replied to these in the seventh, to which again the editor, point by point made his observations. When the letters were published in book format in 1288 B.S. (1881). Rabindranath wrote that he was also including the debate with the editor of *Bharati* as every topic has two sides and readers should see both. However this version of the text was not republished until, with several changes it was printed in *Pashchatya Bhraman* in 1343 (1936) (along with *Europe Jatrir Diary*. The entire debate was dropped in that later version. In the Visva-Bharati translated version I am using, following the first publication, the debate is reproduced in translation.

7 Narasingha P. Sil (2005) cites the names of Ajitkumar Chakravarti, Srikumar Banerjee, Mohitlal Majumdar and Charuchandra Banerjee as critics who find Rabindranath's references to women in his poetry a reflection of an ideal he conceptualized, a Muse who inspired him, or an imaginary figure, a *manasi*.

8   Cited from the poem, 'Aasanka', *Purabi*, Rabindrarachanabali, vol. 14 (109).

REFERENCES

Alam, Fakrul and Radha Chakravarty. eds. 2011. *The Essential Tagore.* Kolkata: Visva-Bharati.

Bhattacharya, Sabyasachi. 2011. *Rabindranath Tagore: An Interpretation.* New Delhi: Penguin.

Chatterjee, Suniti Kumar. 1971. *World Literature and Tagore.* Kolkata: Visva-Bharati.

Dyson, Ketaki Kushari. 2001. 'On the Trail of Rabindranath and Victoria Ocampo', *Parabaas* July 15; http://www.parabaas.com/rabindranath/articles/pKetaki1.html, last accessed on 5 January 2013.

———. 1992. *Rabindranath Tagore, I Won't Let You Go, Selected Poems.* New Delhi: UBSPD.

———. 1997 [1985]. *Rabindranath o Victoria Ocampo'r Sandhane.* Kolkata: Navana.

———. 1988. *In Your Blossoming Flower-Garden: Rabindranath Tagore and Victoria Ocampo.* New Delhi: Sahitya Akademi.

Gombrich, E. H., and Ernst Kris. 1938. 'The Principles of Caricature', *British Journal of Medical Psychology*, 17: 319–42 [Trapp no.1938A.1]. https://gombricharchive.files.wordpress.com/2011/05/showdoc85.pdf accessed on 26 December 2012.

Ramachandran, V.S., and William Hirstein. 1999. 'The Science of Art: A Neurological Theory of Aesthetic Experience', *Journal of Consciousness Studies* 6–7: 15–51.

Sil, Narasingha P. 2005. 'Devotio Humana: Rabindranath's Love Poems Revisited', *Parabaas* 15 February; http://www.parabaas.com/rabindranath/articles/pNarasingha.html, last accessed on 10 January 2013.

Tagore, Rabindranath. 1940. *Amar Chelebela: My Boyhood Days*, trans. Marjorie Sykes. Kolkata: Visva-Bharati, 1997.

———. 1878. *Europe Pravasir Patra: Letters from a Sojourner in Europe*, trans. Manjari Chakravarty. Kolkata: Visva-Bharati, 2008.

CHAPTER 12

Rabindranath Tagore's Travelogues and the Absent Female Voice

Amrit Sen

In 1878, an interesting debate was played out between the young contributor of *Bharati,* Rabindranath Tagore, and its more senior editor, his eldest brother, Dwijendranath, Tagore on the issue of women's emancipation (see also Chapter 11). The young contributor, Rabindranath, had argued that it was futile to expect Indian women, caged in the antahpur and constrained by a lack of education, to provide either intimacy or intellectual companionship. Ruthlessly comparing the denial of privileges to women with homicide, Rabindranath passionately argued that his intention was to generate a debate about the freedom of women and that its need was as urgent as the 'rapidly spreading Brahmoism' (Tagore 1936a [1878]: 88). He also dismissed the unfounded fears of 'female immorality' (ibid.) until women were allowed to venture into the public sphere. The young Rabindranath's critique of the male Bengali outlook drips with a caustic tone:

> I feel it need not be pointed out that to enter into *purdah*, surrounded by walls for the rest of one's lifetime and to sever all contact with the rest of the world—to think this normal is in itself very abnormal (ibid.: 101).

Combined with his critique of the 'hybridized Bengali' (Ingo-Bongo), this was probably one of the earliest and sustained use of satire in colloquial Bengali in the Bengali travelogue. While Rabindranath was critical of most British customs and institutions, the strongest effect of his first encounter with the West seems to have been an interrogation of the 'woman question', a matter which he extensively debated with the editor of *Bharati*, his eldest brother, as just mentioned, in the *Bharati* print space. Yet, even while his later fictional works examine the female voice in some radical detail, his subsequent travelogues hardly ever allow the woman question any significant mention. This essay seeks to examine this silence on the woman question in Rabindranath's travelogues. If the travelogues were some of the most important articulations of Rabindranath's ideas in the public sphere, why did Rabindranath consciously avoid the issue of female agency in his travels?[1]

It would be useful to note here that Rabindranath's radical stance seems to have changed by the time *Europe Jatrir Diary* (1936b [1890]) was published. By the 1890s the debate on the acceptance of western modernity within the national framework was clearly divided into the public and private spheres. As Partha Chatterjee and other theorists have pointed out 'nationalism had in fact resolved the woman question in complete accordance with its preferred goals', (1989: 287) with the confinement of the woman within her home as an iconic indicator of Indian nationhood and its distancing from western modernity. Indrepal Grewal points out that this discourse was used by Indian reformers in an attempt to erase women's sexuality, agency and emerging modernity. Here the tropes of the 'home' and the 'harem' were used in different ways; while Indian women embody the 'home', the free mingling western woman became a symbol of the 'material' and therefore promiscuous as in the trope of the 'harem' (Grewal 1996: 23). In Rabindranath's case, this promiscuity was in the submission to a culture of materialism that treads the non-empathetic exploitative ideology of imperialism and, therefore, needs to be disciplined. At the same time, he was aware of the incursions of modernity within the domestic sphere and the urgency of the home as a site where an understanding of the inclusive nature of Indian nationhood needed to be realized. Thus, Anandamoyee, in Tagore's novel *Gora*, became the ideal vision of Indian womanhood—gentle, nurturing and inclusive, but remaining within her domestic sphere. While Rabindranath's travelogues interrogate ideas of education, nationalism, cosmopolitanism and identity, he sought to reinforce this idea recurrently in the travelogues.

Europe Jatrir Diary seems to reinforce this private–public distinction by arguing for the Englishman's limited understanding of the happiness of the woman in her private sphere. Thus, Rabindranath considers the Hindu *balbidhaba* (child widow) as happier than the English old maid because she has a support system of the joint family, where she can exercise her womanliness: 'The womanliness of our child widows never gets an opportunity to dry up and remain fallow. Her lap is never vacant, her hands are never inactive and her heart is never inactive' (Tagore 1936b [1890]: 45). While Rabindranath is perceptive to note that despite their independence, Englishwomen are still disempowered, he seems to reinforce the binary of the man–woman, public–private with considerable simplicity when he comments: '*Karmakshetre amra karta—antahpure tara katri, amra atithi, tai amader eto ador*' (In the sphere of work we are the lords, in the domestic space they are sovereign, we are merely guests and so we are treated with such great care). (ibid.: 47) Taking this a step further, Rabindranath is sharply critical of the Englishwoman who is callous to the violence against the *pankah* puller as unwomanly:

> What I cannot understand is why your ladies, who are ever ready with their noisy demonstrations of pity . . . do not feel for the wretches who are treated in such heartless manner by their husbands and brothers before their eyes. We thank God that our early marriages and myriad other such social evils have not produced such utter heartlessness in our woman (ibid.: 200).

Meanwhile in 1891, an interesting debate was played out between Krishnabhabini Dasi and Rabindranath in *Sahitya* and *Sadhana*. Krishnabhabini writing in 1891 in *Shikshita Nari* ('The Educated Woman') had argued that western women were empowered in the public sphere through education and had made a difference by participating actively in employment in courts, banks and post offices (Dasi 1891a: 287). Rabindranath protested against this article. While he was not against women education in itself, he was against any eulogization of the unnatural activity of women. Arguing that in the intense competitive world of men, women would lose their natural instincts if they were exposed, Rabindranath wrote: 'Today's women are removing themselves from this ideal: women are great because they are women, if they encroach on the activities of men, they will not be greater; rather the reverse may be true: in this their soft nature, patience and resolution might be disturbed'

(Tagore 1936b [1891]: 90).[2] Krishnabhabini came to a compromise arguing that 'primary' duty of a woman was to her home, but if she was forced to step out into the public sphere by necessity, she should not be chastised (Dasi 1891b: 475).

I refer to this debate in some detail to raise a few questions. Was Rabindranath gravitating towards the nationalist ideology as a factor reinforcing these binaries? Or was this symptomatic of his mistrust of European modernity as avaricious and imperialistic, and therefore to be carefully sifted through? In this context, where would the 'travelling woman' and the 'woman's travelogue' be located? After all, Jnanadanandini's travels to Mumbai and Europe had led to the substantial revision of the Bengali woman's attire of the sari, complete with bodice, petticoat, shoes and socks—an attire that had permitted bhadramahilas to emerge in the public sphere. Do we detect two Rabindranaths here—one who was comfortable with the more radical female presence within the Thakurbari (an exclusive experimental zone) and within his creative world (1892 was when his radically feminist dance-drama *Chitrangada* was published)—the other, the public Rabindranath, aligning himself with the gendered notion of nationalism, latent within the struggle, to carve out a significant matter of actual identity? Or, is Rabindranath already constructing a version of the self that is an 'other' of an aggressive, violent male selfhood that is based on empathy and self- restraint that will be the basis of his universalism?

From 1912, the implications of travel undergoes a fundamental shift in Tagore's consciousness. In his seminal theoretical essay, he accepts the lure of the new as a factor of travel, but defined travel as a *tirtha* (pilgrimages) with a utilitarian purpose:

> I must acknowledge that I am motivated by a sense of profit. . . . If we in turn go to Europe without any prejudice and witness the truth that makes it great, what superior pilgrimage can we think about? (Tagore 1939: 7)

Thus, Rabindranath's future travels are all marked by a *sankalpa* (a purpose) leading to the broadening of the self and its application in his *tirthas—Bharatbarsha* (India) and Shantiniketan. What is interesting is the gendering of this travel in a metaphor. The lure of the land is seen as the caring mother preventing the individual with its diet and lullaby from venturing overseas:

> The land shackles you like a caring mother who never allows her son to
> venture after [something]. It feeds him rice and curry and lulls him to
> sleep in the green shadows. If he wants to move outwards, it threatens
> him with the fear of dire consequences (ibid.: 30).

Clearly travel is seen as a gendered activity—the male encounter
with the modern West. This letter was addressed to the students of
Shantiniketan. We must remember that even in 1912, Rabindranath
had not been successful in his first attempt at setting up a female
student's hostel in Shantiniketan. By contrast, in Bolpur the primary
school was in operation from 1905. In the 1912 travelogue, there
is a record of the necessity to embrace technology, the importance
of a dynamic work ethic, English intellectual and religious circles
and a new education system, but all this is exclusively male in its
content. Henceforth, the presence of the woman question would
remain peripheral in Rabindranath's travelogues. The travelogues
would be clearly public statements by Rabindranath, not intimate
records of experiences.

Tagore uses the presence of the woman interestingly in *Japan
Jatri* (1919). In this text, Tagore does refer to a Japanese woman who
is at par with her male colleagues in terms of her business acumen.
But the thrust of *Japan Jatri* is in its critique of Japan's submission to
materialism and imperial greed. Tagore moves the travelogue to the
aesthetic, citing Japan's alternative sense of heroism.

> I have seen in the conduct of the Japanese their wonderful self-control,
> and what seems to be a sense of forgiveness, or at least of mutual under-
> standing... I shall have to confess that the Japanese possess a monopoly
> of certain elements of heroism (Tagore 1919: 75).

Rabindranath's two addresses in Osaka—'To Women' (5 June
1924) and 'Address to Women' (6 June 1924)—locate this heroism
not in Japanese men but in the women, 'The beauty of sacrifice,
that is the true beauty of woman, and she must know it not for
her own sake only, but for the sake of man.' Rabindranath uses the
legend of Shiva, Parvati and Madana[3] to suggest her capacity to
'save the world from the power of evil' (ibid.). It is interesting how
the woman in Rabindranath's travelogue is strategically used as an
alternative to an aggressive masculinist nationalist doctrine to which

Japan had submitted. Even here, Rabindranath seems to be trapped within the biremes of the public and the private, locked in the hope that the feminine self might contain and discipline the aggressive ruthless masculine self.

As Mandakranta Bose has pointed out, Rabindranath's inclusion of women as students and especially their participation in public dance programmes had been a radical intervention in the educational system in Bengal (2008: 1086) (see also Chapter 2). In *Java Jatrir Patra* Rabindranath clearly articulated the message of the travelogue:

> The civilization of India had once travelled beyond its borders, and outsiders had adopted it. India spread its knowledge in Tibet, Mongolia and the Malayas, tapping into the intrinsic needs of sharing ideas between human beings. On a pilgrimage to see this blossoming, we find that it has not sent a barren message but provided fertile ideas in architecture, sculpture, painting, music and literature. Apart from the wish to collect material for the reconstruction of Indian history and to establish this as a permanent basis of research, I have no other reason for wanting to travel there (Tagore 1935: 6, author's translation).

In the fourteenth letter (addressed to Pratima Devi) and seventeenth letter (addressed to Nirmal Kumari Mahalanobis, who was also known as Rani) Rabindranath refers to the dances by the Javanese women and comments:

> That the dancers are women, there is no difficulty in comprehending. Whether the dancers are male or female; that is immaterial, the beauty of the dance is what counts. It is the body of a woman but the martial role of a man; the contradiction is what makes the performance interesting—the overflowing aesthetic of bravery within the body of feminine grace—not two tigers or lions in conflict, but two dainty flowers with their petals in disarray (Tagore ibid.: 89).

The reference is puzzling—while Tagore is sanctioning woman's participation in the public sphere of performance, he is in effect reinforcing the image of the *kalyanmoyee*—the sacrificing woman; the combative woman is acceptable only in performance and only as artifice. While there are descriptions of villages and religious sites, this travelogue too elides completely the issue of the domestic conditions of Javanese women.

It was in Rabindranath's experiments at Sriniketan that women had a more active role to play from its inception. Led by Gretchen Green, Nanibala Roy and Prabhabati Majumder had started a girl's school by 1913 and were actively campaigning in villages for the improvement of reproductive health of women, especially with training programmes for midwives. Indusudha Ghosh[4] and Pratima Devi, Rabindranath's daughter-in-law, had meanwhile (around 1927), accepted key roles in the crafts departments and the first *Brati Balikas* (lady scouts) were trained in 1927. Consequently, in *Russiar Chithi* (*Letters from Russia*, 1931) Rabindranath mentions the Chechen woman farmer who outlines the role of women in the Russian commune:

> In ten years there has been a change in the condition of the women farmers. We have learnt to depend on ourselves. We spread the word about advantages of women in communes and have established crèches, schools and common kitchens in every commune (Tagore 1931: 49, translation author's).

While Rabindranath noted the similarities between his project at Sriniketan and the Russian experiment, *Letters from Russia* remains remarkably silent about issues of female health and education that were being so urgently discussed at Shantiniketan. Rather, the political dimension of the text seems to imply that the process of change is directed towards the male subject position and female participation or agency is merely peripheral.

Parasya Jatri (1932) is probably the most important text in this context. Rabindranath's utopian projection of the Pehlavi state as a model for Asian modernity includes resistance to British imperialism, the establishment of transnational railway networks, the minimization of religious violence and the nullification of the mullahs; but Rabindranath does not mention Reza Shah Pehlavi's radical step of abolishing the burkha that he saw as an emblem of an obsolete tradition. The women's awakening (1936–41), the more emancipatory marriage law of 1931 and the Second Congress of Eastern Woman in Tehran are milestones in the women's movement which are not even mentioned by Tagore. While the thrust of Tagore's travelogue is the secular credentials of the Pehlavi state, he must have been aware of the impact of the woman's movement in Persia. Considering this was a fertile period where some of his most important radical texts on women appear, one is left wondering about the absence of this detail within the travelogue.

What questions then does the absent female voice in Tagore's travelogues raise? Considering that the travelogues span the period from 1878–1932, Rabindranath seems to have carefully elided this question vis-à-vis travel. In 1936, when *Paschatya Bhraman* was published, the entire debate with Dwijendranath that he had raised as a young man in 1878 was carefully deleted. A glut of women's travel narratives had already appeared in the market and the female traveller was an accepted part of the print space. For Rabindranath, the travelogue was an ideological space specifically testing his ideals of the nation, modernity and international cooperation. In this framework of ideas in the public sphere, the woman was still the 'other' who held social discipline together through her rootedness and stability. Even in his praxis of ideas in Shantiniketan, the woman remained a peripheral presence whose active ventures into the public sphere could be only as a companion, without a great deal of agency. Did Tagore's travelogues locate technology, mass education and secularism as more urgent aspects of his samkalpas in his vision of India's modernity?

In *Kabir Shange Europe* (a record of her sojourn with the poet in 1926) Nirmal Kumari Mahalanobis offers an interesting anecdote where she accepts the challenge of two German males to drink a glass of wine. While Nirmal Kumari was unfazed by the challenge, Rabindranath escorted her with great trepidation to her room, anxious that she might embarrass herself (Mahalanobis 1969). This anxiety about the woman's role in the public sphere vis-à-vis cultural identity marks Rabindranath's travelogues and relegates the woman to a fringe presence.

NOTES

1 Here the author has used agency as a theoretical context to examine Rabindranath's treatment of women in his travelogues.
2 All translations from Tagore's works are authors'.
3 Madana, the God of love and desire, was burnt to ashes when he aimed his arrows at Shiva's feet. When Shiva and Parvati were married he regained his life.

204   *Amrit Sen*

4   Indusudha Ghosh was a student of Kala Bhavana in the 1920s and later taught at Siksha Satra, the vocational school at Sriniketan. She was later arrested for revolutionary activities against the British government.

REFERENCES

Bose, Mandakranta. 2008. 'Indian Modernity and Tagore's Dance', *University of Toronto Quarterly* 77(4), Fall.
Chatterjee, Partha. 1989. 'The Nationalist Resolution of the Women's Question', in *Recasting Women: Essays in Colonial History,* edited by Kumkum Sangari and Sudesh Vaid. New Delhi: Kali for Women.
Dasi, Krishnabhabini 1891a. '*Shikshita Nari*', *Sahitya* Ashwin (mid-September–mid-October).
———. 1891b. '*Shikshita Narir Pratibader Uttar*', *Sahitya* Magh (mid-January–mid-February).
Grewal, Inderpal. 1996. *Home and Harem: Nation, Gender, Empire and the Cultures of Travel.* Durham: Duke University Press.
Mahalanobis, Nirmal Kumari. 1969. *Kobir Shonge Europe- e.* Kolkata: Mitra and Ghosh.
Tagore, Rabindranath. 1963 [1932]. *Parasya Jatri.* Kolkata: Visva-Bharati.
———. 1939 [1912]. *Pather Sanchay.* Kolkata: Visva-Bharati.
———. 1936a [1878]. *Europe-Pravasir Patra.* Kolkata: Visva-Bharati.
———. 1936b [1891]. *Europe Jatrir Diary.* Kolkata: Visva-Bharati.
———. 1935 [1927]. *Java Jatrir Patra.* Kolkata: Visva-Bharati.
———. 1931. *Russiar Chithi* Kolkata: Visva-Bharati.
———. 1919 [1916]. *Japan Jatri.* Kolkata: Visva-Bharati.
———. 1891. 'Letter' in *Sadhana,* Aghrayana (mid-November–mid-December), 90–91.

PART VI

WOMEN IN OTHER ARTS

CHAPTER 13

Gender in Rabindrasangeet

Debashish Raychaudhuri

When Rabindranath started composing lyrics in his teens, little did he know that over the next few decades his prolific musical creations would emerge as one of the salient features and expression of modernity in the Bengali-speaking world. His two thousand plus songs collectively known as Rabindrasangeet (songs of Rabindranath) have been one of the cultural components that formed the identity of the Bengali through the early and middle years of the twentieth century. Even in the present postmodern world of the contemporary Bengali, spread over several corners of the globe, Rabindrasangeet remains to be a staple musical form for 'true blue' Bengalis and answers the needs to connect to the roots of the Bengali diaspora. Interestingly, even their exposure to other forms of music does not dissuade Bengalis away from listening to or singing Rabindrasangeet. Rabindranath had composed his last song in 1941. Despite the time gap, Rabindrasangeet has not become passé. The wisdom of the composer made him pronounce with confidence in his mature years that Bengalis will have to sing his songs forever![1] Scholars and critics have devoted volumes to analyse the reasons for the ever-increasing popularity of this form of art music created in the final decades of the Bengal Renaissance. One of the most common reasons pointed out by them is the variety of emotions that Rabindrasangeet represents, which the present-day listener as well as the singer can easily identify with despite the socio-cultural changes that took place in the seven long decades since Rabindranath passed away in 1941. Having accepted this feature of Rabindrasangeet, I would like to point out another unique aspect of Rabindrasangeet that has made this genre of music a perennial favourite for singers and listeners.

Rabindranath was a modern composer in every sense of the term. Not only were his compositions innovative and eclectic, rich in poetic and emotional content, but he was also extremely careful in the preservation and dissemination of his musical creations. No other composer around Rabindranath's time was as conscious of this aspect as he was. Rabindranath nurtured a faithful band of musically trained followers like Sarala Devi, Indira Devi, Kangali Charan Sen, Dinendranath Tagore, Anadi Dastidar and Shailajaranjan Majumdar, who would immediately write the notation of the songs that they learnt from the composer. He had also encouraged a group of singers to become performers of his songs in gramophone records and live programmes in Shantiniketan and Calcutta. These singers were under his direct tutelage and could imbibe musical nuances that the composer emphasized in the style of singing. Soon a group of singers appeared who were known to the listeners as singers who specialized in singing the songs of Rabindranath. A good number of these artistes were women from respectable upper and middle-class Bengali homes who were close to Shantiniketan or to the extended circle of the Tagore family. They were Sahana Devi, Kanak Das, Rama Majumdar, Sati Devi, Amita Sen, and later, Amala Datta, Amiya Tagore, Kanika Mukherjee (later, Banerjee), Malati Ghoshal, and others. In the 1930s and 1940s when the musical scenario of Calcutta was dominated by professional singers and courtesans, the *baijis*, the introduction of female singers from 'respectable' background was a unique feature indeed! In fact, the Gramophone Company had appointed Dinendranath Tagore, grandson of Dwijendranath Tagore, the eldest brother of Rabindranath, and the 'receptacle' of Rabindranath's songs, as a 'trainer' for artistes not belonging to the Shantiniketan circle. Dinendranath had trained actor Niharbala who had become famous after acting in Rabindranath's play *Chirakumar Sabha*. Since then, a sizable number of women have specialized in singing Rabindrasangeet. In fact, often the women artistes outnumbered men. Even today the number of female exponents of Rabindrasangeet is more than that of the male counterparts. One of the reasons for this is probably that women find a peculiar affinity in the themes of these songs. In the composition of no other Bengali composer has the woman been represented with such a variety of moods and emotions. When I say this, I include the creation of dramatic characters like Chitrangada, Prakriti (in *Chandalika*), Shyama, Kamalika (in *Shapmochan*), I emphasize on the peculiar space that Rabindrasangeet opens up particularly for women belonging to the modern and contemporary world. This space is present not only in his dramatic works but in songs classified under *Puja* (Devotion), *Prem* (Love) and *Prakriti* (Nature) in *Gitabitan*, the compendium of Rabindranath's musical creations. This space constitutes a woman's world, complete with its feminine perspective and reality. It is this unique aspect of Rabindrasangeet that I would like to point out as an important factor for its popularity. The growing self-consciousness of the Bengali woman after independence which finds its representation in the literary and film narratives (for instance, Charulata in *Nashtaneer* (dir Satyajit Ray, 1964), Nita in *Meghe Dhaka Tara* (dir Ritwik Ghatak, 1960), Paromita in *Paromitar Ek Din* (dir Aparna Sen 2000) to name just a few) found expression in Rabindrasangeet. The more self-conscious the woman becomes she finds her thoughts more fully reflected in the songs of Rabindranath. It is this essentially feminine space in Rabindrasangeet that I would like to highlight in this discussion.

Does the space in Rabindrasangeet change its gender? My answer to this question is yes. In my opinion, it is not a singular one! Rather, there are several spaces created by Rabindranath in his songs. Some assume a distinctly and unmistakably masculine voice, others feminine and some remain clearly ambiguous. The first ones where the space is distinctly masculine in characteristics do not surprise us as the creator himself is a man. What surprise us are those lyrics where the space created by Rabindranath is feminine. There the speaker is a woman voicing her feminine thoughts, from a feminine perspective, complete with feminine imagery. How did Rabindranath discover this woman? When did Rabindranath begin to speak through her voice? Or, is it the other way around? Is it a woman who is speaking through Rabindranath's voice, using his language and imagery? We must address these questions in order to solve the mystery.

Rabindranath had started composing songs when he was in his teens. The woman's voice found its place in his lyrics when he started creating the songs for his *Bhanusingha Thakurer Padavali*, a

set of some 22 lyrics written in the Vaishnava padavali style under
the pseudonym 'Bhanusingha' (both Rabi and Bhanu mean the
sun.) The teenager Rabindranath was an avid reader of the lyrics
of Vaishnava poets. It was in the compositions of these medieval
poets that Rabindranath discovered the woman's voice, the voice of
Radha, the beloved and devotee of Lord Krishna. In the Vaishnava
padavali, the poets would imagine themselves a part of the *Vraja-
leela* or the play (of love) in Vraja, the place where Radha and
Krishna would meet along with the male and female companions of
both. Interestingly, the poet would assume the personage of either
Krishna's male friend or Radha's female friend or *sakhi* and advice
or comment on the proceedings at Vraja. The poets of the padavali
are therefore androgynous, assuming either male or female characteristics according to the requirement of their purpose. Moreover,
the poetic convention of the padavali necessitates the poet to assume
any of the three personages: that of a detached onlooker, that of
Radha and that of Krishna. The narrative of the padavali freely
moves between the third person, the second person and the first
person. The first person narrative is either in the voice of Radha
or Krishna. The poet, thus, easily assumes the personality of the
male and the female simultaneously. The following famous verse
by Vidyapati begins with Radha's voice lamenting her loneliness in
the absence of Krishna but ends with the comment of the poet himself: *'E Sakhi hamari dukhera nahi ora/ E bhara badara maha bhadara/
Shunya mandira mora'*:[2]

> O Sakhi, there is no end to my sufferings.
> During this heavy monsoon in the month of Bhadra
> My temple is empty.
> The heavy clouds are thundering
> The world is covered by torrents of rain.
> My love is away, the god of love
> Has pierced my heart with a sharp arrow.
> With constant lightning
> The peacocks are dancing in glee.
> The frogs are intoxicated, the gallinules sing
> My heart is writhing in pain.
> The dark night is stormy.

Lightning restlessly runs across the sky.
Vidyapati asks how would you spend
Your days and nights without Hari.

The young Rabindranath was so fascinated by these verses that he set these lines to tune. When he assumed the pseudonym of Bhanusingha, he immediately picked up this convention of multiple voices in the padavali. Sometimes it is Bhanusingha giving in third person, detached, but sympathetic commentary of Radha's movements, sometimes it is Radha herself speaking in her own voice, with the poet's comment as Bhanusingha at the end of the verse. Thus, there is an easy fluidity in the change of the narrative voice: from the author to the subjects, from the masculine self of the poet to the feminine self of Radha. Rabindranath, thus, apprenticed himself to assume an androgynous role as a poet, right from his teens.

In a way, Rabindranath exercised what John Keats had described as 'negative capability', a poetic capacity to efface one's own mental identity by immersing it sympathetically and spontaneously within the subject described, as Shakespeare was thought to have done. Rabindranath too was a playwright and created innumerable characters as Shakespeare did. The playwright's negation of his own self is required to create an imaginary character. Rabindranath in his *Bhanusingha Thakurer Padavali* happily assumes several characters and gives them a freedom of thought and expression! Thus, these poems have a dramatic quality of dialogues. In one of the verses of *Bhanusingha Thakurer Padavali* we hear the voice of Radha ending with the voice of Bhanusingha: '*Badarabarakhana, niradagarajana, bijulichamakana ghora,/Upekhai kaichhe ao tu kunje nitiniti madhava mor*':[3]

It's raining, clouds thundering and there's constant lightning,
How do you ignore them and regularly come to the bower, O my
Madhava.
When lightning strikes continually, O lord, and when it thunders,
Thinking of you, my beloved, I am tense.
Your dress is wet, O Madhava, with the constant rain,
Why do you neglect your health for me, I am a mere lass.
Come and sit, O lord, on the flower bed and extend your feet.

I shall carefully wipe your feet with my unclasped hair.
Spread your tired limbs, O Vrajasundara, on my breast.
I shall cover your body with the delighted touch of my delicate lotus-
stalk arms.
Bhanu says, O daughter of Brikabhanu, my Kala is an ocean of love
For you, for love he will endure all pains.

These poems of *Bhanusingha Thakurer Padavali* were written intermittently by Rabindranath between his sixteenth and twenty-fifth years. Curiously, in the last verse written when he was twenty-five, the boundary between the voice of Radha and that of the poet fades away. Between these years Rabindranath composed songs for two of his operas, *Valmiki Pratibha* and *Kalmrigaya*, songs for *Nalini*, some Brahmasangeet and a few patriotic songs. These songs, except those sung by the female characters of his plays, do not present the feminine world. The songs of Bhanusingha are the only ones composed by the young Rabindranath where the composer assumes the feminine self. At twenty-five Rabindranath had attained a maturity and depth that surpassed those of the medieval poets. The last of the *Bhanusingha Thakurer Padavali* songs, *'Ko tunhu bolabi moy'*, obfuscates the boundary between the genders: the personage of Radha and the personage of the poet Bhanusingha. In this verse, Shyam or Krishna assumes the form of the mysterious Supreme Being whom the poet addresses. Nowhere in the verse is the name Krishna or Shyam mentioned. In fact, this question of Radha's, *'Ko tunhu bolabi moy'* (Tell me, who are you?) is now more of a quest of Bhanusingha. Here, more than Radha, it is Bhanu who assumes the personage of the devoted lover of that mysterious being! He is the *'virahi'* like Radha. In this last verse, Bhanusingha sheds his objective self and almost identifies with Radha in empathy. Thus, the androgynous self of the poet is established in the following verse: *'Ko tunhu bolabi moy!/Hridaya-maha majhu jagasi anukhan, ankha-upara tunhu rachalahi asana'.*[4]

Tell me, who are you!
You are constantly awake within my mind; you have built a seat on my
eyes,
Your bright eyes do not disappear
From my mind even for an instance! Tell me, who are you!

My heart, like a lotus, trembles at your feet, my eyes fill up with tears
My body, overwhelmed with love, delights in glee
and wants to merge in you! Tell me, who are you!...
The music of your flute is both nectar and poison for me. It breaks my
heart yet steals it too.
Its intense music fills up the world,
And overwhelms my heart. Tell me, who are you!

...

My thirsty eyes look at your face, with your sweet touch Radha is
thrilled,
She fills her heart with the wealth of love,
And places herself at your feet. Tell me, who are you!
I ask everyone, 'Who are you', and wipe my constantly tearful eyes,
Prays Bhanu please clear all doubts—
He wants to spend his life at your feet. Tell me, who are you!

This transformation of the detached narrator into the devoted lover in this last verse of *Bhanusingha Thakurer Padavali* is a vital positional shift on the part of the lyricist that will determine the mood of a good number of songs that he will compose throughout his life. This is the moment that Rabindranath, the lyricist, discovers in him the voice of the devoted lover in search of the 'mysterious one'. Like Radha, this devotee has a feminine self. The mysterious one is often the 'male' entity; Rabindranath addresses him as *sakha* (a male friend), *nath* (lord), *swami* (husband), *prabhu* (master) and *priya* (lover). The speaker in the songs, therefore, assumes a Radha-like feminine self of the seeker. The speaker negates his gender in order to place himself in the position of the devotee *who* is in search of the loved one. Years after the composition of the last verse of *Bhanusingha Thakurer Padavali*, the mature Rabindranath, in 1926, composed another exquisite lyric which draws on the imagery of the flute and its mysterious player. Rabindranath too, has traversed a long way from the world of the medieval padavalis. His quest for the 'mysterious one' has evolved through the agonising years of the '*Gitanjali* phase'. Yet it is interesting to note how the flute and all its associated thoughts resurface in this composition of the 65-year-old composer while he was in Budapest. *Diner belay banshi tomar baji-yechhile anek sure/ Ganer parash prane elo, apni tumi raile dure:*[5]

> Many tunes you played in your flute during the day—
> Your songs touched my heart, yet you were far away.
> I asked the passersby, 'Who played the flute?'
> They confused me with different names, I strayed in search from door
> to door.
> Now the sky has dimmed, the weary day shuts its eyes—
> If you make me wander away my quest will be in vain.
> Come and sit within me—
> Come, play your flute
> Within the recesses of my heart.

The same quest of *'Ko tunhu bolabi moy'* continues here with the mature composer asking the flute player to play his flute within his heart. Here the voice of the seeker assumes a feminine self though Rabindranath never mentions the gender of the flute player or the seeker. However, with the cultural associations it is unlikely that an Indian would identify the flute player as a woman and the seeker a man! Therefore, singers both male and female are free to sing this song, but a woman readily identifies herself as the seeker. It is probably this vague feminine space that often attracts women to sing these songs more spontaneously than men and this probably explains why more women took up singing Rabindranath's compositions than men.

The same year when Rabindranath composed *'Ko tunhu bolabi moy'* he wrote a few more lyrics which present definite male and female perspectives. While *'Ami nishi nishi kata rachiba shayana'*,[6] [How many evenings shall I prepare the nuptial bed] *'ogo shono ke bajay'*[7] (O listen to the flute being played) and *'ogo eto prema-asha'*[8] (How can he ignore my yearnings for love) express the plight of the lovelorn woman like Radha, *'Tumi kon kananer phul'*[9] (O flower, in which garden do you bloom?) is essentially a man's admiration for a woman. The theme of endless waiting for the beloved irrespective of his constancy and expression of unqualified love for him seem to be a constant theme of many songs that speaks in the voice of a woman. For instant *'Amara parana jaha chay'*[10] (You are what my heart desires) or *'Ami nishidina tomay bhalobasi'*[11] (My love for you is constant) express unconditional love for the beloved despite a probable desertion by him! The final verse of *'Amara parana jaha chay'* says: *Jadi ar kare bhalobasho, Jadi ar*

phire nahi aso / Tabe tumi jaha chao tai jeno pao, ami jato dhukha pai go
(If you love someone else and never return to me/ Then let all your
wishes be fulfilled and let me have all the sufferings).
    In *'Ami nishidina tomay bhalobasi'* the speaker says:[12]

> I shall love you always,
> You may love me in your leisure.
> I'll wait here for you forever,
> Come to me when you remember me.

Unqualified, selfless love seems to be a characteristic of woman,
while man's love is a wavering and less sincere one. Is this an
archetype that Rabindranath picked up from the Vaishnava poets?
Probably, yes. His keen observation of the man–woman relationship in his contemporary social and family circles could also
have prompted him to form this idea. In general, the women created by Rabindranath are serious and sincere in love and forgiv-
ing and generous in betrayal. The songs mentioned earlier were
all written in his youth, when he had lived in the company of
his sisters-in-law Jnanadanandini and Kadambari and his wife,
Mrinalini. Simultaneously, he had temporary but a passing close
friendship with Ana Turkhud[13] in Bombay and the daughters of
Dr. Scott in London. He had also observed his sisters, and later,
his daughters as they grew up and numerous women of the family
and social circles. Three of his nieces, Indira, Pratibha and Sarala,
who were often his associates in musical, dramatic and literary
activities, were particularly close to him. His amused observation
of his wife's continuous tête-à- tête with her female friend, Amala
Das,[14] led to the creation of *'Olo sai, olo sai, amar ichche kare toder
mato maner katha kai'*[15] (O dear friend, I wish I could, like you, con-
fide my secrets to you) in 1895![16] These exposures to the world of
women in real life and those of the fictional worlds of literature
and Vaishnava padavali helped Rabindranath create a woman's
world complete with feminine details and thought process. His
song *'Amar man manena—dinarajani'*[17] (1893) (Day and night, my
mind would not rest) is a purely feminine expression of a girl newly
introduced to love. These lyrics surprise us when we know that
the lyricist is a man. Songs like these are numerous. Rabindranath

constantly refers back to the romantic world of the flute, the bower, Krishna and Radha, their 'sakhis', and all the related associations while creating songs like '*Ekhano tare chokhe dekhini*'[18] (I have not seen him yet, only heard his flute), '*Sakhi, amari duare keno asilo*'[19] (O dear, why did the beggar appear at my door), or '*Aji je rajani jay*'[20] (How can I return to this fleeting evening) (all composed in 1893). In 1894 he composed an extremely poignant song '*Eso eso phire eso*'[21] (Please come back to me) which implores the *bandhu* to return to the speaker in a language that surpasses any traditional padavali in its emotional and poetic content. There is no mention of any Radha or Krishna in the text but the 'bandhu' is adorned with a variety of epithets like *nishthura* (cruel), *natha* (lord), *karuna komala*' (compassionate and soft), *sajala jalada snigdha kanta* (the one with the soft hues of the rain-bearing clouds), *sundara* (beautiful), *nitisukha* (constant bliss), *chiradukha* (eternal agony), *saba sukha dukha manthana dhana* (treasure churned out of all sorrows and joy), *chira banchhita* (the eternally desired one), *chita sanchita* (saved in the heart), *chanchala* (restless), *chirantana* (eternal), And what is most important, Rabindranath successfully turns this into a modern poem of longing spoken by a woman: *Amar bakshe phiriya eso, / Amar chakshe phiriya eso,*[22]

> Return to my heart,
> Return to my eyes,
> Infuse my awakening and my conduct,
> Infuse my smile and my tears,
> Infuse my whole world with your presence.

One may argue that in the duality between the devotee and the deity, the devotee takes up the feminine space! But even then there is no denying that the speaker of these words is a woman and therefore this song should be ideally suitable for a female voice. However, one is struck by the performance of this song: Rabindranath as a singer had performed this favourite song a number of times. Only four days after the composition of this song Rabindranath had visited Ranaghat where he was a guest at Nabinchandra Sen's house. There he had sung this song and later also sent him a copy of the lyrics. Despite definite feminine images the composer himself sang this song and was much appreciated.

This should not give the impression that Rabindranath was composing songs which presented only the feminine perspective. This was a time when he also composed several songs which have definite male perspective. Songs like *'Ami chini go chini tomare'*[23] (I know who you are, O woman beyond the Sindhu) or *'Tumi rabe nirabe'*[24] (You'll reside in the silence of my heart) or *'Se ase dhire'*[25] (She comes slowly) or *'Akula keshe ase'*[26] (She appears in dishevelled hair) shared an unambiguous male attitude, addressed to female subjects and all composed in 1895. Simultaneously, Rabindranath composed songs like *'Tumi jeyo na ekhani'*[27] (O don't leave as yet) or *'Ohe sundara mama grihe aji'*[28] (O beauteous one, it is a festive evening in my house) with definite feminine imagery. In *'Ohe sundara mama'* the hostess is inviting the precious guest, the *'hridi ballava'* or the sweetheart. In the final stanza, she mentions with a feminine declension of the adjective *'lina'* that she will sit at the feet of the beloved and play the golden veena, thus specifying the gender of the speaker.

For the next few years, Rabindranath composed several songs with clear gender identity; some feminine, some masculine. The number of masculine songs outnumbered the feminine ones. The 'masculine' songs were often light and flirtatious in mood like *'Mana mandira sundari! Mani manjira gunjari'*[29] (The beauty of the temple of my mind). However, after the death of Mrinalini, his wife, in 1902, the 'masculine' songs disappeared. For the next few years, Rabindranath would have to go through a trying and agonizing time as a young widower with the responsibility of five children, constantly juggling with the problems at his estates, the uncertainties of his newly founded school and paucity of funds to support all these. Soon, within five years of his wife's death, Rabindranath was bereft of his two children, his father and a close associate. In his public life he was in the middle of the tremendous political upheaval initiated by the Partition of Bengal (1905) and Tagore was deeply involved in the Anti-Partition movement. This was the period when he was composing lyrics for *Gitanjali, Gitali* and *Gitimalya*,[30] writing *Gora*[31] and *Raja*.[32] These troubled times made him look inwards. The voice of often a playful male lover, found in the songs composed in the final few years of the nineteenth century, totally disappeared from the songs composed in the first decade of the twentieth century.

In his youth, Rabindranath had composed a poem entitled *'Vaishnav kabita'*[33] (in *Sonar Tari*) where he wrote: *Debatare jaha dite pari, dii tai / Priyajane jaha dite pai / Tai dii debatare:*

> All that I can offer to the deity, I offer
> To my love. All that I can offer to my love
> I offer to the deity; what else can I give?
> I make divinity my lover and my lover divine.

In the songs composed during the first decade of the twentieth century, Rabindranath addressed divinity as lover with all his multidimensional identities which are essentially that of a male: a friend, a lover, a husband, a lord, a cruel taskmaster, a terrible foe, a gentle father. The speaker, however, assumed a feminine identity to complete the lover–beloved and divinity–devotee dualism. The male poet exercised his negative capability to leave his 'male' self and enter wilfully into a 'female' space that is inhabited by the *virahi*, the submissive, enduring and tearful devotee waiting patiently for a union with the divine lover much like the androgynous self of the Vaishnav poet. In a 1904 composition, *'Darao amar ankhira age'*,[34] (Stand in front of my eyes) he writes: *'Darao jekhane virahi e hiya tomari lagiya ekela jage'* (Appear where my ever-waiting heart is awake alone for you). In several songs of *Gitanjali*, this analogy is continued: *'Se je pashe ese basechhila tabu jagini, ki ghum tore peyechhila hatabhagini'*[35] (He came and sat beside me, yet I didn't awake, What What deep sleep had overpowered you O ill-fated woman!). The theme of union with the mysterious one is amplified in a 1906 song, *'Amar godhuli lagan elo bujhi kachhe'*[36] (The dusk falls, the moment of my marriage draws near) which elaborately mentions 'marriage'. The dusk is identified as the moment of death of the mortal self and union with the divine. This imagery of marriage of the poet's feminine self with the male identity of the divine continues in songs like *'Maharaja e ki saje'*[37] (1909) (O maharaja, how majestically you arrive in my heart), *'Tomay amay milan habe bale'*[38] (1913) (The sky is full of light, for we will unite), *'Amar din phuralo'*[39] (My day comes to an end) and *'Ebar rangiye gelo hridaygagan'*[40] (1919) (My heart is flushed with the colour of the dusk). These songs depict and suggest a bridal identity of the speaker and a groom-like identity of the 'mysterious' one.

Rabindranath's self as a devotee has found a dramatic projection in two of his characters from his play *Raja*[41] (1910): Surangama and Thakurda. While Surangama depicts all the characteristics of a female devotee, Thakurda is a depiction of the male devotee. One may even look at Rabindranath's songs expressing devotion, composed during the first two decades of the twentieth century, as songs by Surangama or Thakurda. These two characters were, in a way, projections of the poet's own self during this period.

The male perspective and the man's voice return in the seasonal and love songs of the poet during the 1920s and 1930s. Instances can be numerous. However, love songs like *'Sei bhalo sei bhalo'*[42] (So let it be thus) or *'Tomara giti jagalo smriti'*[43] (Your song awakens memory) or monsoon songs like *'Mane holo jano periye elem'*[44] (It seems I have traversed endless miles), *'Barshana mandrita andhakare'*[45] (In the darkness sonorous with rain) or *'Amar priyar chhaya'*[46] (The shadow of my beloved) depict a man's perspective and are addressed to a woman. This is not to say that the feminine space and the woman's voice disappeared from Rabindranath's songs composed in the final two decades of his life. On the contrary, the feminine space remains firm and stable and the woman's voice is heard with greater sophistication than ever before in exquisite compositions like *'Dip nibe gechhe mamo'*[47] (My lamp has been put out), *'Amar jadi bela'*[48] (1921) (If my hours are spent), *Ami sandhyadiper shikha'*[49] (I am the flame of the evening lamp), *'Dinashesher ranga mukul'*,[50] (1924) (The blazing blossom blooms in the mind as the day ends), *'Amar jvaleni alo'*[51] (My lamp did not light), *'O amar dhyaneri dhan'*[52] (O the treasure of my mind), *'Se amar gopan katha'*[53] (Listen to my secret), *'Sakhi, andhare ekela ghare'*[54] (1926) (O friend, I am alone in a dark room), *'Jani tumi phire asibe'*[55] (I know you will return), *'Rangiye diye jao'*[56] (1927) (Make me glow with your love before you depart)', *'Aro kichhukshan nahoy'*[57] (Why not sit for a while by me), *'Hay atithi, ekhani ki holo'*[58] (1928) (Alas, my guest, has the time to leave, *'Mallikabane jakhan pratham dhoreche koli)'*[59] (1930) (jasmine buds bloomed in my garden for the first time), *'Tumi kon bhanganero pathe ele'*[60] (You have come on a path of destruction) (1939), and so on. I am not citing examples from the plays which will have many more songs for the woman's voice. Notably, the three protagonists of the final three dance dramas of Rabindranath are all women: Shyama, Chandalika and Chitrangada.

Clearly, the poet gives free rein to his imaginative and artistic self which was divided between both male and female entities as a creative composer. Following Rabindranath's example later composers of Bengali songs like Atul Prasad Sen and Kazi Nazrul Islam and the *adhunik* (modern) lyricists of the post-Tagore period composed songs from both male and female perspectives. The concept of gender in modern Bengali songs appeared with Rabindranath who opened up complex, psychological space for composers and singers to explore and rediscover facets of the composer. Tagore scholars may probe into the gender of Rabindranath's musical compositions to further interpret and understand the poet.

NOTES

1 '*Kintu ami jantum Bangladeshe amar gaan gaowaboi…E na geye upay ki. Amar gaan gaitei hobe—sob kichhute.*' (I knew with certainty that Bengal shall sing my songs. There's no way they could avoid it. They'll have to sing my songs in every aspect of their lives.) Rani Chanda (2011): 125.

2 All translations used in this essay are by the author. Cited here is the full poem:

> *E Sakhi hamari dukhera nahi ora.*
> *E bhara badara maha bhadara*
> *Shunya mandira mora.*
> *Jhampi Ghana garajanti santati*
> *Bhuvana bhari barikhantiya.*
> *Kanta pahuna kama daruna*
> *Saghane khara shara hantiya.*
> *Kulisha shata shata pata-modita*
> *Mayura nachata matiya.*
> *Matta daduri dake dahuki*
> *Phati yayata chhatiya.*
> *Timira digbhari ghora yamini*
> *Athira bijurika pantiya.*
> *Vidyapati kaha kaichhe gongayabi*
> *Hari bine dina ratiya.*

3   Citing the full poem:

> *Badarabarakhana, niradagarajana, bijulichamakana ghora,*
> *Upekhai kaichhe ao tu kunje nitiniti madhava mor.*
> *Ghana ghana chapala chamakay yaba pahu, bajarapata yaba hoya,*
> *Tunhuka bata taba samarayi priyatama, dara ati lagata moya.*
> *Angabasana taba bhinkhata Madhava, Ghana Ghana barakhata meha,*
> *Kshudra bali ham, hamko lagaya kaha upekhabi deha.*
> *Baisa baisa, pahu, kusumashayana-para padayuga deha pasari.*
> *Sikta charana taba mochhaba yatane kuntalabhara ughari.*
> *Shranta anga taba he Vrajasundara, rakha baksha-para mora.*
> *Tanu taba gheraba pulakita parashe bahumrinalaka dora.*
> *Bhanu kahe, Brikabhanunandini, premasindhu mama kala*
> *Tonhara lagaya premaka lagaya saba kuchha sahabe jwala.*

4   The full poem:

> *Ko tunhu bolabi moy!*
> *Hridaya-maha majhu jagasi anukhan, ankha-upara tunhu rachalahi asana,*
> *Aruna nayana taba marama-sange mama*
> *Nimikha na antara hoya. Ko tunhu bolabi moy!*
> *Hridayakamala taba charane talamala, nayanayugala mama uchhale*
> *chhalachhala*
> *Premapurna tanu pulake dhaladhala*
> *Chahe milaite toy! Ko tunhu bolabi moy!*
> *Bansaridhwani tuha amiya garala re hridaya bidarayi hridaya harala re,*
> *Akula kakali bhuvana bharala re,*
> *Utala prana utaroy. Ko tunhu bolabi moy!*
> *...*
> *Trishita ankhi taba mukha-'para viharai, madhura parasha taba, radha*
> *shiharai,*
> *Premaratana bhari hridaya prana lai*
> *Padatale apana khoy. Ko tunhu bolabi moy!*
> *'Ko tunhu' 'ko tunhu' sabajana puchayi, anudina saghana nayanajala*
> *muchhayi,*
> *Jhache Bhanu saba sangshaya ghuchayi—*
> *Janama charana—para goya. Ko tunhu bolabi moy.*

5   Song no. 603, (Puja) *Gitabitan* (2004): 237:

> *Diner belay banshi tomar bajiyechhile anek sure—*
> *Ganer parash prane elo, apni tumi raile dure.*
> *Shudhai jata pather loke 'Ei banshiti bajalo ke'—*
> *Nanan name bholay tara, nanan dware berai ghure.*
> *Ekhan akash mlan holo, klanta diba chakshu boje—*
> *Pathe pathe pherao yadi marba tabe mithya khonje.*
> *Bahir chhere bhitarete apni laho asan pete—*
> *Tomar banshi bajao asi*
> *Amar praner antahpure.*

6   Song no. 303 (Prem) *Gitabitan* (2004): 391.
7   Song no. 300 (Prem) *Gitabitan* (2004): 390.
8   Song no. 302 (Prem) *Gitabitan* (2004): 391.
9   Song no. 363 (Prem) *Gitabitan* (2004): 413–14.
10 Song no. 142 (Prem) *Gitabitan* (2004): 326.
11 Song no. 143 (Prem) *Gitabitan* (2004): 327.
12 *Ami nishidina tomay bhalobasi, / Tumi abasaramata basiyo / Nishidina hethay base achhi, / Tomar jakhan mane pare asiyo.*
13 Ana Turkhud [1861–91] was the daughter of a prominent Marathi social reformer and physician Dr. Atmaram Pandurang [1823–98]. Rabindranath met her in 1878 in Bombay before he left for England. She is also mentioned in Chapter 11, note 4. Rabindranath named her 'Nalini', wrote poems with Nalini as a character, started teaching her Bengali. "Nalini" used to acquaint Rabindranath with western manners, as she had already studied in England, brushed up Rabindranath's conversational English, and tried singing the young composer's songs in Bengali. The young Rabindranath was particularly fascinated by her. For further details, see Pal (1990).
14 Amala Das, sister of Chittaranjan Das, was a close friend of the Tagores and a singer in her own right.
15 Song no. 81 (Prem) *Gitabitan* (2004): 304–5.
16 Sahana Devi, the famous singer, writes about Amala Das, who was her aunt (mother's sister): 'My mashima (aunt) was closest to the poet's wife Mrinalini Devi. She used to call her "kakima". A song by Rabindranath that records the intimate moments of tete-a-tete between the two friends is *"Olo soi, olo soi"*. My mashima talked about this song and I have also heard her singing this song' (1961): 229.

17   Song no. 58 (Prem) *Gitabitan* (2004): 295.
18   Song no. 367 (Prem) *Gitabitan* (2004): 415.
19   Song no. 150 (Prem) *Gitabitan* (2004): 330.
20   Song no. 247 (Prem) *Gitabitan* (2004): 370.
21   Song no. 252 (Prem) *Gitabitan* (2004): 372.
22   The poem:

> *Amar bakshe phiriya eso,*
> *Amar chakshe phiriya eso,*
> *Amar shayane swapane basane bhushane nikhila bhubane eso.*
> *Amar mukher hasite eso,*
> *Amar chokher salile eso,*
> *Amar adare amar chhalane amar abhimane phire eso.*

23   Song no. 86 (Prem) *Gitabitan* (2004): 306.
24   Song no. 367 (Prem) *Gitabitan* (2004): 415.
25   Song no. 140 (Prem) *Gitabitan* (2004): 326.
26   Song no. 153 (Prem) *Gitabitan* (2004): 331.
27   Song no. 152 (Prem) *Gitabitan* (2004): 330.
28   Song no. 187 (Prem) *Gitabitan* (2004): 345.
29   Song no. 82 (Natya geeti) *Gitabitan* (2004): 796.
30   *Gitanjali* (1910) *Gitali, Gitimalya* (1914) are collection of verses most of which are songs set to tune by the poet. These are significant compositions anthologized in *Gitabitan,* the comprehensive collection of Rabindrasangeet or 'songs of Rabindanath'.
31   *Gora,* a novel by Rabindranath was published in 1910.
32   *Raja,* one of the dramatic works by Rabindranath published in 1911.
33   *Sonar Tari,* Tagore (1961): 367: *Debatare jaha dite pari, dii tai/ Priyajane jaha dite pai/ Tai dii debatare; ar paba kotha?/ Debatare priya kari, priyere debata.*
34   Song no. 101 (Puja) *Gitabitan* (2004): 47.
35   Song no. 267 (Prem) *Gitabitan* (2004): 378.
36   Song no. 65 (Puja) *Gitabitan* (2004): 65.
37   Song no. 522 (Puja) *Gitabitan* (2004): 206.
38   Song no. 34 (Puja) *Gitabitan* (2004): 19.
39   Song no. 36 (Prakriti) *Gitabitan* (2004): 442.
40   Song no. 568 (Puja) *Gitabitan* (2004): 223.
41   *Raja,* first published on 6 January 1911 by Indian Publishing House, Calcutta.

42 Song no. 190 (Prem) *Gitabitan* (2004): 346.
43 Song no. 253 (Prem) *Gitabitan* (2004): 373.
44 Song no. 115 (Prakriti) *Gitabitan* (2004): 471.
45 Song no. 107 (Prem) *Gitabitan* (2004): 313.
46 Song no. 124 (Prakriti) *Gitabitan* (2004): 474.
47 Song no. 287 (Prem) *Gitabitan* (2004): 385.
48 Song no. 76 (Prem) *Gitabitan* (2004): 302.
49 Song no. 96 (Bichitra) *Gitabitan* (2004): 586.
50 Song no. 101 (Prem) *Gitabitan* (2004): 311.
51 Song no. 257 (Prem) *Gitabitan* (2004): 375.
52 Song no. 185 (Prem) *Gitabitan* (2004): 344.
53 Song no. 117 (Prem) *Gitabitan* (2004): 317.
54 Song no. 281 (Prem) *Gitabitan* (2004): 383.
55 Song no. 178 (Prem) *Gitabitan* (2004): 341.
56 Song no. 16 (Bichitra) *Gitabitan* (2004): 550.
57 Song no. 50 (Prem) *Gitabitan* (2004): 292.
58 Song no. 163 (Prem) *Gitabitan* (2004): 335.
59 Song no. 249 (Prakriti) *Gitabitan* (2004): 526.
60 Song no. 221 (Prem) *Gitabitan* (2004): 359.

REFERENCES

Chanda, Rani. 2011. *Alapchari Rabindranath.* Shantiniketan: Visva-Bharati.
Devi, Sahana. 1961 (1368 BS). *Kabir Sangsparshe', Rabindrayan,* edited by Pulinbihari Sen, vol. 2. Kolkata: Baksahitya.
Pal, Prashanta Kumar. 1990. *Rabijibani,* vol. 2. Kolkata: Ananda Publishers.
Tagore, Rabindranath. 2004. *Gitabitan.* Shantiniketan: Visva-Bharati.
———. 1961. *Rabindra Rachanabali,* Centenary Edition, vol. 1. Calcutta: West Bengal Government.

CHAPTER 14

Breaking the Mould: Paintings by Rabindranath Tagore

Tapati Gupta

Rabindranath Tagore did not ever have much formal training in art. Yet what a versatile artist he turned out to be! He grew up in a family that was extremely conscious of the best of both worlds: the indigenous culture, its art and literature, as well as the western culture imported by the British Raj. The nationalistic urge that led him to encourage nephew Abanindranath to delve into the form and medium of Indian tradition also drew him to distil the essence of the modernist European Expressionism[1] which he mingled with deep individual apprehension.

Between the years 1927–28, Tagore started painting regularly and prolifically and this activity continued till his last days. He is said to have produced over 2,500 landscapes, faces and sketches. He was immensely attracted not only to European Expressionism but also primitive art and Japanese art. Distortion of form, aberrant use of colour and sensitive handling of lines characterized his paintings. The same influences were operative in Europe at the time. Breaking away from conventional form, his paintings had a strange surrealism and bizarre expression that were very new to Indian art at the time.

During his tour of France in the spring of 1930, Tagore the poet-artist was advised by some art critics of local newspapers to hold an exhibition in Paris. In May 1930, the first exhibition of his paintings in was held at the Gallerie Pigalle in Paris, and the show travelled to different countries in Europe in the same year. His home town Calcutta hosted the exhibition in 1931.

Sudha Basu (2011: 85) points out that after the exhibition in Germany in 1930, the German press showered overwhelming accolades on Tagore, pointing out similarities between the art of contemporary European and German Expressionist artists, and that of Tagore who had penetrated outer reality to arrive at the essence of being. His animals reminded one of Christian Morgenstern's art; his shadowy human figures reminded one of Munch; the free play of his fancy is reminiscent of Paul Klee, while his groups of heads were reminiscent of Emil Nolde.

It is true that Rabindranath Tagore's eclecticism led to his amalgamation of diverse influences in his artistic output. But whatever cultural values he accepted as his raw material, it was turned into creations uniquely his own. Basu also mentions a more perceptive though 'orientalist' trend in German appraisal of Tagore: Tagore's poetical vision is unique and not imitative of any Occidental school (ibid.: 85). Basu's observations significantly underline the ambivalent sources of Tagore's art, which combines the pictorial values of home and the world, and seizes the inwardness and spiritual values found in both.

Most critics today seek to connect his paintings to his writings. But in my opinion the paintings impact strongly upon modern Indian art and have independent significance. *Rabindra Chitravali,* the four-volume publication of his artistic output (Visva-Bharati and Government of India, Ministry of Culture 1911) would doubtless help open new windows upon Tagore the artist, by making the public aware of the variety in his visual output, his expertise in handling form and colour, his mingling of the corporeal with the conceptual.[2]

Some basic observations on his art, I feel, would not be out of place here. The inner eye peeps through his landscapes suggesting a dream world of lyricism; obviously an inner eye has penetrated the mystery of nature. His animals, so grotesque and weird, reassert modernistic notions of beauty and ugliness. The sensuous and visual worlds resonate with a spirituality which both renounces as well as embraces the material world. Western style collaborates with eastern stylization. The doodles re-create the lines of his written poetry and re-invent a new text. The portraits gaze at us with psychological intensity. His palette is restricted, his lines simple, but his vision is complex. It transgresses the borders of narrow nationalism and trumpets the destruction of the restrictive borders of clime and time.

Tagore's paintings need to be seen as having independent value as art and not as an adjunct to his output as a writer. The art historian should definitely take into account Tagore's affinity with the German Expressionists, whose works he saw during his trips to Europe and whose exhibition was also held in Calcutta. At the same time, one should take note of Tagore's originality in defying the canons of art, the social relevance of his paintings of women, and his attitude to gender. This chapter is in the nature of an enquiry and does not seek to arrive at a definitive assessment or straitjacket Tagore into any aesthetic ideology. Here, I will concentrate only on his paintings of women and hope to indicate the iconoclastic nature of his art, his approach to conventions of taste regarding beauty and gender, and his countering of the nationalistic ideology of 'Mother India'/Mother Goddess.

'Women have the vital power more strongly in them than men have,' says Tagore in his essay, 'Woman'.[3] And what he says about beauty is also worth quoting: 'Beauty is not a mere fact; it cannot be accounted for, it cannot be surveyed and mapped. It is an expression'.[4] Representation of the vital power required a more vital language than the decorative style of the Bengal School[5] artists or Raja Ravi Verma's[6] or Hemendranath Majumdar's[7] mimetic and volumetric approach to the human form. The West was, by then, getting accustomed to Expressionist and Fauvistic[8] distortions in form and colour and was ready to accept the modernism of the Indian poet as evidenced in the exhibition in Paris. To people at home, perhaps, Tagore's paintings were uncomfortably different (Basu 2011: 121).

The question at the core of this investigation should be why are the women he painted so enigmatic? Is it because of the 'no-place' they 'inhabit'? Tagore spoke of the importance of woman in the domestic space which is their safeguard against the void. In the paintings, they are in an alternative place/space—a romantic mental space where there is freedom of self-expression. I may begin with Casey's opening question:

> Can you imagine what it would be like if there were no places in the world? None whatsoever! An utter placeless void! I suspect that you will not succeed in this thought-experiment, which is not just difficult to perform (can you really eliminate any trace of place from your experience of

things) but also disturbing . . . Our lives are so place-oriented and place-
saturated (1993: ix).

'The Greek word *atopos* (literally, "no place") means "bizarre" or
"strange". No wonder we feel estranged when we are out of place'
(ibid.: x). Yet this is the first impression evoked by some of the paintings. They float about de-contextualized. There is no mythological
or historical background, no firm 'earth-footing' to give them perspective. Although the veiled women suggest Bengali social context,
for example, in the portrait, Plate 168 (A Veiled Woman)[9] and Plate
225 (A Woman's Face with a Red Bordered Veil), both in *Rabindra
Chitravali* vol. 3, and similar such portraits, there is no narratologi-
cal or domestic ambience or interaction with a familiar environment. But they create an alternative place/space of their own and
therein differ from contemporary representations by other artists of
his time. I beg to differ from Sudha Basu who thinks that most of
the women he paints belong to the upper class sophisticated stra-
tum of society (Basu 2011: 54). I suppose the enigma that shrouds
them, the simple oval shape that envelops their facial form gives to
many of them a dignity that is essential to their self-identity, the
poet's conception of feminine identity rather than physical or social
identity. It endows them with a subjective personality transcending
the restrictive norms of womanly existence. Technically, these faces
achieve a rare competence in the minimalist mode of painting. But
there is great variety in his depiction of women. Gendered notions
of beauty are also deconstructed in some of those faces. I would
illustrate the point with a few examples. In Plate 331 (Face of a Dark
Veiled Woman), in *Rabindra Chitravali* vol. 3, it seems that Tagore
contests the usual association of women and fair complexion. Yet
the dark woman here with her head tilted to one side is quite an
individual and no less feminine. Again in Plate 73 (Face of a Girl in
Profile), *Chitravali,* vol. 2, it is no accident that the nose protrudes
horizontally from the girl's face defying all classical and common-
sensical norms of harmony. Plate 250 (Nude Bust), in vol. 3 of the
same publication, startles with its boldness. The woman unabash-
edly flaunts her bare body while her eyes stand out sharply from her
dark face with an indifferent, far-away look. She is the new diva of
a new age.

These women were at odds with the traditional notions of Indian beauty as well as with the colonial naturalistic representation. Nineteenth-century Britain, with its naturalistic Royal Academy style was what the British sought to impose upon India through the art schools they set up. The Tagore family artists, Rabindranath, Gaganendranath and Abanindranath, were conscious of the need to contribute to the resurgence of the cultural nationalism of the Bengal Renaissance through not only literature but also painting, indigenous craft, architecture and home décor, as evidenced in the architecture of the Uttarayan complex in Shantiniketan; artist architect Surendranath Kar,[10] artist Nandalal Bose[11] and others also contributed to the efforts. British dismissal of Indian art and aesthetics also made the Indian artists' and art critics' position unenviable.

John Ruskin believed 'the Indian will not draw a form of nature but an amalgamation of monstrous objects'. He said of Indian art, 'To all facts and forms of nature it wilfully and resolutely opposes itself, it will not draw a man but an eight armed monster, it will not draw a flower but only a spiral or a zig zag'[12] The critic George Birdwood[13] made the provocative comment that in the East artists produced pictures and sculptures as works of art but they did not know what beauty was.[14] Birdwood believed that the future of Indian artisans may be redeemed by western design instruction. The 1886 Colonial and Indian Exhibition in London had only reinforced this idea of the passive type of Indian craftsmanship—skilled, but neither creative nor modern.[15] British 'orientalism' and chauvinism justified the need for British rule in every aspect of Indian life including art.

So the Indians fought back. In Bengal, Annada Prasad Bagchi started the first art magazine called the *Shilpa Pushpanjali*. *The Times of India* ran a vigorous art column from the early 1900s in Bombay. The Bengali journals *Prabashi,* edited by Ramananda Chatterjee, and *Bharati*, run by the Tagores, were also influential. These journals took up the challenge of questioning colonial stereotypes. By the 1900s the emphasis was firmly on nationalism. Artists started defying western influence. Words like 'Hindu' and 'Aryan' became current. If Indian art was judged to be unscientific by Europeans, Indian artists and critics now upheld its spiritual qualities. Again art was considered a binding force in a nation so divided in its languages and desperately in need of unity against the British. Of course there were unintended ironies. The first book of artistic nationalism, *The Rise of the Fine Arts and Artistic Skills of the Aryans* by Shyamacharan Srimani[16] in 1874 was dedicated to Locke. However, Indian assertions were important. In 1920, the Indian Society for Oriental Art brought out *Rupam,* an English art journal edited by O.C. Ganguly.[17] In its pages, writers like Coomaraswamy,[18] Ganguly and Asit Haldar[19] fought the theory held by Vincent Smith and James Ferguson that Indian art imitated and descended from the Greco-Roman tradition. By 1905, when Abanindranath had painted *Bharat Mata* or Mother India, the idea of the potential new nation had taken root. Abanindranath's followers continued in this quest for the historical and mythical subject that suggested a composite, grand past. His followers spread the idea of a nationalist art across the length and breadth of India.[20]

Tagore fully approved of the endeavour to promote cultural nationalism through art. By the time Tagore started painting, the Bengal School led by Abanindranath Tagore had already launched its revivalist movement. Nevertheless, Rabindranath was not in favour of the narrow restrictions of nationalism. He advised Gaganendranath[21] to open his windows to the world. The latter's individualistic cubistic paintings had the full approbation of Rabindranath.

As I have already pointed out, Tagore himself, due to his numerous trips abroad, was fully aware of the style and mood of European Expressionism of the early twentieth century. He also felt its deep angst. In Europe there was pre-war and inter-war social unrest. Did Tagore also feel disturbed by the emerging narrow nationalism at home, radical and violent freedom fighting activities, the idealization of woman as a politically motivated goddess, a stereotype, a mother goddess figure without real autonomy? Indianness for Tagore was not a mechanical attempt to re-create the past tradition. In fact, Indianness, he felt was a misnomer, a forcefully concocted appellation. Art, according to him, should be, like poetry, an outpouring of the soul. He understood art as essentially musical and rhythmic, at par with the life that runs through nature, and conscious of an evolving holistic rhythm. One is reminded of the words of Paul Klee, an artist who sought to combine in his work the values of music and painting:

May I use a simile, the simile of the tree? . . .

. . . From the root the sap flows to the artist, flows through him, flows to his eye.

Thus he stands as the trunk of the tree.

As, in full view of the world, the crown of the tree unfolds and spreads in time and in space, so with his work.

. . .

. . . standing at his appointed place, the trunk of the tree, he does nothing other than gather and pass on what comes to him from the depths. He neither serves nor rules—he transmits (1966: 14–15).

Ironically, against the backdrop of the resurgence of a nationalistic movement, Tagore's art seemed strange and outlandish to viewers used to the pretty ornamentation and stylized romanticism of the Bengal School. Rabindranath wanted to embrace world aesthetic values and included both the West and the East in his ken. He was consciously or unconsciously unifying through his work the ethos of the modernist, not the naturalistic corporeal West, a West that met the East in its attempt to free art from mere naturalistic representation, thereby readjusting his vision to suit his purpose of subjective self-realization. His women also sought to share this realization.

He evoked not only a new style of a new era in painting; it also connoted a new intensity of focus. The fragmentariness of the compositions evokes evanescence and instantaneous spiritual–intellectual gratification. His paintings belonged to the last phase of his career. The new style of his later poems was also boldly stark. But in this essay, I am not making an attempt to connect his paintings with his poetry but discuss him as a painter and gauge his art–historical contribution towards the evolution of an Indian modernity in art.[22] I have narrowed down the focus to his paintings of women, his deconstruction of the accepted mould.

These paintings exhibit his alliance with the opposite sex, penetrating their consciousness and losing himself in the 'other', acknowledging his own androgynous creative self.[23] One is struck by the starkness and economy, the volume less, immaterial bodies and faces of enigmatic women, both beckoning and receding, the eyes expressing a variety of emotions and moods. It does not matter whom the eyes belonged to or whether what haunted Tagore was the gaze of a particular person. The eyes, the most expressive organ of the human body are more than bodily organs. They express the soul, the soul of the artist in different moments of identification with the subject he paints. His faces are not portraits, unlike the labelled and identifiable portraits of his elder brother Jyotirindranath Tagore. It would be unfair to connect them with the face of Victoria Ocampo or Kadambari Devi. Ocampo's visage, from what appears in photographs, was of a different mould altogether. Had Tagore wanted to represent in his paintings a particular individual from among the many women of his acquaintance, he would not have hesitated to do so. But nowhere is there any record of him doing so. When he composed songs on the other hand, he often had particular voices in mind. He would for instance often send for Sahana Devi[24] to teach her the particular lyrics he had just composed with Sahana Devi's voice in mind! His paintings were an intimate and private occupation, whimsical, emotional and surrealistic. Hence, he never gave titles to his paintings.

Tagore's women strike different and various moods and postures: some dreamy, some bold, some turn away from the world, some asexual, others enjoy male company. They are not all young and pretty. Some are wrinkled like dry vegetables, for instance, Plate 196, vol. 2 [25] 'Head of an Old Woman'. What is striking here is that even age is not marginalized; her eyes impress their own thoughts on us. Some are incarnations of his soul be they curvilinear or angular, for example, Plates 45, 'Woman with a Mirror' and 398 'Woman with Basket'.[26] Here totality is created through geometry of form. The spirit, not flesh is stressed. Familiar actions are de-familiarized, romantically, expressionistically. In the latter instance, the familiar icon of a woman carrying a basket is made unfamiliar as if in a dream. The worldly context recedes into non-context. There are ethnic types, for example, Plate 266 (vol. 2) 'Woman in Profile with Ornate Headdress'. The strange headgear indicates the poet's awareness of different cultures, the post-colonial inclusivity of his world view. Since space does not permit multiple examples, suffice it to say that Tagore's visual imagination ranged over various character types of both men and women. In his depiction of women, he moves away from the conventional stereotype. The reader will have a fair idea of the variety from the prints in *Rabindra Chitravali*.

Although not schooled in the western academic anatomical perfection, the poet often displays his virtuosity in depicting women in various postures: squatting in typical Indian style and sitting in various angles on settees, chairs and on the ground. Sometimes geometrical shapes determine the contours in harsh strength of lines. This is the new visual idiom of the new age. In a Giacometti-like elongated stylized 'mother and child',[27] the child becomes one with the flesh of the mother's thigh. The essence of motherhood is etched into line drawings connoting the warmth of the womb in tightly constructed circular space, tensioning both mother and child in embryonic togetherness, symbolizing modernist primevality as in the print given below (Image 14.1).

Men and women are found in intimate embrace and rhythmic camaraderie. The women are here on equal terms with the men. Woman becomes part of the environment when in line drawings

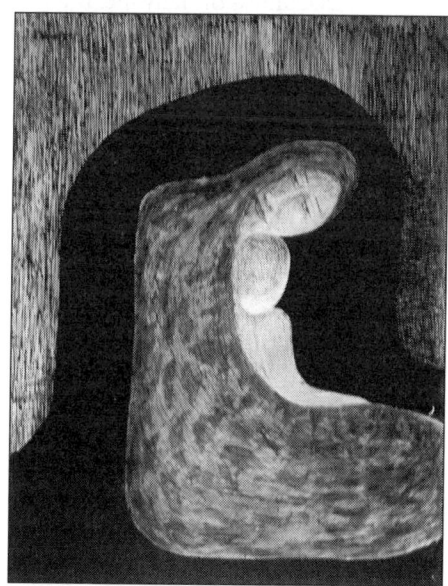

Image 14.1: 'Mother and Child'.

Source: Plate 346, *Rabindra Chitravali*, vol. 3; reproduced with permission from Visva-Bharati.

she is seen pushing through driving rain (Plate 24, vol. 3) or merged
in body and soul into what appears like a cross-section of a piece
of wood. An example is the ink on paper woodcut in Image 14.2
which seems to symbolize an ecological awareness binding nature
and the human. Woman becomes part of the natural environment,
elemental and empowered.

Tagore believed that the artist expresses the mood of the moment.
'One can only express the condition of just a moment in nature. The
moment a smile appears on a beautiful face, that moment is captured in art. 'That moment is evanescent and vanishes soon after,'
he comments in his essay, 'Sangeet o Kavita' (Song and Poetry).[28]
Fragmentariness and evanescence co-relate with the metaphysics of
moving time gyrating towards a still centre. It is like nature; there
is movement and stasis. There is no attempt to create monumental-
ity in his paintings. The women come and go in a criss-crossing of
vision and imagination. The material he uses—pastel, water colour,
coloured ink—have the casualness of daily life. But like the objects of
daily life that acquire emotional significance, his paintings reverber-
ate with a soul of their own; particularly the women.

Image 14.2: 'Seated Woman'.

Source: Plate 282, *Rabindra Chitravali*, vol. 3; reproduced with permission from
Visva-Bharati.

As I mentioned in my article (2006), Tagore had always been fascinated by the expressive quality of lines. In a letter to Ramananda Chatterjee he wrote: 'The subject matter of a poem can be traced back to some dim thought in the mind . . . . While painting the process adopted by me is quite the reverse. First, there is the hint of a line, then the line becomes a form' (ibid.: 159).[29] From a very young age he learnt to observe the world as a spectacle made up of line and shape. In his Chinese ink drawings, the lines criss-cross and cross-hatch, creating a sense of movement and a unity in diversity. Just as in his landscapes, he seeks to distil the essence of nature rather than its details so too in his line drawings he expresses the essence of all creation, that is, rhythm. In a famous pen and ink drawing, Plate 202, 'Swirling Female Figure' (*Chitravali,* vol. 3), out of moving curves arises the form of a woman who seems to be Tagore's vision of the incarnation of imagination. She holds together the sky, earth and water; she is concrete yet ethereal. The swiftness of the lines often makes forms appear like a momentary vision. Perhaps such images were his way of personifying the poetry he has been creating with black ink and paper? His awareness of rhythm in all art was the factor that led to his unified awareness of poetry, music and painting.

The quest for rhythm and essence seems to me to be the motivating force of his paintings. This is the quest that lends character to Chinese and Japanese art which fascinated Tagore. An eclectic in the cultural field his base, Shantiniketan, was the meeting place of great minds, of the East as well as the West. It would be a half-truth to say he was impressed by western modernism and modernism alone. Naturalism and volumetric approach to form had never been the mark of traditional eastern/Indian art.

In Tagore, there is both stasis and movement, scintillating dynamism as well as piercing stillness: in those strange grimacing creatures, the placid sunset trees and sad, soul-piercing eyes; in the expressionist loud hues and the swirling lines creating new horizons of knowledge and self-realization. His paintings have a closed and flat perspective. This is not only the new style of a new era in modernist painting; it also connotes a new intensity of focus, eliminating redundant details, moving towards abstraction. This flatness is part of the eastern tradition also.

Tagore's women marked a remarkable departure from the conceptualized Mother India figure of India's great nationalistic era—the concept of Bharat Mata or woman-as-nation, as visualized by Abanindranath in his painting *Bharat Mata* 1902–05. 'A unique icon of the woman is introduced early in the twentieth century, investing her with the powers of the new goddess' (Sen 2002: 17). Sister Nivedita in *Prabashi* wrote: 'We have here a picture which bids fair to prove the beginning of a new age of Indian art' (ibid.: 28). Nivedita finds the image typically Indian, the *shankha*, that is, the white bangles made of conch shell, she wears in her arms, the four arms, the pale lotuses What I find here is ambivalence. Here is woman as a goddess. What is significant is the way her docility and chastity are highlighted. She is wearing the conventional red and white bangles that Bengali wives wear, wives who are characterised as *shahadharmini* Her doubly idealized status secures the political-emotive purpose. But she is treated as an object (ibid.: 19). As Tagore observes, in India the idea of woman is associated with the Devi. Womanliness is synonymous with godliness.

Yet how is it that Tagore does not paint such goddesses? Why does he have this urge to create an alternative? Why should he deviate from his own stated ideal? Is he painting Mother India in pain? Perhaps this is the sentiment evoked in his song *'keno cheye aachho go ma'* (why are you staring, O Mother)? In fact he is painting the antithesis of a goddess. If Edvard Munch's[30] famous expressionist painting 'The Scream' shouts at social injustice, so do Tagore's women, only less loudly. In Abanindranath's *Bharat Mata* the references are objective. His Bharat Mata wears vermillion in her hair, the mark of marriage, yet also a saffron sari, the symbol of religiosity. We wonder at her actual identity. Is she human or divine? Virgin or married? She appears to be the goddess mother in the guise of the docile Indian wife who mingles desire with devotion. She is coy, as in tradition, does not raise her eyes to the viewer. On the other hand, the women in Tagore's paintings look at the gazer pleadingly, being bold as well as demure. They emerge as individuals demanding serious attention. Traditionally women have been the object of male gaze; yet here they stare out at *us*. We can actually exchange looks with them.

In Tagore's paintings woman is dethroned from the status of the mother goddess or Mother India. Woman here is not utilized or commodified. She is her own self, perhaps pained at her social condition of being an object. She longs to achieve subjecthood and it seems she has succeeded. In his novel *Ghare-Baire*, Tagore is against the iconization of woman as Mother India.

Woman is powerfully subjectified in Tagore's paintings. Tagore's women, stylistically expressionist, are politically disempowered yet romantically empowered. Although many of the women in Rabindranath's paintings are asexual in appeal many also have a latent subtle sexuality. They are a contrast to traditional representations of women in every way. They are not, for instance, fleshy as Hemendranath Majumdar's are, or situated in a womanly environment as Ravi Verma's women are.

Here we cite a few examples. In Hemen Majumdar's oil painting, 'Girl with Pitcher: Woman after Bath' the sensuous appeal valorizes the male gaze. The presentation is naturalistic. The focus is on the external. In Tagore's paintings of women, the body is sucked inwards into the soul. In Majumdar as in Ravi Verma, the body bulges outwards from the inward. Ravi Verma's women are sensuous and sensual, contextualized in mythology, history, society and custom. Western naturalism and norms of composition, as well as volumetric representation characterize his art.

Tagore is ahead of his times in depicting the physical and mental energies that lie dormant in woman but not through naturalism or ideology. He enters the woman's consciousness. He is one of India's first feminists, radically breaking the mould, and most so, in his paintings.

Tagore's last words in 'Woman and Home' (Tagore 1980: 166) is worth quoting by way of conclusion.

> At least the present age has sent its cry to women, asking her to come out from her segregation in order to restore the spiritual supremacy of all that is human in the world of humanity. She has been aroused to remember that womanliness is not chiefly decorative. It is like that vital health, which not only imparts the bloom of beauty to the body, but joy to the mind and perfection to life.

NOTES

1   German expressionism in art is a term associated with a school of art originating in Germany, in the years immediately preceding World War I. It began mainly in Berlin. It was characterized by a distortionist avant-garde non-naturalistic style expressive of intense individualism, angst and even spiritualism of a non-traditional kind.

2   I have referred to plates from these volumes; it was unfortunately not possible to reproduce them.

3   'Woman', *Personality* (Tagore 1917): 174.

4   'What Is Art? Tagore (1917): 34.

5   The Bengal School was a nationalistic and revivalist art movement whose principal proponent was Abanindranath Tagore. The artists who adhered to this movement were motivated chiefly by Mughal miniature art which was noted for its flat picture plane and vertical perspective and obliteration of perspective.

6   Raja Ravi Verma (1848–1906) was an Indian artist of great repute. In his paintings, he depicted scenes from Indian literature and mythology. The subject matter, though Indian, was fused with the technique of European academic art.

7   Hemendranath Majumdar (1894–1948), an Indian painter, who worked in the western academic style. He sought to highlight women in their sensuous beauty in realistic mode.

8   Adjective derived from Fauvism which was an art movement originating in France, around 1905. Its adherents were mainly Matisse, Derain and Vlaminck. The characteristics of their work were: use of pure brilliant colours, rough brushstrokes, thick outlines and two dimensionality.

9   The titles are given by editor R. Siva Kumar for the convenience of readers of *Rabindra Chitravali*. Tagore never gave any titles to his paintings. Siva Kumar's titles are to be found in the *Catalogue* to the publication.

10 Surendranath Kar (1892–1970). He was an artist, architect and art teacher in Tagore's Shantiniketan. He accompanied Tagore on most of his overseas visits. He was known for his fusion of western and eastern architectural styles.

11 Nandalal Bose (1882–1966), was a pupil of Abanindranath Tagore and a key figure in modern Indian art. He was an art teacher in Shantiniketan and lived there till his death.

12   John Ruskin, vol. 16 (1905): 265.

13   George Christopher Molesworth Birdwood (1832–1917) was an art critic who delivered a lecture on western and eastern art in which he harshly criticized eastern art. His remarks deeply pained and disgusted Ananda Coomaraswamy.

14   'The Challenge of Ignorance', http//www.freeindia.org/biographies/greatpersonalities/ananda/; accessed on 5 July 2016.

15   Colonial and Indian Exhibition, Colonial and Indian Exhibition (Anon 1886).

16   Srimani's book titled *Suksa Shilper Utpatti o Aryajatir Shilpa-chaturi* was the first work on the history of art written in Bengali and of cultural nationalism.

17   O.C. Ganguly (1881–1974), was an artist, art critic and art teacher. He founded the art journal *Rupam*.

18   Ananda Coomaraswamy (1877–1947), a Sri Lankan Tamil, was philosopher and historian of Indian art. He was largely responsible for introducing Indian art to the West.

19   Asit Kumar Haldar (1890–1964) was an artist of the Bengal School and art teacher in Shantiniketan.

20   It is interesting to note a reaction to Tagore's art published in *The Daily Telegraph* and *Morning Post,* 8 August 1941, p. 6, Col. 4, titled *Subconscious Art,* written the day after the poet's death by one Peterborough:

> Only a few years ago Tagore suddenly dawned on the art world as an experimenter in black and white. No one understood his pictures, which had no titles and were said to be impressions of the artist's subconscious mind.... it used to be thought that Mr. Churchill had turned to art fairly late in life... he was then 41, but Tagore was over 70 when he began. I have seen a couple of his strange productions in the Croydon Town Hall—of all unexpected place (cited from Kundu et al. 1990).

If this smacks of the colonizer's impishness, the Briton's pragmatism, it is also a measure of Tagore's irresistibility; a world personality in the truest sense.

21   Letter to Gaganendranath, *Visva-Bharati Patrika* Magh–Chaitra (mid-January to mid-April), 1353 B.S. (1947): 134–35.

22   This topic has been discussed in Gupta (2006): 149–62.

23 Tagore's androgynous self is suggested by many poems, songs and
    fiction in his oeuvre where he effectively speaks from the woman's
    point of view, sharing her sentiments and gaze. Prashanta Pal in his
    Bengali work *Rabijibani* (2003: 19) has cited an interesting comment
    made by Amitalal Basu on the first day's acting of Tagore's *Bisarjan*
    (on Saturday 25 August 1923. It appeared in *The Indian Daily News*, on
    4 September as '*Visarjan*'—An Appreciation.':

    > ...In endowing Robi Babu with a great mind, Providence seems to
    > have prepared a special mould to cast the golden casket in which
    > that mind was to find its home. There is, in the masculine frame of
    > Rabindranath, such a judicious admixture of the feminine, that the
    > product almost approaches the Divine. He sighs, murmurs, wails,
    > kneels, claps his hands, draws out his long vowels; and we feel that
    > the woman peeps out, without making effeminate, the poetry of
    > his presentation.

    In his paintings, he enters the woman's psyche, becoming them, while
    retaining his self-identity, even giving it a new colour; post-colonial
    gendering of the self, transcending social barriers and creating subjects
    of a modern discourse. One may safely assume that Tagore assumed
    a radical role in gender matters and it was a uniquely politico-social
    stance.

24 Sahana Devi (1897–1990), was a talented singer of Tagore songs. She
    had learnt directly from Tagore and had lived in Shantiniketan for
    some years.

25 All illustrations are from *Rabindra Chitravali*.

26 Both in *Rabindra Chitravali*, vol. 3.

27 Alberto Giacometti (1901–66), Swiss sculptor, painter, draughtsman.
    His sculptures were noted for their distinctive stylized, elongated
    forms.

28 Tagore (1988); translation author's.

29 The letter to Chatterjee is dated 28 May, 1930 and translated by Khitish
    Roy.

30 Edvard Munch (1863–1944) Norwegian artist and printmaker. His
    interest was in psychological themes which he treated in the Symbolist
    style. His works had a great influence on the German Expressionists.
    'The Scream' is his most famous painting.

REFERENCES

Anon, 1887. *Report of the Royal Commission for the Colonial and Indian Exhibition*. London: William Clowes & Sons.

————. 1886. *Colonial and Indian Exhibition*. Empire of India: Special Catalogue of Exhibits by the Government of India and Private Exhibitors. London: William Clowes & Sons.

Basu, Sudha. 2011. *Rupshilpi Rabindranath*. Kolkata: Pustak Bipani.

Casey, E.S. 1993. *Getting Back into Place, Toward a Renewed Understanding of the Place-World*. Bloomington, IN.: Indiana University Press.

Gupta, Tapati. 2006. 'A Unifying Experience: Rabindranath the Poet-Artist', in *Tagore and Modernity*. Edited by Krishna Sen and Tapati Gupta. Kolkata: Das Gupta & Co.

Klee, Paul. 1966. *On Modern Art*. London: Faber & Faber.

Kumar, Siva (ed.). 2011. *Rabindra Chitravali, Paintings by Rabindranath Tagore*, vols 1–4. Kolkata: Pratikshan, with Visva-Bharati and Government of India, Ministry of Culture.

Kundu, Kalyan, Sakti Bhattacharya, Kalyan Sircar (eds). 1990. *Rabindranath and the British Press 1912–1941*. London: The Tagore Centre (UK).

Pal, Prashanta Kumar. 2003. *Rabijibani*, vol. 9. Kolkata: Ananda Publishers.

Royle, J.R. 1887. *Report on the Indian Section of the Colonial and Indian Exhibition 1886*. London: William Clowes & Sons.

Ruskin, John, 1905. *The Complete Works of John Ruskin*. New York: Thomas Y. Crowell.

Sen, Geeti. 2002. *Feminine Fables: Imaging the Indian Woman in Painting, Photography and Cinema*. Ahmedabad: Mapin.

Tagore, Rabindranath. 1988. *'Sangeet o Kavita'*, *Rabindra Rachanabali*, vol. 15. 125th Rabindrajayanti edition. Kolkata Visva-Bharati: 75–78.

————. 1980 [922]. *Creative Unity*. Macmillan Pocket edition. New Delhi: Macmillan.

————. 1917. *Personality*. New Delhi: Macmillan Pocket Edition.

CHAPTER 15

Women in Tagore's Dance-Dramas

Amita Dutt

Tagore's views on women, their nature and their position in society have been voiced—directly or indirectly—in a large number of his publications: his essays, letters, novels, short stories, poems, dramas, operas and his dance-dramas. He viewed women as affectionate and passionate beings and often stated that they could contribute a great deal to society if they were emancipated from the narrow confines of their domestic boundaries. Although many of his poetic and lyrical dramas have been staged by infusing them with dance, his true dance-dramas are the trio that was composed in the last decade of his life, that is, *Chandalika* (1935), *Chitrangada* (1937) and *Shyama* (1939). These are all remodelled on earlier dramatic or poetic pieces ('*Chandalika*', '*Chitra*', '*Parishod*') and the differences lie partly in the style of composition and to some extent in the lyrics expressing Tagore's social and philosophical views. Why these three are specifically labelled as his 'dance-dramas' is because in them dance is an integral and not a sporadic component of the entire composition. The dramatis personae express themselves through dance and the lyrics are consciously made dramatic so that no separate dialogue needs to be included. And Tagore himself states in his introduction to *Chitrangada* that his compositions should be judged as songs written to accompany dance and not for their intrinsic poetic merit.[1] I have chosen Tagore's dance-dramas to delve into his thoughts on women for two reasons. As a dancer, expression through dance comes to me most naturally. Again, since this trio came towards the last phase of Tagore's life, we may state that they voice his final views on the topic. All the three dance-dramas have as their protagonist a woman after whose name the composition is titled.

Again, in keeping with Tagore's opinion of the fairer sex, they are all women of affection and are in love. It is their passion and their all-encompassing love that not only sustain the drama but also act as the agent of change both in their character as well as in our outlook on the subject.

Chandalika revolves around the issue of caste distinctions and the problem of the untouchables. But is this the only conflict portrayed in the dance-drama? If so, then the piece would have come to an end with its climax in the scene in which the Buddhist monk Ananda accepts water from the untouchable girl Prakriti and blesses her saying: *Je manav ami sei manav tumi kanya, sei bari tirthabari, jaha tripta kore trishitere* (You are of the same humankind as I am. And that water is sacred that gives satisfaction to the thirsty) (Tagore 1991: 173; see also Chapter 4).[2] *Chandalika* is much more than a mere exploration of the problems of untouchables. In fact, Tagore simultaneously addresses two problems that his contemporary society was ridden with: that of the low caste and of the weaker sex. The heroine in her anguish symbolizes both.

The dance-drama analyses the two central women characters who, belonging to two different generations, have disparate views about life and society. Mother Maya had faced a lot of persecution and has come to terms with her plight. She is no rebel like her daughter. Rather, her outlook is conventional and conservative. Prakriti, the daughter, cannot and does not accept the inane dictum of society that persecutes her for no fault of hers. She questions her plight and compares herself to a flower which, though born amidst the dust, is considered to be worthy of divine offering: *Phool bole dhanya ami matir pore* (The flower considers itself to be blessed. Although it has risen from the ground, it is worthy of God) (ibid.: 174).[3]

The dance-drama begins in spring when the flowers are abloom and when young women are buying garlands and bangles to ensnare their lovers. But Prakriti is deprived of all such privileges which higher caste women enjoy. She is immersed in contemplation regarding her predicament only to be reminded by her mother that she should go about her daily chores and not waste time with useless lamenting. Soon appears the Buddhist monk with his message of love, peace and equality. The words '*Kalyan hok tabo kalyani*' (Blessed be you O blessed one) (ibid.: 173) leave her mesmerized. Her ecstasy is reflected in her dance to the powerful song that describes her joy and exultation at the monk's acceptance of her offering of water: '*Sudhu ekti gandush jal/Aha nilen tar karaputer kamalkalikay*' (Only a handful of water, which he took with the lotus fingers of his palms. My well became an endless ocean. Here, I see the waves dancing. They dance across my whole being. My mind sways in ecstasy. O what great joy, what great joy, what ultimate freedom') (ibid.: 173).

But the dance-drama does not end here. Prakriti is a young woman full of passion and zest for life just like her counterparts from high society who were trying to empower their lovers. And so she wants to know why the monk chose her, from amidst this wide world, to give him water: *Shiure uthlo deha amar,/chamke uthlo pran* (My body started shivering and my soul startled...Is there no water in the whole city? Why did he come near my well?) (ibid.: 176).

Her obsession for the monk grows intense. And when she finds him again she is perturbed because the saint is oblivious of her presence. She is determined to have the monk within her grasp and when she discovers that her mother knows magic, she cajoles and pesters her till she finally succumbs to her desire and uses heinous black magic to ensnare him: *Por tui sob cheye nisthoor mantra/Pake pake dag diye/Joraye dhoruk or monke* (Recite your most cruel chants. Let it coil around him and ensnare him. Wherever he goes, may he never be able to avoid me...I will not admit defeat. I will lure him with my magic. Entrap him within my laughter and tears) (ibid.: 180).

But a new revelation dawns on Prakriti when she sees her monk's plight after he was exposed to the magic and made captive for her wiles: *Lajja, chi chi lajja.../Buk phete jay, jay go* (Shame, disgrace and shame... My heart breaks asunder) (ibid.: 182).

In her state of maturity she wants to set him free, and mother and daughter ask for his forgiveness: *Prabhu, eshechho uddharite amay,/Dile taar ato mulya,/Nile taar ato dukkho.* (You have come to save me,/You have paid such a grave price,/You have embraced my sorrow) (ibid.: 186). The words reiterated by the monk—'*Kalyan hok tabo kalyani*' (Be blessed you blessed lady)—acquire a new meaning and significance for her.

This dance-drama highlights through rhythmic body movement and gesture the plight of the untouchable, the obsessed and the outcaste and again through dance reveals how Prakriti's realization and final emancipation are achieved. We learn from the article of Sukriti Chakraborty (1996) published in *Desh* that when *Chandalika* was first performed, Tagore's granddaughter Nandita performed the role of Prakriti in the Manipuri dance style. There was also a touch of Kandian dance (Kandy Dance of Sri Lanka), especially in the enactments of the songs in which Prakriti voiced her anger and rebellion. The Kandy dance was taught by Shantidev Ghosh who had been sent to Sri Lanka by Tagore to learn the dance form (Chakraborty 1996: 28). Sukriti Chakraborty enlightens us further regarding the dance of the other characters. The role of the Mother or Chandalini was performed by Mrinalini Sarabhai in the Bharatnatyam style with touches of Kathakali and folk dance forms. The roles of Ananda, Doiwala and Churiwala were performed by Kelu Nair, Nileshwar Mukherjee and the Japanese student Maki (ibid. 1996: 31–32). Kelu Nair taught Kathakali and Nileshwar Mukherjee Manipuri dance at Shantiniketan. So we can assume that these dance styles were employed in their delineations and obviously Maki danced in his own Japanese style, a style that was appreciated by Tagore.

As a Kathak dancer, I have experimented with this dance-drama using my dance style to portray the characters and their interactions. Being trained in both the Lucknow and Jaipur Gharana styles of Kathak, I had the liberty to choose from both the graceful, subtle and sophisticated style of the Lucknow Gharana and the vigorous, powerful and energetic style of the Jaipur Gharana. Moreover, I had an added advantage as Kathak employs both Lok Dharmi and Natya Dharmi Abhinaya, meaning natural and stylized methods of communicating. I have choreographed the opening scene employing the graceful Lucknow style but added rhythmic pieces from the repertoire of both the Gharanas as I wanted to give the impression of cultured high-caste maidens dancing. The roles of the Doi-wala (Yogurt-seller) and Churi-wala (Bangle-vendor) were composed more in the folk spirit as the characters represented villagers. Incidentally, Kathak also employs folk elements as a result of the influence of the Raas Leela of Mathura and Vrindavan. In my choreographed presentation, Prakriti performs basically in the Kathak style, but there is a rustic charm that envelops her delineations, as compared to the stylized enactments of the high caste women who deride her (see Image 15.1).

Image 15.1: Amita Dutt explaining her ideas before her performance of Tagore's *Chandalika*.

Courtesy: Chandrava Chakravarty.

The Mother's enactments are rather loud, bereft of the subtle sophistication of the Lucknow Gharana. And when she dances in order to caste the magic spell on Ananda, the vigorous, powerful and gripping abstract dance style of the Jaipur Gharana adds the right touch (Images 15.2, 15.3 and 15.4). Having read that Tagore had been deeply impressed by the Shadow Dance that he saw in Java, I employed this dance to show the agony of Ananda when he is being tormented by Black Magic (Tagore 1985: 97). A sharp light helped to create the illusion of the tormented soul as his shadow fell on the large white screen. And this eerie portrayal of the agonized soul contrasted with the enactments of the Mother and Prakriti who

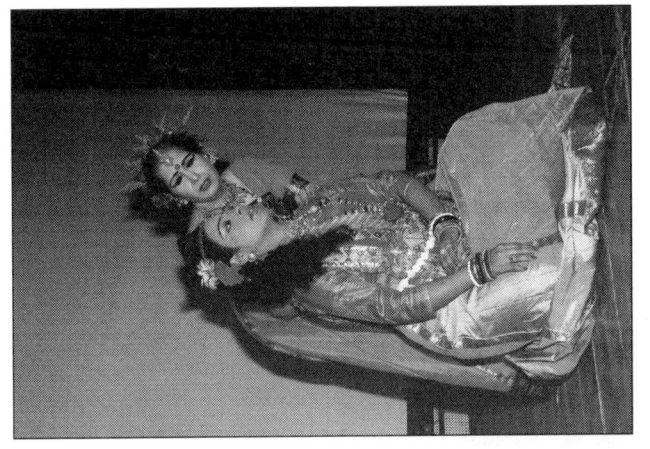

Images 15.2 and 15.3: Prakriti telling her mother about the Buddhist monk Ananda.

Courtesy: Chandrava Chakravarty.

Image 15.4: Prakriti forcing her mother to practise black magic on Ananda.
Courtesy: Chandrava Chakravarty.

were in full spot light in front of the screen. Prakriti's songs are so rich and varied in content, thought, rhythm, melody and emotions that it was both a challenge and a pleasure to choreograph her dances. The touching *'Phul bole dhanya ami, dhanya ami matir pore'* (Tagore 1991: 174) gives scope for the portrayal of subtle sensitivity while *'E notun janma, notun janma, notun janma aamar'* (this is a new birth, new birth, my new birth) (ibid.: 176) brings out her spirit of hope and joy. Her determination and resolve find expression in *'Na, kichui thakbe na.'* (No, nothing will remain) (ibid.: 176) and this contrasts sharply with her final realization in *'Prabhu eshecho uddharite amay'* (O Master, you have come to rescue me) (ibid.: 186). All these songs are performed through Kathak but the styles differ in keeping with the spirit of the song.

I have also tried to creatively use lighting techniques to highlight Prakriti's giving of water to Ananda and receiving his blessing, where a pin focus contrasts sharply with the rest of the stage which is in total darkness. The use of strobe lighting enhances the magic dance of the Mother and her companions. The dance-drama makes ample use of different coloured lights and Ananda is always given an amber halo. Maybe, this choreography differs from the one designed at Shantiniketan in front of Tagore. But I have kept in mind the

fact that Tagore was more interested in true portrayals of his sentiments than in the grammar of dance styles. I have used Kathak as
my training has been in this dance style. But while choreographing
I have been more involved with Tagore's ideas and sentiments than
with the grammatical details of Kathak. My analysis here comes
as an afterthought. While creating I was engrossed in the spirit of
Tagore's dance-drama *Chandalika*.

The dance-drama *Chitrangada* directly explores the ideal of
womanhood and women's position in society. Both the heroine
Chitrangada and the hero Arjun, and we along with them, explore
what qualities a true woman should possess and what her position
should be in society. The dance-drama opens with Chitrangada's
negation of her innate womanhood. Her father, unable to accept
the fact that she was born as a woman in his royal lineage, nur-
tures and trains her to become a man, learning all the princely arts.
Chitrangada, too, accepts this situation and so behaves as if she
were a prince. Once, while hunting she encounters the great Arjun,
the Pandava prince, and is immediately mesmerized by him. Arjun,
not realizing that she is a woman, laughs and tells her to go back
with her companions to her mother's lap as she is just a young boy.
To Arjun the whole episode is ludicrous: '*Oho ki adbhut koutuk!*'
(O what a wondrous comedy) (ibid.: 148). Chitrangada is humili-
ated because Arjun does not even condescend to fight with her, but
instead just forgives her. Gradually, her womanly instincts get the
better of her and the first flowering of love overpowers her. She
realizes that her life had been arid and effete and implores nature
to augment it: *Ore jhar neme aay, aay re amar/ Sukno patar dale...*(O
storm, come and drench my bough of dry leaves) (ibid.: 149). Her
friends also realize the change in her and marvel at it: *Sakhi ki dekha
dekhile tumi!* (O friend, whom did you encounter? Your earlier self
is laid waste just by one glance?) (ibid.). Chitrangada, her womanly
and passionate instincts now unbridled, offers herself as a woman
in love to Arjun: *Ami tomare koribo nibedan/ Amar hridoy, pran mon*
(I will offer to you my heart, my soul, my mind) (ibid.: 151) only
to be spurned by him. Chitrangada, in her agony, realizes that it is
she who is to be blamed for this predicament, for she had always
overlooked her femininity. She chastises her armour that represents
masculinity: *Hay hay, narire korechi byartho/ Dirghakal jibone amar*

(Alas! I have denied my womanhood for years. Shame on my bow and arrow! Shame on my muscular strength!) (ibid.).

In her agony, Chitrangada is determined to entice Arjun and so seeks the assistance of the God of Love Madana (Cupid) to make her a proper woman–charming, coy and beautiful—at least for one year, admitting that up to now she had overlooked the dainty arts.

Arjun is immediately attracted to this beauty and does not know whether it is real or just an apparition Arjun impulsively offers his love to her and is impatient to do so. He feels that she epitomizes womanhood. But Chitrangada reminds him that this is not her real self. She, too, feels that she is cheating herself and Arjun: *Se ami je ami noi* (But that is not the real me. It is not my true self. It is the artifice of some god. O God, how long will you make me play this trick?) (ibid.: 157). Arjun is impressed and tells the beautiful female apparition with whom he is having a dalliance that he is intrigued by the enigmatic Chitrangada who is at once powerful and loving.

But the new Chitrangada reminds him that Princess Chitrangada is not attractive. She is devoid of feminine beauty and charm: *Chi chi kutshit kurup se* (O no. She is hideous and repulsive. She cannot pierce the heart of a man with her sidelong glances. She knows no coyness or timidity. Nor does she indulge in cruel though charming dalliance) (ibid.: 160). But Arjun expresses his impatience to find the princess who is at once energetic and competent and not a mere medium for the satisfaction of carnal desires. Chitrangada is happy that finally Arjun has discovered her true worth: *'Bhagyabati se je'*, (She is lucky that finally she is welcome in a hero's consciousness) (ibid.: 161). The final verdict on the true virtue and calibre of a woman is made through Chitrangada's statement: *Ami Chitrangada, ami rajendranandini.* (I am Chitrangada, the emperor's daughter. I am no goddess; nor an ordinary woman. I am not she who you will pray to and keep on a raised platform. I am not she who you will throw behind with disdain. If you can keep me by your side in troubled and joyous times, if you permit me to be your partner in all your endeavours, then you will know the real me. I am Princess Chitrangada) (ibid.: 164).

We know that the original Chitrangada of the *Mahabharata* never really became a life partner of Arjun. They lived together for some time and their son joined the Pandavas in the Kurukshetra war. In fact, in Tagore's poem *'Chitra'*, Chitrangada promises that she will offer her son who is now blossoming within her to Arjun. But in the dance-drama, there is no reference to the son or any form of supplication before a husband. In the last phase of his life, Tagore having met and interacted with many women of substance, wanted a woman to be a man's equal in personal and social life. In fact, this dance-drama states through powerful songs, dance and music, Tagore's final view of an ideal woman: *'Ramaneer mon bholabar cholakala/Dur kore diye uthiya dnarak naree,/ Saral unnata beerjabanta antarer bole... / Jano se samman pay purusher'* (Leaving aside pleasant coquetry woman should make her presence felt in the power of a simple, enlightened and ennobled mind so that she extracts respect from men) (ibid.: 162).

The songs match the differing moods of the dramatis personae as they undergo change and gain maturity. This dance-drama embodies Tagore's—perhaps final—views on the ideal man–woman relationship. We learn from Chakraborty's article in the journal *Desh* that the first staging of *Chitrangada* was preceded by a preparation period that covered three to four months. Tagore composed the songs and taught them to eminent singers and Santidev Ghosh inspired the dance gurus to compose the dance pieces which were finalized only after Santidev Ghosh and then Tagore himself expressed their approval. Even after the vocal and dance pieces were set, there was a rehearsal period of one and a half months in front of Tagore (Chakraborty 1996: 30–31). We learn from Santidev Ghosh's account that in the first few stage shows of *Chitrangada*, the dance was almost entirely based on Manipuri with occasional poses and gestures from folk dance forms. But during 1939–40, the dance of Arjun was set to the Kathakali dance style. In 1940, the Japanese student Maki enacted the role of Madana (Cupid) with élan (Ghosh 1983: 222–23). It is my personal belief that the young energetic tomboyish Chitrangada's dance was inspired by the martial dance of two young ladies that Tagore had seen in Java where two young women, dressed in the attire of women, had performed the roles of Arjun and Subol. Tagore commented that their dance was virile and vigorous but one could easily make out that they were young women. In fact, there was no attempt at hiding the truth through camouflage (Tagore 1985: 92). Tagore had probably remembered this dance which left such a lasting impression on him that he had designed Chitrangada's earlier dance pieces accordingly. While choreographing this drama, I have used different dance styles as there were gurus, students and performers of various dance styles at Rabindra Bharati University. I recreated the tomboyish Chitrangada, especially when she goes hunting, by employing Chau dance which relies heavily on martial tactics. Madana was portrayed in the Odissi style and Arjun in the Bharatanatyam. The beautiful Chitrangada's movements blended Lucknow Kathak and Manipuri, incidentally both styles are equally lilting and graceful. The final Chitrangada rises above any particular dance style and in her portrayal, it is more the beauty of gestures that accompany powerful words and music.

Although *Chitrangada* explores the idea of womanhood, we may also state that here Tagore is more concerned with a woman in relation to a man, than with her own individual identity. And so we have *Shyama*, where the issue of crime, punishment and forgiveness are explored, this time the issues going beyond masculinity and femininity, though they all stem from the central issue of love; and that too of a woman who is the protagonist of the dance-drama.

The heroine Shyama is a court dancer. In ancient India women of this category were educated and respected, and enjoyed a great deal of freedom which their counterparts in domestic life did not. They were free to choose their lovers and had a lot of sway politically and socially. Shyama is a vain and callous beauty who is quite conscious of her own attractiveness and is amused by the love and dedication that the young Uttiya has for her. But when she sets eyes on the foreigner Bajrasen, love dawns on her for the first time. She is shocked at the idea of Bajrasena being taken captive and being sent to the gallows. Using her charm she requests the warden to let him live for a while. In the meantime Shyama knows that some drastic and perhaps miraculous action has to take place in order to save Bajrasena. And Uttiya comes stating that his concern is not for right or wrong but only for her. He offers to take the burden of Bajrasena's supposed crime on his shoulders and believes that at least Shyama will remember him for his sacrifice even as she enjoys Bajrasena's love: *Nyay anyay jani ne, jani ne, jani ne* (I am not concerned with right and wrong or virtue and crime. I only know you, O beautiful one! Your lover, whom you will save by taking my life as a pawn—with him, I will reside in your heart, tied through the bond of death) (Tagore 1991: 194).

Freed and grateful, Bajrasena leaves the city with Shyama and they enjoy their love for each other, although Shyama—the wondrous court dancer—is being looked out for by the warden. Even in the ecstasy of her love for Bajrasena, she is tormented with the thoughts of her own crime in sacrificing Uttiya. Bajrasena is intrigued and coaxes her to reveal the secret of her magical ploy. When she finally tells him the truth, Bajrasena holds her in aversion. She pleads, in vain, for forgiveness. Bajrasena, however, realizes later that his inability to forgive Shyama is his greatest crime: *Khomite parilam na je / Khomo he mamo dinata* (I could not forgive her; forgive this wretchedness in me, O Saviour of all sinners! I know you will forgive her, the hapless soul who is now suppliant at your feet. But you will never pardon my inability to condone, O refuge of all sinners!) (ibid.: 202).

Though the focal issue in this dance-drama is crime, punishment and forgiveness, the drama is also valuable as a study of the complexity of woman's love. It is the passionate frenzy of a woman that led her to indulge in her crime. She was totally blind in her love for Bajrasena. Not only did she sacrifice Uttiya but also gave up her life of opulence and comfort as a respected court dancer to go with Bajrasena into a life full of uncertainties.

In fact, the differing natures of a woman and a man are beautifully highlighted by Tagore in *Shyama*. Shyama is not bound by society. She willingly embraces her life with Bajrasena and her actions and their outcome are very much her own doing. When she has chosen the love of her life, she is willing to suffer all tribulations on account of him. The dance-drama *Shyama*, as we learn from the writings of Santidev Ghosh (1983) and Sukriti Chakraborty (1996: 29), incorporated the greatest number of dance styles: Bajrasena—performed by Mrinalini Sarabhai—danced the Bharatanatyam form; Shyama—performed by Nandita—and her friends in the Manipuri; the Kotwal—performed by Anangalal of Sri Lanka—in the Kathakali and Kandy; the Guard (Prahari)—performed by Kelu Nair—in the Kathakali; Uttiya—performed by Asha Ojha—in the Kathak; and the villagers in the folk dance styles (Ghosh 1983: 222–23). In choreographing *Shyama*, I have not tried to compartmentalize different dance styles. I composed just as the images of dance appeared in my mind's eye. The dance is a visual rendering of my interpretation of Tagore's *Shyama*. Of course, some styles do dominate. The main characters—Shyama, Bajrasena and Uttiya, as well as Shyama's companions all dance Kathak while the Kotwal and Prahari perform a blend of Kathakali and Chau. The villagers perform folk dance movements.

The women in Tagore's dance-dramas are all independent beings with minds of their own. Tagore shows how these women's passionate love make them indulge in inexplicable activities, not in keeping with their character. And the underlying thoughts of Tagore come to the forefront through the very womanly, I will not call it feminine, actions of these women. In fact, Tagore has said that it is love and passion, or emotions that control a woman and that over-power her intellect and powers of reasoning.[4] And this explains why Prakriti in *Chandalika* wanted to ensnare and hold captive the monk who redeemed her; why Chitrangada wanted to give up all her labo-riously attained princely qualities to become a sensual waif and why Shyama could sacrifice Uttiya to free Bajrasena. And all this could be competently conveyed to the audience as Tagore blended visual images of dance with his compelling poetic outpourings.

NOTES

1 The major part of this volume is composed in the form of songs and the songs are designed for dance. It is important to remember that in this type of composition melody far surpasses language… This type of composition should not be judged by the principles of poetry designed for recitation (cited from Introduction to *Chitrangada*, Tagore 1991; translation author's). *Ei granther adhikanshai gane rachita, ebong se gan nacher upayogi. E katha mone rakha kartavya je, jatiya rachanay swabhabatai sur bhasa ke bahu dur atikram kore thake… kavya-abrittir adarshe ei shrenir rachana bicharya noi.*

2 All quotations from *Chandalika*, *Chitrangada* and *Shyama* are from *Rabindra Rachanavali*, vol. 13. All translations of Tagore's lyrics in this article are the author's.

3 *Gitabitan* (Prem), song no. 538.

4 '*Soubhagyakrame strilok ke kakhono bahire giya kartavya khujite hoi na…se jakhani bhalobasite arambha kore takhoni tahar kartavya arombho hoi…takhoni*

tahar samasta charitra udbhinno hoia uthite thake.' (Fortunately, a woman does not have to venture out in order to seek her duty... As soon as she experiences love, immediately her duty begins...Then only her entire nature starts evolving.)

REFERENCES

Chakraborty, Sukriti. 1996. *'Natarajer Natyashale'*, *Desh* 64 (4), 28 December.
Ghosh, Santidev. 1983. *Gurudev Rabindranath o Adhunik Bharatiya Nritya.*
    Kolkata: Ananda Publishers.
Tagore, Rabindranath. 1991. *Rabindra Rachanabali,* vol. 13. Kolkata:
    Visva-Bharati.
———. 1986. *'Panchabhut'*. *Rabindra Rachanavali*, vol. 1. Kolkata:
    Visva-Bharati.
———. 1985. *Java Jatrir Patra.* 4th edition. Kolkata, Visva-Bharati.

CHAPTER 16

Tagore's New Woman and the Contradictions of Patriarchy: Adapting *Char Adhyay* as *Elar Char Adhyay*

Sneha Kar Chaudhuri

This chapter addresses the rich use of Tagore's works in Bengali film adaptations. This preoccupation clearly extends the ways in which Tagore's women have been seen and depicted by those film makers who have re-read and re-invented Tagore's women and his views on them. The chapter, therefore, goes beyond just Tagore's views and his multifarious representations of women and includes how his women have been re-presented in the various screen adaptations of his novels. The aim of this chapter is to add to the possibilities in which Tagore read women through the postmodern cinematic gaze of the film director's re-interpretations of Tagore's women and the consequent additions and modifications such film adaptations have made to this thought-provoking subject.

There is a long-established tradition in Bengali mainstream and parallel cinema to represent the splendour and simplicity of Tagoreana in their deliberately stylized period films. Incidentally, the most prominent and canonical films have particularly meant to focus on the many instances of female livelihoods in nineteenth-century colonial Bengal as found in Tagore's vast and boundless *ouevre*. From Satyajit Ray's incisive and sympathetic focus on Tagore's women in films like the Tagore trilogy *Teen Kanya* (*Postmaster*, 'Monihara'– The Lost Jewels and *Samapti*–The Conclusion, 1961), *Charulata* (1964) and *Ghare-Baire* (1984) to Rituparno Ghosh's opulent re-invention of Tagore's women in *Chokher Bali* (2003) and *Noukadubi* (2011), we come across several cinematic adaptations of Tagore that reinforce the relevance of Tagore's views on womanhood and his enigmatic representation of the 'weaker sex' coming to terms with the rigid boundaries of colonial patriarchy. The example from retro-Tagore films that I have chosen to base my essay on is a screen adaptation of Tagore's last novel *Char Adhyay* (1934) by Bappaditya Bandopadhyay in his film *Elar Char Adhyay* (2012). This film failed to receive much commercial success and to rise up to the bar set by Ray and Ghosh, but its contribution lies in attempting to bring on screen Ela, one of the most recalcitrant and emancipated heroines of Tagore. Instead of focusing on Tagore's domestic women at the thresholds of rebellion and conformity like Ray and Ghosh, *Elar Char Adhyay* revolves around the so-called New Woman question in colonial Bengal and the tragic struggle of the female protagonist with the manifold contradictions of orthodox patriarchy, nationalism and the public sphere.

It is perhaps no coincidence that the reiterated focus of most Bengali film makers has been on the struggles and problems of Tagore's women in the confines of the private sphere. The nineteenth-century Bengal Renaissance, despite its claims to intellectual emancipation and to be a confluence of the best ideas of the East and the West, was also a period when the issue of female liberation brought out the deeply entrenched conservatism and ambivalences of traditional Hindu upper-caste patriarchy. While on the one hand, there was an increasing social need felt by the educated sections of the society to further the cause of women for the regeneration of colonial India, on the other hand, the weight of tradition deterred such enlightened thinking about the 'weaker sex' to get materialized in concrete social changes. Regarding the so-called woman question even the most notable Bengali scholars and thinkers of the age like Raja Rammohan Roy posited conformist views uplifting the image of the chaste, domesticated and self-sacrificing women as ideal. The ubiquity of female conduct literature of the time testifies to the fact that the most learned men of the Bengal Renaissance felt comfortable to applaud the image of the age-old *grihalakshmi*, steadfast in her selflessness, spirituality and piousness. In opposition to the profanity, coarseness and restlessness that characterized some of the European *bibis*, the *adarsha Hindu nari* was the very embodiment of household peace, love and virtue (Deb 2009: 3). Thus, in the very image of the ideal upper-caste Hindu woman we observe a prominent synthesis of the Puranic religious idealiza-tion of female sublimity and the concurrent need to re-designate her exalted place in the hallowed domestic sphere that both nurtured and protected her spiritualized purity. Tanika Sarkar, therefore, suc-cinctly brings out the inherent paradoxes of late nineteenth-century colonial patriarchy when she makes the following observation:

> If the household was the embryonic nation, then the woman was the true patriotic subject. The male body, having passed through the grind of Western education, office, routine, and forced urbanization, having being marked with the loss of traditional sports and martial activities, was sup-posedly remade in an attenuated, emasculated form by colonialism. The female body, on the other hand, was still pure and unmarked, loyal to the rule of the Shastras (2003: 43).

The assigning of the sanctified and well-protected private sphere to Bengali women was commensurate with the nationalistic project of resisting forces of western modernity that argued for the equal rights and opportunities for women in the public sphere.

In Bengali literature of the nineteenth century, there was a con-scious attempt to emulate this nationalistic enterprise of empower-ing women within the household. They were also warned against the blind imitation of their impious and iconoclastic western coun-terparts. Caught in this cross-current of tradition and modernity, Tagore's representation of women became saddled with the many contradictions that dominated the intellectual climate of his genera-tion. Thus, Tagore's basic authorial intention in his representation of the many facets of his domesticated women was to highlight the myriad problems that arose out of the conflict between a woman's desire and her responsibilities, her expectations and her limited scope circumscribed by the politics of the private sphere. Tagore's quasi-conservative attitude in appropriating women as creatures of the household is undercut by his deep respect for the educated and talented *navinas* in his own family—Jnanadanandini Devi and Kadambari Devi (Deb 2010: 84–86) and his repeated support for the cause of female education, empowerment and liberation through his various writings, his involvement with female literacy in Shantiniketan and his ideological support for the new age Brahmo, educated and enlightened woman. Ela's characterization and destiny in *Char Adhyay* is deeply inflected by this inherently ambivalent attitude that Tagore had towards female emancipation both in theory and in practice.

It must be also acknowledged that Tagore's representation of women and the deeply entrenched sexual politics of the private sphere were inspired from his readings in and awareness of western literature and thought. For example, he was very much aware of the emergence of the new woman in late Victorian England, a class of women who have turned patriarchy on its head by choosing to be independent, educated and self-sufficing. Most of these urban and self-reliant women engendered doubt and scepticism in conservative circles and their proximity with the activities of the public sphere, especially men, were perceived as anarchic and licentious (Larson 2002: 167–68). Even the 'social purity' school of new woman thinkers like Sarah Grand[1] promoted the importance for chastity and sexual restraint for women asserting their role in social eugenics, and this moral conservatism clashed with the 'free love' school represented by the likes of George Sand, Annie Besant and Olive Schreiner,[2] who preferred female sexual emancipation. The moral undercurrent of a transitional society was either to ignore the rise of such women power in society or to label them as fallen and recalcitrant in dire need of conformity and subservience to the traditional public/private divide perpetuated by western patriarchy. Thus, the image of the educated and liberated new woman in the context of European societies itself was problematized by a liberal need to provide women with equal rights and the failure to bear and accept the consequences of such liberal policies. Even these emancipated women saw themselves as either unable to identify with the conservative womenfolk around them or completely at odds with the self-interests and hypocrisy of the men related to them. The problem of these women is their very newness—their non-assimilative tendencies and the hostile undertones of a society apparently advocating change but unable to come to terms with the problems that arise consequently. In such contexts, the fates of such women are subject to neglect, ignominy and lack of conventional respectability or even frustration, desperation, suicide and death. Literary examples of such women can be found in novels like George Gissing's *The Odd Women* (1893), Thomas Hardy's *Jude the Obscure* (1895) and the Sarah Grand trilogy (1888–97), where the 'new woman' characters suffer social ignominy and neglect and reflect the real-life experiences of such women in late Victorian society.

Though published in 1934, *Char Adhyay* cannot be identified with the major trends of the experimental novels of the modern period but has prominent ideological links with this very belated Victorian novelistic response to the enigmatic figure of the free-thinking women of the period, the Bengali 'new woman' or the *navina*. Tagore is like those very sympathetic but self-contradictory western male thinkers and writers like George Gissing and Thomas Hardy who had a very positive impression about these new women and simultaneously entertained doubts about their position and importance within patriarchy.

The chapter is divided into four sections; each recounting one major life-defining aspect of the heroine's existence. The narrative mode is realistic and the authorial intent is to analyse the rich interactions of his enlightened heroine Ela with the many forces of colonial modernity in her time. Pivoting on Ela's tryst with her family and the forces of a transitional pre-independent Hindu patriarchy, the plot of the novel re-contextualizes the European new woman in terms of her social mobility, well-defined individuality and active love life as in the cases of George Eliot and Victoria Woodhull among others, thereby making her a Bengali version of a modern, educated young lady who wants to actively engage with a profession and participate in the Swadeshi movement of her times. In this passionate engagement with the freedom struggle of the country, Ela discovers her love, her true identity and the stark realities of her encounters with the forces of Indian nationalism, and ultimately dies, living up to her ideals of passion, courage and honesty. Instead of imitating western situations and problems, Tagore shows the failure and frustration of a woman ahead of her times in the troubled waters of colonial Bengal.

Ela works for Indranath's armed nationalist group and vows to observe celibacy as is the rule set by the latter for all members of that secret organization. Ela's life remains pretty placid at this stage before the entry of Atindra (Antu) whom Ela sees arriving at one of the rain-drenched river ghats. She gets instantly attracted to him and life turns more beautiful as well as topsy-turvy because the feeling of first love colours her with a certain sense of hope and passion. But with the stern and anti-romantic Indranath lurking in the background, Ela's love life is doomed from the very beginning. She has committed herself to her country and has also taken vows of celibacy as was usual with the members of Indranath's group; and fears the fate of co-patriot Uma being forced into an arranged marriage for her growing intimacy with Sukumar. Hence, Ela finds it convenient to mingle her love for Antu with her love for the motherland. She repeatedly expresses her determination to merge her love for her motherland with her love for this boy younger than her. Her first reaction when she encounters Antu is, therefore, imbued with a sense of noble purpose; she wants to draw him to her world and her mission. In the second section of the novel, she describes the moment later to him with vivid confidence:

> Oh, I've told you so many times. For quite some time I had been looking at you again and again from the corner of the deck. I forgot to notice whether anyone else was observing it. In my life that is the most wonderful moment of eternal recognition. My heart said, wherefrom has come this man of remote species, not made of any known measure, a lotus with hundred petals in the middle of moss. Then and there I vowed to myself that I'll have to draw this rare man not only towards me, but to all of us (Tagore 2010; 1934: 3).[3]

Ela's will power and autonomy in the love plot unsettles the standard image of the Bengali upper-class woman as coy, uneducated and domesticated. Her assertiveness and open-minded devotion to a public cause is rather expressive of the emergence of a new kind of womanhood in the context of a largely regressive social environment. In her mores and manners she is unconventional, a khaddar-clad nationalist refusing to confine herself to the petty domestic world. Her life is shown as torn between her desire to unite with Antu and her vows of sacrifice and celibacy made at the altar of Indian armed nationalism. She wants to remain with Antu though she is also honestly critical of the wife's role and position in a Hindu household dominated by base kitchen politics, victimization and discrimination spearheaded by the mother-in-law. She does not want to confine Antu to the limits of a married domestic life as in her description it is a woman's God-gifted physical beauty that diverts men from the other noble purposes of their lives. In the second section of the novel, she strongly disapproves of the attractions and the pleasures of married domesticity, an aspect that women can cater to and that which easily pushes men towards boredom and mediocrity:

> You are not like anyone – you are tremendous. It is only because of the distance I am from you that has made me see your enlightened presence. I fear to imagine that I will enwrap you with my ordinariness. How will you develop in the everyday pettiness of my domestic life! How will I make you realize that when I lift my face how high up I see you? The sole dependence/means of women are on the nitty-gritty of their lives; there are girls who are perhaps not afraid to stifle the lives of men like you with that burden; I'm aware of so many tragedies they have caused. I've seen before my eyes how the web of creepers do not allow the tree to grow; those women feel that it is enough to cling (ibid.: 6).

Ela strongly resents the lack of self-reliance of the average Bengali housewife and her inability to liberate her male partner from the quotidian routine of their daily lives. What she says is very unusual in an age where women were expected to be mere submissive dependents on men, her voice is that of a woman who has transcended such mortal weaknesses and has dedicated herself to the country's freedom. She finds it ennobling to become a mother, a sister and a daughter serving the freedom fighters (ibid.: 7). For her, romantic love is inseparable from her impassioned sense of patriotism.

However, Antu's responses to Ela's distinctive personality, her towering passion and her overwhelming presence in his life are fraught with typical male chauvinistic contradictions. While recalling her first encounter with him, he cannot stop dwelling upon Ela's bold and unwomanly approach and keeps chiding her for being very headstrong and unbending. Antu is quite traditional, and he also largely finds it difficult to accept Ela's fiery presence and initially wants her to give up her oath of celibacy. He strongly disapproves of Ela's sacrificial role and her persistent desire to dedicate and inspire him for the cause of the nation (see ibid.: 2: 8). Tagore also depicts Antu's ambivalence at accepting her much emancipated love for when Ela comes searching after him in his secret hideout he remarks that she resembles the traditional Bengali ideal griha-lakshmi (ibid.: 5). Antu's sentiments for Ela, however, deep-rooted, are also intricately enmeshed with his political mission. He is drawn towards the mission of serving the nation-state in order to retain his proximity with his beloved. On the contrary, the mean-minded Batu and the cunning and domineering Indranath feel an intense urge to dominate and defeat Ela as they find her individuality inimical to standard male expectations from women. The distinctive attitudes of these three men towards Ela prove how the personal imbricates the political and vice versa. Ela's death is expressive of patriarchy's failure to absorb and tolerate strong and independent women like Ela within the folds of conventionality.

Ela is like a moral touchstone figure of innocence and simplicity against whom are measured all the evils of the world. Ela's initiation into the Swadeshi movement is through the shrewd and conniving Indranath who heads a group of freedom fighters, who unfortunately often spy and act against each other. Through Indranath's group, Tagore has presented to us the images of perverted and distorted nationalism that was dominated by selfishness, malice and rivalry, and which made these young men fight against each other instead of serving the goal of national freedom. Indranath is strongly reminiscent of the rakish demagogue and false patriot Sandip in *Ghare-Baire* (1916), the fallen and self-seeking nationalist who seduces the malleable Bimala. In the third section of the novel, Atindra voices his protest against such harmful power-mongers camouflaging as Swadeshis; they are men polluting the noble mission of Indian independence with their lust for corruption and dominance:

> Today I'll acknowledge to you that I'm not the kind of patriot that you know of. For those who do not accept that there is something greater than patriotism, to them it is equivalent to riding the crocodile's back like a boat to cross the river. Falsehood, meanness, mutual mistrust, conspiracy for power and espionage will one day drag them below the mire. I can see that clearly. In this vortex of an ugly world where I'm inhaling the poisoned air of falsehood day in and day out, my nature will not be able to preserve that manhood that can do something great for the world (ibid.: 9).

This is a very significant statement from the idealistic Antu inspired by Ela to join Indranath's gang in relation to the hypocrisy and opportunism that his comrades practised in the name of jingoism, thereby, killing the soul of the country to save its life (ibid.: 9). Ela repents that she has been instrumental in forcing Antu into this situation and wants to move away from this dangerous group, but to no effect. Ela's realization comes too late and Batu, lusting for her, conspires to kill the lovers. Ela's noble aspiration to fight for her country is doomed by her failure to see through the astute hypocrisy of Indranath's false rhetoric and heroic nationalism and subdue Batu's unscrupulous desire for her. Ela and Antu both court death as a kind of sublime release from the failures and frustrations of their honest, dynamic and idealistic lives. In the fourth and final section of the novel, Antu encourages her to think of death fearlessly in lieu of a life that has never fulfilled her aspirations:

> [You] coward! Why do you see death as a route to escape? Death is the most certain thing – it is the ultimate ocean for all the moving rivers of life, it is the unending confluence of all the truth and falsity, good and bad in our lives. Tonight we together are caught in the wide embrace of that greatness—reminding me of the lines from Ibsen—

> 'Upwards,
> Towards the peaks,
> Towards the stars,
> Towards the vast silence.' (ibid.: 2)

Patriarchy survives. Nationalism rages. But Ela dies. This tragic ending leaves many questions unanswered. The socio-cultural environment in which the novel is set is not conducive to support the survival of Ela and the success of her relationship with Antu. Tagore is sympathetic in his depiction of the spirited heroine but does not know how to rescue her from the clutches of orthodoxy and repression that defined her times, and hence cannot grant her a future life. Tagore's literary celebration and exaltation of Ela's proto-feministic courage, wisdom and dignity is ironically underscored by his awareness of the turbulent and hostile social ethos that determined her tragic destiny.

Bappaditya Bandopadhyay's big screen adaptation of Tagore's novel was released in 2012 with the title *Elar Char Adhyay*, claiming in the opening credits that it is due to copyright issues that the title had to be changed. Changing the title, however, has major implications in terms of the adaptational strategies of the novelistic text on celluloid. It is the director's explicit adaptational technique to foreground the life and times of Ela (played by Paoli Dam), a woman much ahead of her times and acting as an inspirational presence with her boldness, moral integrity, undying love and sacrifice. Released during the season of Tagore's one hundred and fiftieth birth anniversary celebrations, this film reminds us of Tagore's ability to portray womanhood at its strongest. It is the second attempt to bring this novel on screen after Kumar Shahani's film on this novel released in 1997, with a script by the lone English translator of this work, the established scholar Rimli Bhattacharya. Crafted as a faithful homage to Tagore, Bandopadhyay's film reverentially highlights the broadness of the writer's creativity when he brings alive such a dynamic and feisty character like Ela who has the capacity to inspire the woman of today to think differently and to forge her well-defined identity in a world dominated by men.

The film is a rather conservative adaptation of Tagore's last novel in the sense that it most closely adheres to the novel. It is, however, not the weakness but the strength of the script that it foregrounds Tagore's emancipated gender ideology in the context of female enlightenment, education and participation in Indian nationalistic movements. It emphasizes how Tagore's novel underscores the scope, possibility and importance of women's liberation and despite its tragic ending reinforces the belief in an evolving womanhood that transcends conventional vulnerabilities and drawbacks. William Shakespeare's works are widely adapted in western popular and intellectual cinema, yet those revivals are not always so uniformly respectful towards the original source text. But with Tagore, Bengali directors have always been very cautious and respectful, and this film is not an exception. In this respect, Bandopadhyay's adaptation can be best described in the words of John Ellis: 'Adaptation into another medium becomes a means of prolonging the pleasure of the original presentation, and repeating the production of a memory' (1982: 4–5). The film endorses the commonly held view among the Bengali intelligentsia about the relevance of Tagore's thinking on womanhood and his unforgettable literary women, and attempts to re-live the emergence of modern Bengali female

subjectivity through liberated women like Ela. Thus, in its attempt
to value representational 'authenticity' the film becomes, according
to Julie Sanders 'a far from neutral, indeed highly active, mode of
being, far removed from the unimaginative act of imitation, copy-
ing, or repetition' (2007: 24). In other words, the 'pastiche' mode
that the director uses allows him to make 'an extended imitation'
(ibid.: 163) of Tagore's style, but it does not reduce the scope of
offering a valuable social message through the film or the narrativ-
ization also firmly establishes the relevance of the vision of womanhood as portrayed through Ela. In fact, it is the very iconic status of
the original novelistic text that makes it most suitable for adaptation.
Sanders aptly clarifies this point:

> Canonicity, it has been posited, is almost a required feature of the raw
> material for adaptation and appropriation. If the implied pleasure
> involved in the action of assessing the similarities and differences between
> texts, between source and imitation,...as fundamental to the reading and
> spectating experience of adaptation, is to be [made] possible it requires
> prior knowledge of the text(s) being assimilated, absorbed, reworked, and
> refashioned by the adaptive process (2007: 120).

The film carefully narrates the four major phases, encounters
and men in Ela's life. By centring the narrative on Ela's rise and
fall, the director also foregrounds the hopes and impediments of a
Bengali new woman coming to terms with the limits of her social
scope and opportunities in a context rife with the struggle for the
country's independence and a newly acquired interpretation of the
Bengal Renaissance. The film depicts a period of emancipation
and the struggle to achieve freedom on all fronts from the shackles of conservatism and foreign rule. In such a milieu, the voice
of women repressed by religion, social norms and patriarchy tried
to achieve as much freedom and rights that the transitional times
offered.

Ela's life from the very beginning is subject to such struggles
with forces of opposition within and without her family. The film
begins with Ela strongly refusing to behave normatively as her
mother, forcing the latter to complain to her indulgent and liberal
father. The next set of opposition comes from her uncle's flamboyant wife objecting to her un-feminine individuality and forcing

her husband to shun the responsibility of providing money and support for Ela. As the heroine of the narrative Ela is a troublesome and strong presence in a family of conservative upper-class Hindus where all the women in her family are properly domesticated, uneducated, pious and are mere ornamental appendages to a comfortably rich household. Ela's mother is worried about her bent on education and her refusal to settle as a housewife and her uncle's wife is openly critical about her non-conformist attitude. But her uncle and her father do not discourage or deter her in her ways and she gradually starts to work in a school and associate herself with a clandestine group of militant nationalists fighting the British Raj. Ela clearly refuses an arranged marriage and opts for a career in school teaching and maintains close proximity with Indranath (played by Indraneel Sengupta) and his gang of men working as armed Swadeshis for India's independence. Ela as a new woman figure is at the receiving end of a typically colonial socio-political dynamic; her experiences are both distinct from as well as similar to her western counterparts.

In adding this sub-plot concerning Ela's relationship with her family members, the director makes a significant addition: what is merely implied in Tagore's novel is episodically narrated in the film to provide a more well-articulated context for Ela's rebellious engagement with the deterministic limits of Hindu patriarchal family values. Veteran Bengali director Goutam Ghose praises the innovative cinematic narratology of the film:

> Tagore's *Char Adhyay* is a very complex novel and the dialogue sometimes gets slightly discursive; so it's not so easy to interpret in cinema. But he [Bappaditya Bandopadhyay] did it very intelligently. He didn't want to tell a complex story in a linear form rather he has put Ela in different situations, so that's why, though the film begins from the end [in the text] you don't feel uncomfortable. It is not pronounced, it is quite cinematic. It's like a rondo in a music piece where you come back to the tonic....
>
> A lot of people may question what had happened to Ela's parents [played by Dipankar De and Srilekha Mukherjee] suddenly because after a point they are not there in the film. I don't think that a director should always follow the typical style of storytelling where you have to show everything. That's why I thought that the film is like a musical movement (Ghose 2013).

The family's confounded and often adverse reactions to Ela's strong individuality sets pace for a narrative rich with the typical conflicts of a navina's trajectory in a hypocritical male-dominated social environment. Tagore's novel about Ela's life does not have the traditional linearity of realistic plot construction, it is a rather selective narration of four most significant encounters and episodes in the protagonist's life. In the film, Ela's adult years are narrated in flashback starting with the family sub-plot and then moving towards the Indranath and Atindra episodes. The first shot in the film where Ela lies dead is then repeated in the end to show the complete story of Ela's love, longing, patriotism and death. Bandopadhyay re-adjusts the sequencing of the episodes in the novel to make the narrative a more straightforward and simplified life history of his central female character.

The general thrust of Tagore's narrative is well brought out by Bandopadhyay—the novel is predominantly about Ela's undying and uncompromising love for Atindra (played by Vikram Chatterjee). The film is a slow-paced, lyrical and romantic interpretation of a predominantly political narrative. The purity of the lovers is offset with the cold-blooded selfishness of two other men in Ela's life—Indranath and Batu. Indranath sees her as his 'muse' and Batu is too vulgar and offensive in his pursuit. On the contrary, Antu and Ela are poetic, self-effacing and idealistic lovers. The director magnifies the romantic context of the original narrative by using the famous Tagore song from the *Puja* section of the *Gitabitan* entitled '*Majhe Majhe Tobo Dekha Pai*' ('Sometimes I can see you'; translation author's) and making it a passionate refrain of doomed love. In the song, Tagore had imagined himself as the devotee who never gets a permanent glimpse of his beloved God due to his worldly diversions, but longs to undo his individuality and merge his self with the Almighty. As is very common in Bengali celluloid adaptations, the director re-contextualizes and improvises upon this devotional song using it as a deeply romantic refrain in the entire film. The song's hauntingly elegiac tone depicts the sublime misery and hopelessness as well as the profound ecstasy and contentment of Ela's love for Antu. In fact, not only the song, but the director's extensive focus on the Ela–Antu romance brings to the forefront her dilemmas as a woman torn between the callings of her desire and spirit. Again, the '*Aye tobe sahachori*' ('Come then, my companion', translation author's) song is colourfully shot to lend more vibrancy to her work as a school teacher. The dancing children and their playful moves lend hope, cheerfulness and joy to Ela's otherwise drab and stern personality. The English party song is lavishly shot to contrast Ela's simplicity with the expensive and hollow Anglophile lifestyle of her other family members and that is a sequence wholly invented by the film maker. Bandopadhyay's effective use of Tagore songs and appropriate background music undoes the monotony attached to watching this film that has minimalist historical grandeur in its use of sets and costumes. Film critic Shoma A. Chatterjee (2013) similarly thinks that 'Gaurav Chatterjee's music reflects Tagore's secular philosophy with three songs placed in keeping with the mood of a given sequence. There is an English song in the party scene while the fakir number suggests Ela's mother's orthodox attitude in contrast to Ela's progressive ideology'.

The overtly sexual treatment that the director grants to the Ela–Antu relationship establishes Ela's bold articulation of her physical passion for the opposite sex. Like Binodini's guilty seduction of Mahendra in Rituparno Ghosh's *Choker Bali*, Ela's approach towards Antu in their very first meeting underscores their ability to take more agency and expressiveness in a typical man–woman relationship. Lack of conventional inhibitions allows Ela to close in upon Antu and express her intense longing for him. In the penultimate scene where Ela realizes that death is close on its heels she demands and then relishes the last kiss together. Ela's sexual boldness foregrounds her ability to come to terms with her physicality in a way that even married women of her times were wary to express. In fact, it is the problematic repression of female sexual desire within stringent and suffocating patriarchal marriages that Ela wants to reject openly for a life of free love and passionate togetherness. The director here deliberately goes much beyond what the original text intended to state about Ela's sexual desires and thus expresses her physicality in a very bold manner that sometimes appears unconvincing and anachronistic in a historical narrative.

In the novel, Tagore provides muted hints regarding Ela's uninhibited sexuality, while as a contemporary director Bandopadhyay depicts the sexual overtones of Ela's passion with necessary poise and intensity. It is important to realize the contrasting approaches to Ela's sexual freedom in Tagore's novel and Bandopadhyay's film

version of it. The love-making scenes in the film do not exist to tit-
illate the audience or act as any commercial ruse to lend any sen-
sational effect to a very bleak narrative, they unlock the silence of
the Victorianized Tagore narrative regarding Ela's active love life
that celebrated the warmth and spontaneity of her emancipated
subjectivity. In the moral parlance of her own times, she is very
anti-conventional, unchaste and impure, tainted by her exposure
to education, her male co-patriots and the exigencies of the public
sphere. Her purity emerges from her innocent ardour to fight for the
country's independence and her ability to love beyond all bounds. In
the film her image has never been deliberately eroticized to cater to
the audience's gaze; rather her sexuality is depicted in contrast to the
paradoxically de-sexualized image of the-then Bengali housewife.
She is not the ordinary Bengali woman living up to the standards
of a spiritualized and domesticated femininity, her discovery of her
selfhood and her love enables her to realize the sublime and spiritual
side to her apparently non-conformist existence.

   Elar Char Adhyay is a cross-historical tribute to Tagore's celebration of women power in an age and society where the concept
of womanhood was caught in a cusp of tradition and modernity.
Produced and conceived in 2012, the film harks back upon a historically bygone era rife with nationalism, political unrest and the
possibilities of female empowerment. Like the novel, the film shows
the hopes and failures of thinking, educated and recalcitrant female
subjectivity as every moment of the reception of the film's text, in
Sanders's opinion, is both 'individual and distinct, albeit governed
by manifold conventions and traditions, by prior knowledges and
previous texts' (2007: 81). Sanders correctly points out that in every
adaptation the quintessential aspect is the combination of the layers
of the old and new ways of looking at the source text that ultimately
transforms our reception of both the original and its reproduction.
The transposition of the written text to a visual text is a significant
cultural moment rejuvenating our contact with Tagore's intellectual imaginary. On the whole, Tagore's enigmatic understanding
of female liberation is conveyed with a trans-historical urgency and
immediacy in the film to lend universal relevance to his vision of
femininity with which all contemporary thinking minds can con-
templatively engage.

NOTES

1   Sarah Grand (1854–1943) is a leading novelist and social thinker of the late Victorian period. She is well-known for her incisive and spirited treatment of the 'New Woman' issues and characters in her novels like *Idealia* (London: W.W. Allen, 1888), *The Heavenly Twins* (London: Heinemann, 1893) and *The Beth Book* (London: Heinemann, 1897). She is conservative in the sense that she endorsed the importance of female sexual morality and fidelity and subscribed to the 'social purity' school.

2   George Sand (1804–76), Annie Besant (1847–1933) and Olive Schreiner (1855–1920) are some of the well-known names who were associated with the 'New Woman' issue in their various capacities as novelists and social activists. They largely promoted what can be termed as 'free love', that is, sexual relations without marriage and were less conservative in their approach towards the 'new woman' question.

3   All translations of Tagore's novel *Char Adhyay* are by the author.

REFERENCES

Chatterjee, Shoma A. 2013. 'Review of *Elar Char Adhyay*', http://directorbappadityabandopadhyay.blogspot.in/search/label/Elar%20Char%20Adhyay; last accessed on 25 October 2013.

Deb, Chitra. 2010. *Women of the Tagore Household*. Translated by Smita Chowdhury and Sona Roy. New Delhi: Penguin.

———. 2009. *Antapurer Antakatha*. Kolkata: Ananda Publishers.

Ellis, John. 1982. 'The Literary Adaptation: An Introduction', *Screen*, 23(1): 3–5.

Ghose, Goutam. 2013. 'Review of *Elar Char Adhyay*', http://directorbappadityabandopadhyay.blogspot.in/search/label/Elar%20Char%20Adhyay; last accessed on 25 October 2013.

Larson, Jill. 2002. 'Sexual Ethics in Fiction by Thomas Hardy and the New Woman Writers', in *Rereading Victorian Fiction*. edited by Alice Jenkins and Juliet John. Basingstoke: Palgrave Macmillan.

Sanders, Julie. 2007. *Adaptation and Appropriation*. Oxford and New York: Routledge.

Sarkar, Tanika. 2003. *Hindu Wife, Hindu Nation: Community, Religion and Cultural Nationalism*. Delhi: Permanent Black.

Tagore, Rabindranath. *Char Adhyay*, (e-book) http://bdbks.blogspot.in/
2010/08/char-adhyay-by-rabindranath-tagore.html; last accessed on
1 January 2013.

———. 2012 (1934). *Four Chapters*, translated by Rimli Bhattacharya,
Rabindranath Tagore Omnibus II. Delhi: Rupa Publications.

About the Editors and Contributors

EDITORS

Chandrava Charkravarty is Professor, Department of English, West Bengal State University; her interests are the complex connections between gender construction, identity and nation-building in various forms of canonical and non-canonical texts. Among her recent books is *Gendering the Nation: Identity Politics and the English Stage of the Long Eighteenth Century* (2013). Recent articles are 'The "King" in Rabindranath Tagore's Drama', in the *Politics and Reception of Rabindranath Tagore's Drama*, A. Bhattacharya and M. Renganathan, eds (2015); 'Connecting Hemispheres, Playing with Distance: Rammohan Roy, an Indian Transnationalist', in *The Idea of Experience of Distance in the International Enlightenment,* Kevin Cope, ed. (forthcoming).

Sneha Kar Chaudhuri is Assistant Professor of English, West Bengal State University and Guest Faculty at Department of English, Jadavpur University; formerly Assistant Editor and current Editorial Board member of *Neo-Victorian Studies*, UK. Her areas of specialization include Neo-Victorian Studies, Victorian literature, postmodern and post-colonial fiction. Her post-doctoral research interests are Adaptation Studies, Gender Studies, Trauma Studies, and popular culture and films.

CONTRIBUTORS

Jasodhara Bagchi was a distinguished scholar and an activist, Founder-Director and Professor Emerita, School of Women's Studies, Jadavpur University; former Chairperson, West Bengal Commission for Women; among her many publications are *Changing Status of Women in West Bengal, 1970–2000: The Challenges Ahead* (2005) and *Interrogating Motherhood* (2016).

Malini Bhattacharya was formerly Professor of English, Department of English, Jadavpur University; former Director of School of Women's Studies, Jadavpur University; former member, National Commission for Women; former Chairperson, West Bengal Commission for Women. Among her edited books are *Globalization: Perspectives in Women's Studies* (2004); and co-edited *Talking of Power: Early Writings of Bengali Women* (2003).

Nandini Bhattacharya is Professor, Department of English and Culture Studies, The University of Burdwan, West Bengal, India. Her areas of scholarly interest are Translation Studies, Cultural Studies, Literary Historiography; nineteenth-century colonial Bengali and Hindi Literature; Gandhi and caste studies; genocide studies. She has edited Rabindranath Tagore's *Gora: A Critical Companion* (2015) and *The Annotated Kankabati* (2016).

Mandakranta Bose is Professor Emerita at the Institute of Asian Research, University of British Columbia, where she was Director of the Centre for India and South Asia Research and taught in the Departments of Religious Study and Women's Studies till her retirement. Her publications are numerous and spread over several scholarly fields, among her books are *Women in the Hindu Tradition: Rules, Roles and Exceptions* (2010) *Saṅgītanārāyaṇa: A Critical Edition* (2009).

Tirthankar Bose taught British Renaissance literature at several universities in India before moving to Simon Fraser University, Canada. In addition to Renaissance drama and poetry, his research interest includes nineteenth-century British literature of imperialism and late nineteenth to mid-twentieth centuries Bengali literature. For several years now his work has centred on Milton and Tagore.

Supriya Chaudhuri is Professor Emerita, Department of English, Jadavpur University, Kolkata. Her research interests include Renaissance Studies, critical theory, fiction, cultural history, cinema and translation. She has translated extensively from Rabindranath Tagore for the Oxford Tagore Translations series, and her translation of *Jogajog* (relationships) was listed among TLS Books of the Year in

2008. Among her recent publications are co-authored, *Conversations with Jacqueline Rose* (2010) and the entry on 'Modernisms in India' in the *Oxford Handbook of Modernisms*, edited by Peter Brooker et al. (2010).

Uma Das Gupta is an independent scholar, formerly Research Professor, Indian Statistical Institute, Kolkata; formerly head of the United States Educational Foundation in India for the Eastern Region, known for her distinguished scholarship on Tagore. Among her books are: *Rabindranath Tagore: A Biography* (2004), *The Oxford India Tagore: Selected Writings on Education and Nationalism* (2009).

Sanjukta Dasgupta is Professor, Department of English and currently Dean, Faculty of Arts, Calcutta University, teaches English, American literature and New Literatures. She is a poet, critic and translator and her articles, poems, short stories and translations have been published in journals of distinction in India and abroad. Among her books are *Radical Rabindranath: Nation, Family, Gender Post-colonial Readings of Tagore's Fiction and Film* (2013); co-edited *The Indian Family in Transition* (2007), is the Managing Editor of *FAMILIES: A Journal of Representations*.

Dipannita Datta is a postdoctoral research scholar and translator, teaching English at the Centre for Book Publishing, University of Calcutta, and is a guest lecturer at the Centre for Translation, Jadavpur University. Among her publications are 'Features and Literary Criticism' in *Sunil Gangopadhyay: A Reader* (2009); *Breaking the Silence* (2011) and *Colonial and Modern Feminist: Ashapurna Devi* (in press).

Amita Dutt is a scholar, performer and an innovative choreographer, one of the leading exponents of Kathak; she was formerly the Uday Shankar Professor of Dance and Dean of the Faculty Council of Studies in Fine Arts, Rabindra Bharati University, Kolkata. She has a wide range of publications on various aspects of dance, contributed to cultural encyclopedias and has also a series of CDs on dance training produced by the UGC Consortium for Education Communication.

Jayati Gupta is Tagore National Fellow for Cultural Research, Government of India (2015–17); she was formerly Professor of English, of West Bengal State University. She specializes in eighteenth-century English literature and travel writings, and literatures of the marginalized. Among her books is *Victorian Literature and Modern Indian Literature* (2014).

Tapati Gupta is an art critic and Professor of English, Department of English, University of Calcutta; visiting professor at the Ibsen Centre, Oslo. Her publications include 'From Proscenium to Paddy Fields: Utpal Dutt's Shakespeare Jatra' in *Re-playing Shakespeare in Asia*, Poonam Trivedi and Minami Riyuta, eds. (2010); co-edited *To Times in Hope: Essays in Memory of Subodhchandra Sengupta* (2012).

Debashish Raychaudhuri is a well-known exponent of Rabindrasangeet, a writer and an Associate Professor of English at Anandamohan College of the City group of colleges, Kolkata.

Amrit Sen is Professor of English at Visva-Bharati; among his publications are *The Narcissistic Mode: Metafiction as a Strategy in Moll Flanders, Tom Jones and Tristram Shandy* (2007) and 'The Pen Employ'd in Finishing her Story: Moll Flanders as Early Metafiction', in *Penguin Critical Edition of Moll Flanders*, Jayati Gupta, ed. (2006).